What Works in Writing Instruction

NCTE Editorial Board

What Works in Writing Instruction

Research and Practices

Deborah Dean
Brigham Young University

NATIONAL COUNCIL OF TEACHERS OF ENGLISH
1111 W. KENYON ROAD, URBANA, ILLINOIS 61801-1096

Copy Editor: JAS Group

Production Editor: Carol Roehm

Interior Design: Jenny Jensen Greenleaf

Cover Design: Pat Mayer

Cover Image: iStockphoto.com/Elena Ray

NCTE Stock Number: 52119

Library of Congress Cataloging-in-Publication Data

Dean, Deborah, 1952–
    What works in writing instruction : research and practices / Deborah Dean.
        p. cm.
    Includes bibliographical references and index.
    ISBN 978-0-8141-5211-9 ((pbk))
    1. English language—Composition and exercises—Study and teaching (Secondary)
I. National Council of Teachers of English. II. Title.
    LB1631.D2945 2010
    808'.0420712—dc22
                                                                2010028165

Contents

ACKNOWLEDGMENTS vii

INTRODUCTION. ix

CHAPTER 1   Writing Strategies. 1

CHAPTER 2   Summarization. 19

CHAPTER 3   Collaborative Writing. 35

CHAPTER 4   Specific Product Goals. 55

CHAPTER 5   Word Processing. 71

CHAPTER 6   Sentence Combining 86

CHAPTER 7   Prewriting 99

CHAPTER 8   Inquiry Activities 117

CHAPTER 9   Process Writing Approach 133

CHAPTER 10   Study of Models 151

CHAPTER 11   Writing for Content Learning. 168

CHAPTER 12   Putting Everything Together 182

WORKS CITED 195

INDEX 209

AUTHOR 217

Acknowledgments

As a teacher, I always wonder if what I choose to do in my classroom is the best choice. There isn't enough time to waste any by using ineffective practices or strategies. But sometimes, I am just not sure. What does research say? Often one research report contradicts another. Or what seems to be working in my classroom doesn't seem to be supported by research—or, worse, what research says should work isn't working for me . . . or at least it doesn't seem to be working. For these reasons, I was pleased to see the *Writing Next* report with its broad review of research. Although I am aware of the limitations of the report, it is still a solid starting place from which to build. For that, I'd like to acknowledge the researchers whose work informed the *Writing Next* report and Graham and Perin, whose own research gave us the results.

As always, I need to acknowledge students, past and present, whose faces and lives linger in my mind many years after they leave my classes. I think of them—their needs and their responses to the choices I made in our classroom— and hope they know that my memories of them are always part of the choices I make with subsequent students. Those memories are why I try to teach from a more informed position with each passing year. They are the reason I keep learning about what I can do to make writing instruction more effective. I see you in my mind—and you inspire me.

I am able to write because I have so much support. Colleagues who are ready to read a draft and give good, honest feedback are invaluable. Thank you, especially, Jon Ostenson, for multiple readings of this manuscript—it was long work and not always at convenient times. Karen Brown and Chris Crowe gave very helpful feedback on a particularly challenging chapter; even though the feedback was meant to be part of a demonstration of providing writing feedback for our summer institute, it was still extremely useful in moving me past a particularly problematic spot.

Working with NCTE is always a pleasure. The staff is always so professional and helpful. A special thanks to Bonny Graham for envisioning this book as more than I did in its early stages and to Carol Roehm for working so patiently through computer glitches in the later stages.

Last, but not by any means least, thanks to my family for their continued and enthusiastic support. Work from and stories about three of my granddaughters shows up in this book—they are so excited to be in print!—but they and my children and other grandchildren are part of my understanding of writing: watching them teaches me. Also, I have to acknowledge that when I write, it means I can't do as much of other things I'd like to do with them—watch as many movies, go for as many walks, make as many batches of cookies, read as many stories. Thank you to my family for understanding those limitations during writing times. I promise we'll get back to those things now—at least until the next deadline! Finally, and always, a thank you to David. He gives up the most and is always the most supportive. Nothing would happen without him.

Introduction

Writing well is not just an option for young people—it is a necessity. Along with reading comprehension, writing skill is a predictor of academic success and a basic requirement for participation in civic life and in the global economy. Yet every year in the United States large numbers of adolescents graduate from high school unable to write at the basic levels required by colleges or employers. In addition, every school day 7,000 young people drop out of high school [. . .] many of them because they lack the basic literacy skills to meet the growing demands of the high school curriculum.

—WRITING NEXT, *Steve Graham and Dolores Perin 3*

The claim that students' writing skills (and, consequently, writing instruction) are in a crisis has been raised for over a hundred years. The epigraph that begins this introduction is the opening text of the Executive Summary of *Writing Next* (Graham and Perin 2007 3), and reflects the continuation of those claims. The *Writing Next* report identifies current studies to support its assertion of a serious continuing problem with writing and writing instruction. These recent studies and their findings suggest that, even if we aren't getting any worse, we aren't doing as much as we could to provide students with the best writing instruction possible. That's where the recommendations summarized in the Graham and Perin report come in.

Writing Next provides the first large-scale review of writing instruction since Hillocks's report in 1986—and a lot about writing and writing instruction has changed in those twenty-plus years. Graham and Perin use meta-analysis, a "large-scale statistical review of research" (4), to determine what teachers can depend on as research-proven elements of effective instruction. Through their analysis, the authors found eleven such elements:

1. writing strategies

2. summarization

3. collaborative writing

4. specific product goals

5. word processing

6. sentence combining

7. prewriting

8. inquiry activities

9. process writing approach

10. study of models

11. writing for content learning

These elements, we know now from research, can improve students' writing.

How can the results of the Graham and Perin report benefit writing instruction? Mostly the answer to that question has to do with teachers, because they can make a huge difference to students and their writing. In fact, "teacher expertise is the most significant factor in student success" (National 59). What teachers know and how they put their knowledge to use is crucial—that's why knowing these eleven elements provides such a good foundation for effective instruction. Teachers tell me that they are having their students write more than they used to, and that's a good response to recommendations made in recent years that encourage more writing in schools. But Graham and Perin's review of research shows uneven findings on the effectiveness of simply *causing* more writing. In fact, the authors suggest (and I agree) that "providing more opportunities to write without effective instruction and motivation is not enough to improve writing quality" (*Writing Next* 26). We must get students writing, true. But we must also provide them with instruction about writing if we expect them to develop as they can. Teachers make a difference, and with the help of these eleven elements, we can begin to make an even bigger one.

Regarding the eleven elements, Graham and Perin provide a caveat: "All of the elements are supported by rigorous research, but [. . .] even when used together, they do not constitute a full writing curriculum" (*Writing Next* 4). This is important to remember. What it means is that teachers must consider how to use the different elements in varying degrees to address the specific needs of students in their classrooms. Graham and Perin acknowledge that "researchers do not know what combination or how much of each of the recommended activities is needed to maximize writing instruction for adolescents in general or low-achieving writers in particular" (12). There isn't a one-size-fits-all program. Instead, these principles or elements *contribute to* an effective program, and effective writing curricula should reflect these elements to varying degrees. Again, teacher knowledge—also of students—is essential in using the report's findings to improve student writing.

One limitation of the *Writing Next* report is that it doesn't recognize other practices that might benefit instruction, either because sufficient research isn't available, or because the studies that are currently available don't fit into a report like this one. Such practices might include instruction in text structure or vocabulary, for instance, or teachers' use of rubrics and structured responses to student writing. Even the workshop approach, very popular with teachers, isn't represented in this report. All of these practices *might* be beneficial elements of effective writing instruction, but *Writing Next*, based as it is on the meta-analysis of specific types of studies, cannot recommend them. For these reasons, the authors acknowledge that the eleven elements don't constitute a complete writing curriculum. Instead, "educators need to test mixes of intervention elements to find the ones that work best for students with different needs" (12). Teachers who know their students will realize that some current practices *do* work; teachers should not disregard their own professional knowledge simply because an element of instruction does not show up in this report.

Additionally, these eleven elements don't represent a single theoretical approach or ideology. Although some elements grow out of specific theoretical foundations, they don't necessarily still represent those. Because they represent different theories, beliefs, and practices, the eleven elements cannot *alone* be a curriculum. Instead, depending on how they are used, the elements can *serve* a curriculum: they can work on behalf of almost any approach that is theoretically sound. Teachers should be aware of this possibility—and should use the elements in ways that best serve the needs of their own situations and students. Because the elements don't represent a single theory or philosophy, they can help teachers who use any of a number of philosophical approaches. That said, these elements are not simple add-ons or Band-Aids. They should be considered thoughtfully in relation to teachers' already effective practices.

What follows in this book is an explanation of the elements reported in *Writing Next* to be effective, with each element presented in one of the next eleven chapters. Although I have organized the chapters in the order mentioned in *Writing Next*, they may be read in any order that seems best to the reader. Each of the eleven chapters first provides an overview of the element, with some explanation of the history and ideas behind it. As I investigated the research and history associated with the elements, I found that many (if not all) had been used in classrooms, some for a long time. I also discovered that teachers had reported varying success with the elements—and unsuccessful uses seemed to be related to the way that the element had been implemented. When teachers found success, certain specific principles had been part of their practice. So the second section of each chapter lists and explains the principles that research suggests should be practiced for the element to achieve its greatest benefits.

Following the principles section of each chapter, I include classroom applications of the element that teachers can use or adapt to their own situations. Many of the applications come from my own experience teaching grades 7–12, but some are also from other teachers' experiences as well. The applications are explained in detail to help teachers envision how to implement or adapt the practice in some way in their classes. Finally, each chapter concludes with an annotated bibliography of additional resources for teachers who would like more information on that specific element. If an element is not practiced by a teacher, or is unfamiliar, the ideas and books suggested at the end of each chapter should provide both a place to start implementation and the resources to learn more.

My intent is for readers to choose individual paths through this book—each person finding a path that fits her or his needs. If an element is new or little known, I hope all the sections of a chapter will provide the necessary foundation to begin to implement that practice. If an element is already in place in a teacher's classroom, I hope the principles section might present some ideas for refining the approach or the applications section provide some new ways to use it. The references at the end of each chapter, I hope, will provide a stepping-off point for teachers to generate more ideas for implementing the element effectively with their own students.

Although the first eleven chapters might be read in any order, the last chapter of the book serves a concluding purpose to all: it ties together the eleven elements, explaining principles that seem to repeat themselves throughout the elements and suggesting ways for all eleven to work together in a classroom. Ultimately, I hope that this book in its entirety supports teachers in their desire to help students write more, and write more effectively.

Writing Strategies

Strategic writing instruction is a creative business.

—*James Collins*

Overview

I was watching my four-year-old granddaughter write a "book." At her request, I had stapled together several pieces of paper for her, and then she had proceeded to tell me what she was going to write on each page. She knew the correspondence between sounds and letters, but at one point she stopped in the middle of a word, said the letter she needed next, "*E*," and pointed to a word carved out of wood that was part of the room's decor. "There's an *e*," she said. "It's silent." Then she bent to her paper to write the *e*.

Another granddaughter is also a "book" writer (see Figure 1.1). When she wrote her first book at age seven, she had her mother staple together several pieces of paper. Talking to me on the phone, my granddaughter said she was writing a book that was going to be thirteen pages long. She explained that the first page would have the title and a picture, and she told me her work schedule (so many pages a day) and the shape of the story (so many sentences on a page). Both of these girls, even as beginning writers, show that they are strategic writers: they use models, they make plans, and they talk about their writing with another writer.

I, too, am a strategic writer, using similar strategies at some times, and (I hope!) using more sophisticated strategies at others. More important, I am aware of the strategies I use, and I use them fairly consciously. As I've written the various chapters of this book, I've used many strategies that served me well in prior writing experiences. For the most part, I conducted my research by

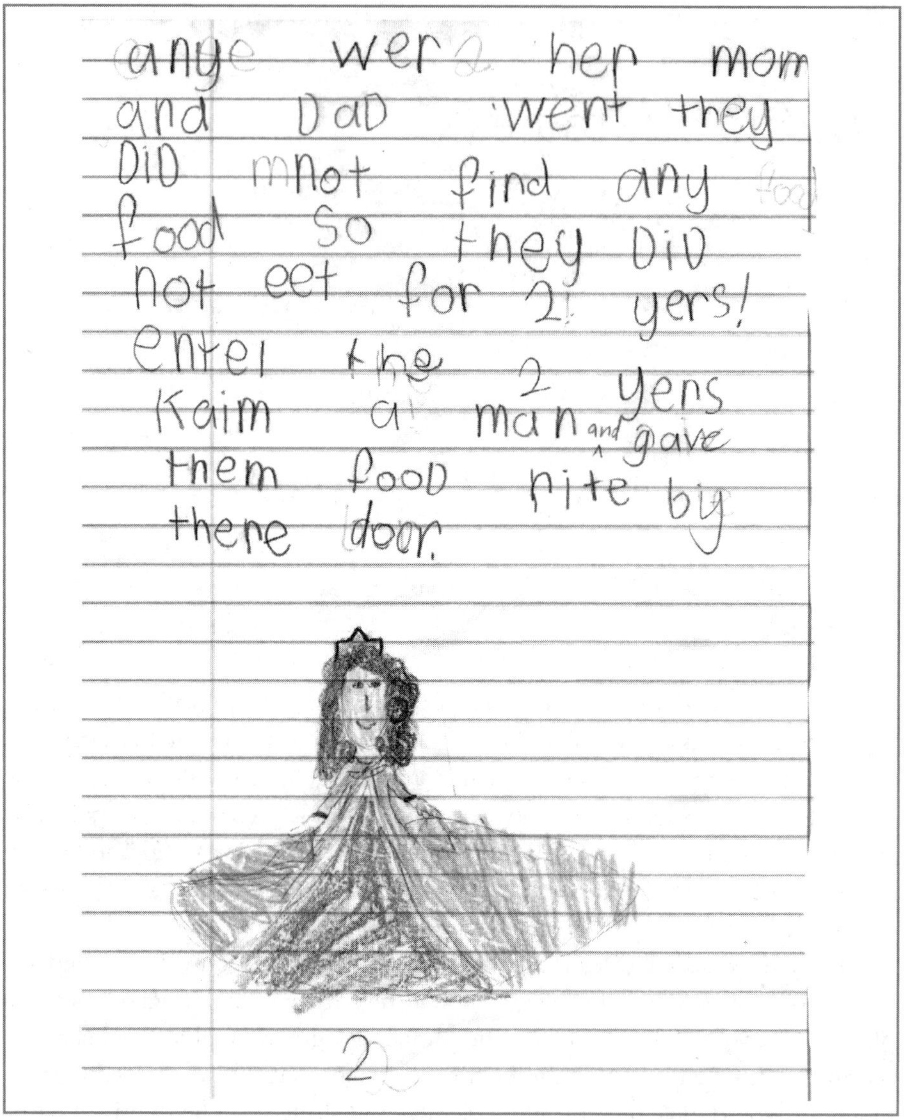

anye wer her mom
and Dad went they
DID mnot find any
food so they DiD
not eet for 2! yers!
enrel the 2 yers
Kaim a man and gave
them food rite by
there door.

2

FIGURE 1.1. A page from my granddaughter's book.

doing traditional **inquiry** in journals and databases (and googling key terms). I also used the references listed in the articles and books I found to gather more information on key questions. I took **notes** in a Word document, **reviewed** them several times to determine key themes and patterns, and wrote an **outline** by hand. Then, after I had drafted it on the computer, I **read my writing aloud**, making changes as I went. Eventually I printed a **hard copy** to continue revision, and I **asked colleagues to read** parts or all of a draft. I also set **deadlines** for different aspects of my writing, **monitoring** my progress in meeting those goals, **adjusting** when needed, and **rewarding** myself when I reached certain goals: a soft drink if I wrote for two hours straight; lunch with a friend when note-taking for a chapter was done; thirty minutes of reading for pleasure if I met my daily writing goals. And as I prepared to draft this chapter, I was tempted to employ avoidance strategies: extra and unnecessary reviews of my notes, a glance at my email, getting that bottle of water I might need later, and so on. All of these are strategies that I've used in the past.

Beyond the strategies I've used before, I have adapted and developed new strategies that helped me with this specific writing task. I wrote the chapters **not in the order** they are found in the book, but in an order that fit my schedule and my own inclinations. For chapters on topics referencing research that was less familiar to me, I **reviewed my notes** several more times than usual—**annotating** them with a code to help me identify patterns or themes. For several chapters that I wrote later in the process, rather than work from a handwritten outline as I had earlier, I began inserting a **rough outline** (as a series of headings) in the Word document; this would eventually become the chapter. I found that **drafting at home** was more effective for me than it had been in the past, when I did most of my writing in my office. I used more self-regulating strategies this time, partly because of the size of the project, and partly because so many unexpected events arose during the time I had scheduled to complete the draft, requiring me to **revise my original interim deadlines**. Because I have experience with writing, and because I wanted to complete the project (even if at times the writing seemed so difficult that I tried to avoid it), I was willing to use old strategies and devise new ones to help me accomplish my goal: writing this book. And that's exactly what writing strategies (some of which I have just highlighted) are supposed to do. They are supposed to help writers accomplish their writing goals more effectively.

Collins reminds us that there is no "master list of [. . .] strategies" (210). There are some that many people find helpful, and some that are more helpful to a specific individual or task. Strategies all serve to solve problems in writing—if by *problems*, we mean the questions or challenges that can occur during the writing process. Researchers classify strategies in three broad categories: (1) cognitive learning strategies, (2) writing strategies, and (3) self-regulatory strategies. Cognitive learning strategies encourage learning in general, but also aid writing. Writing strategies connect specifically to writing tasks. Self-regulatory strategies help writers stay with a task and find ways to be successful with it. Students need to learn and use strategies in each of these categories in order to develop as writers. I noted a variety of strategies in my description of my work, and if I were to classify them, I would label them as follows (Table 1.1):

TABLE 1.1. Types of Strategies for Writing

Cognitive Learning	Writing	Self-Regulatory
Inquiry in journals/books	Outlining by hand	Setting deadlines
Note-taking	Drafting on computer	Monitoring progress
Reviewing notes	Reading aloud	Adjusting deadlines
Annotating notes	Asking colleagues to review	Rewarding myself
	Outlining on computer	Selecting a different order
		Adding additional rereadings
		Drafting at home

Before we teach writing strategies, we should acknowledge that students may come to us unaware of the strategies they already possess; it's our job to help them identify and make controllable any effective strategies they already use. Sometimes students' writing strategies can be tricky to identify because they are invisible; even experienced writers may be unaware of many of their own strategies. Part of our teaching may involve helping students recognize their invisible strategies. In explaining another aspect of strategies, Pressley, Harris, and Marks inform us that they "are not rigidly formulated, exacting cognitive rules; rather, they entail personal interpretation" (16), revealing that the same or similar strategy may look different when different people use it. That ability to be individualized makes writing strategies powerful for writers, and is something both teachers and students need to remember: strategies should be personalized.

Many benefits result from teaching students to use strategies in writing. First, when we participate in any purposeful and goal-directed activity, especially writing, the employment of strategies can help us accomplish our goals more effectively. We want that for our students. Our experience as teachers shows us that use of effective strategies can be a distinguishing characteristic between experienced and novice writers, and we want our students to develop as writers. Additionally, strategy instruction can also "increase knowledge about the characteristics of good writing and form positive attitudes about writing and [students'] writing capabilities" (Graham, Harris, and Troia 2). We have probably all observed how students with few strategies approach a writing task: they may begin writing what comes to mind (what Scardamalia and Bereiter call *knowledge telling*) or they may never complete the writing task. They don't know what to do: how to question the task or situation; how to gather the requisite information; how to learn the expected structure of the writing; how to revise to ensure a quality written product. They have no effective strategies to use. Yet, with instruction, students can become strategic writers.

Strategic writers are prepared to write in all situations and in multiple genres. Some teachers, in support of a natural development approach to writing, believe that getting students to write often is all that is needed to help them develop as writers. And frequent writing is certainly an important element of writing development. But as Graham and Harris point out, "Frequent and extended writing is necessary but not sufficient for promoting writing development" ("It Can Be Taught" 417). Students need more. They need strategies. And instruction in strategies provides the essential extra element for developing writers by moving them beyond putting words on paper to considering the cognitive processes involved—and the tools that will help them address those processes. Strategy instruction helps students learn multiple methods for solving a variety of problems they may face in all kinds of writing situations, not just the kind of writing they do for school. Helping students learn and practice strategies, as well as the regulatory practices that will help them apply those strategies effectively in a variety of future situations, is at the heart of strategy instruction.

One challenge of strategy instruction is *transfer*, the use of strategies in situations beyond the one where students initially learn the strategy. In my own experience, students seem so trained to see strategies as attached to specific products that they don't even consider transfer. Troia explains that one difficulty with transfer might be that students may not be mindful enough to realize that we expect them to transfer strategies. That's a possibility. In some ways, the constructs of school encourage students to compartmentalize, so they do it even when we don't want them to. Being strategic writers also requires effort—and sometimes students don't want to put out the effort to be strategic. Sometimes they aren't interested enough in the writing to care. But sometimes, they just don't see any value in writing in general. Whatever the reason, transfer of strategy use can be challenging.

Strategy instruction is problematic for some researchers because of its use of explicit instruction, something they see as counter to more student-centered teaching, such as process approaches or constructivism. Pressley, Harris, and Marks counter these criticisms by asserting that "[g]ood strategy instruction could never be cookie-cutter, one-size-fits-all teaching as implied in constructivist educator critiques of strategy teaching" (13). In good strategy instruction, students construct knowledge through their interactions with a knowledgeable adult (the teacher) and with peers; we model and explain strategies, and then encourage students to individualize them as they apply them in a variety of situations. These are certainly constructivist behaviors. Collins explains that "the only important difference between good strategy instruction and the generally accepted tenets of constructivist pedagogy is in the degree of explicitness strategy instructors bring to what is being learned" (62). When explicitness is enhanced by multiple interactions and adaptations, this issue is of less concern.

Two primary models for strategy instruction have been proposed. The one most referenced in research studies is Self-Regulated Strategy Development (SRSD). It has six defined steps that include building background knowledge, discussing and modeling the strategy, memorizing it (because most of the tested strategies are based on acronyms), and then supporting its practice until students' independent use is possible (Graham, Harris, and Troia). Despite its well-defined procedure, Sexton, Harris, and Graham encourage teachers to adapt SRSD instruction to meet the needs of their students, showing their awareness of the need for adaptation after explicit instruction (308). In a second model, Collins proposes a more general plan that includes identifying a strategy worth teaching, introducing it through modeling, and then providing scaffolding while students learn the strategy until they can use it independently (64).

Although these frameworks offer different options for strategy instruction, they share common features that help us understand how best to teach writing strategies. They both emphasize *modeling* on the part of the teacher and *practice* on the part of students, practice that is *supported* in the beginning and then moved to independence with time. They both also recognize that we need to help students see the *variety* of strategies available to them, and see how the strategies can be *individualized* by writers in different situations. These are key features that should be found in all writing strategy instruction.

Embedded in both models of strategy instruction is a key factor in strategic writing instruction: the recognition of different kinds of knowledge in learning writing strategies. These three kinds of knowledge are declarative, procedural, and conditional. Declarative knowledge involves the "what" of a strategy: what it is, and what it is supposed to do. Collins notes that "declarative knowledge gives us information" (53). In the SRSD model, this is included in the first stage of building background knowledge, and might involve our explaining the strategy to the students and noting what it can do for a writer. It might include our modeling the strategy for the students. But declarative knowledge can also be engaged by having students deliberately work through a strategy as a class or in small groups, and then discussing what they see as its structure and purpose. In this way, we can guide students to understand the value of a strategy through their involvement with it, not only as something we say is useful.

Procedural knowledge is the "how" of a strategy: how it works. And procedural knowledge is best obtained by practicing a strategy. All models of strategy instruction urge the practice of strategies in pursuit of authentic goals (that is, related to a writing task, not just as stand-alone practices) and in conjunction with support from an experienced user of the strategy. In fact, some research suggests that teachers who don't use the strategies themselves might be less effective in their instruction because they can't be as supportive of students' gaining procedural knowledge of a strategy. In other words, even we need procedural knowledge. Mostly, procedural knowledge means that students need to "feel" how a strategy works for them, not just to learn how it works once, but also to know how it might be useful for them in other situations.

Conditional knowledge is the knowledge that relates to transfer—and that is essential to strategy instruction. It is the "when" of a strategy: when—or in what other situations—might this strategy help me? As Collins states, "It is conditional knowledge that helps orchestrate declarative and procedural knowledge to achieve goals. Control over performance resides in the combination of declarative, procedural, and conditional knowledge" (53). The point of strategy instruction is not for students to be able to use a strategy on the writing task under consideration during the strategy practice, but for them to be able to use it independently in other writing situations. And that is what conditional knowledge can do for them. Good strategy instruction, then, would include all three elements in teaching practices.

Some traps show up in strategy instruction, however, that we need to recognize. One has to do with the form that strategies take. For instance, some strategies are practiced using graphic organizers or other handouts. The problem is that students may view the handout itself as the strategy, and not realize that the strategy is the *thinking* that the handout is meant to teach. In other words, if I want to teach my students a planning strategy for a compare-contrast essay, I might have them use a Venn diagram to organize their ideas. But the diagram itself is not the strategy; instead, the strategy is the way the diagram asks students to think of how the items under consideration are similar or different. Students need to see the activity/handout/practice as a way of thinking, not as simply a thing to do because we ask it of them. The handout with the two overlapping circles is only a tool to implement the thinking that is the real strategy.

Overall, then, a key to teaching writing with a strategic approach is to remember that the focus is not on teaching strategies, but on helping students become strategic writers who are able to use and adapt strategies to their individual needs and purposes. It's important to remember that there is no "set of strategies that guarantee effective writing" (Graham and Harris, *Making* ix). Instead, we must see that strategies vary by the needs of writers (both beginning and more experienced) and the writing tasks they engage. As students and teachers learn to approach writing tasks with a strategic mindset, they are likely to discover and create many meaningful strategies to help them solve their writing problems.

Principles

Context

To be effective, strategy instruction should occur in authentic contexts that are responsive to students' needs. If strategies are taught in isolation, it's possible that students will see them "reduced to a set of memorized writing principles, scripts, or rules" (Englert et al. 364). This is the exact opposite of what strategy instruction is supposed to teach. To provide an effective context for writing strategy instruction, we should (1) make sure strategy instruction fits into the larger curriculum, (2) create an effective classroom environment, and (3) carefully design the kinds of tasks for which students are asked to use strategies.

In terms of curricular design, strategy instruction works especially well when combined with a process approach to writing. Teachers who approach writing instruction from a process perspective already have an effective curricular context in place. When we incorporate strategy instruction with a process approach, students benefit because they can see the effects of strategy use throughout the various aspects of the writing process. Because strategy instruction provides explicit teaching about goals, skills, and processes, it can supplement the benefits available from a process approach: "Where process teaching believes writing abilities are naturally acquired by everyone, strategic writing instruction ensures that they will be learned, even when acquisition is difficult" (Collins x). Together, strategy instruction and process can create an instructional context that engages and meets the learning needs of a wide variety of students. Together they can enhance students' acquisition of strategies to aid their writing development.

Some of the context important to strategy instruction also involves the classroom environment, including the teacher's place in it. Graham and Harris assert that strategy instruction should be "responsive to the teacher's understanding of the learners and the task" (*Making* 41). For that to be the case, we must be attentive to what students need as they work through writing tasks. This could include, according to Pressley, Harris, and Marks, making sure that "students know that failures to understand are natural and that seeking clarification is intelligent" (14). For students to know that failures may be part of the learning process, the classroom must be a supportive, predictable place that values students' efforts. Creating this climate may not be easy. Sometimes I have shared my own "false starts" (failures?) as a way for students to see that I understand the difficulty of writing well and the importance of trying again and again until something works. My own struggles help them see that it's okay to not always "get it right" at first.

As part of the classroom context, Garner suggests that a teacher's overall classroom philosophy also has some influence on the effectiveness of strategic instruction. In general, when students believe that effort can improve performance, and that there is value in learning and trying, they use strategies more than when they think the intent of the class is for students to compete with other students or to perform tasks that don't require much effort (521). So the overall impression that students have of the class might enhance or detract from strategy instruction. What matters in our class? Or what do students think matters? Effort or outcome, learning or competition? Students' sense of the value of effort is certainly conveyed in many subtle ways, but it can also be conveyed by specific classroom practices. For instance, if we provide opportunities for writing that allows students to take risks without fear of failure, they are more likely to see effort and learning as valued. Additionally, I have found that allowing (even encouraging) revisions after the grade has been given helps students see that learning to write is a continuing process rather than a one-shot exercise. Such practices help create a context in which students are more likely to use writing strategies.

We also should ensure that students see the classroom environment as a place where they can work on writing in a social setting. When strategies are taught in isolation, outside of social situations, they risk becoming just "things to do," not ways to solve problems. In fact, Collins asserts that "no amount of strategic writing instruction will help if students are not full participants in classroom communities" (213). We help to create this social context for learning strategies by encouraging students to see writing as a social act, and by encouraging students to work with each other and with us in their writing and learning. Such social interaction allows students to consider the impact that environmental strategies have on writing, as they learn how others in their groups prefer to write. Additionally, writing with others (in one way or another) can encourage the use of self-regulatory strategies, as students set goals and monitor their progress toward those goals. Cognitive learning strategies, such as inquiry and review of learning prior to writing, are enhanced through the talk that is essential to social interaction.

The kinds of assignments that we give constitute another element of the context of strategy learning because they influence how effectively students will learn a strategic approach to writing. For one thing, if students aren't interested in the task, if it isn't engaging, they will be unlikely to do the kind of thinking that allows for strategic approaches, even if they do complete the task. Paris and Paris note that assignments designed to engage strategic behavior are those that

1. are intrinsically interesting;
2. allow personal ownership to some extent;
3. connect to students' lives outside of school;
4. promote collaboration;
5. encourage quality writing through high expectations;
6. provide "consistent support for students to meet those expectations" (93).

In other words, creating effective writing tasks to encourage strategy use is not a simple matter. Some tasks that might meet these criteria are explained throughout this book, but one example might be students' creation of a public service announcement. Gardner suggests having students choose a topic or issue or idea, conduct inquiry, and then create public service announcements that would be broadcast each morning for a month along with the daily intercom announcements (80). In groups, students could create a month-long series of such announcements, all different but related. An assignment of this nature meets all the requirements of the Paris and Paris list—and encourages students to use strategies as they complete it.

To encourage strategy use, assignments can't be too familiar or easy. If students can complete an assignment without much thought, they are unlikely to use the kind of thoughtfulness that makes strategies useful. Graham and Harris suggest that writing about personal experience, for example, may be one of these assignments that doesn't encourage strategic behavior because of its familiarity or ease ("It Can Be Taught" 417). Even with a familiar assignment, though, we can "pump it up" to make it more complex and therefore encourage strategy use. For example, with personal narratives, a genre that students are more familiar with, requiring them to add informative content or present the narrative as a digital story could encourage strategy use. Assignments, then, should be a little beyond the range of what students are used to doing, both in content and genre, so that students need to stretch a bit. At the same time, they can't be so difficult as to overwhelm students. Strategies help writers solve problems, but if a writing task either doesn't present a problem or presents too many problems, it's unlikely to promote strategic behaviors.

Scaffolding

Scaffolding is an essential component of effective strategy instruction that begins with teacher instruction in and modeling of the target strategies; it continues with collaboration between the teacher and students, as students practice the target strategies.

To begin scaffolding, we must engage students. This can happen from either of two directions: (1) the teacher shows how the strategy relates to the task students are working on, or (2) the teacher explains the purpose of the strategy in general, and then lets students use it to complete a writing task. Some explanation of a strategy can happen through direct instruction in mini-lessons, but it can also happen in small-group discussions as students discover some elements of a strategy together. Sometimes I ask students to work through a strategy first, and then, after they've experienced it, we discuss its effectiveness and use in other situations. At other times I might introduce a strategy by name, explain how I think it will help students in their writing, and then let them practice it—first as a class and then individually. Either way, talking about a strategy is an important element of scaffolding toward students' eventual use of it.

Teacher modeling is another essential element of the scaffolding needed for effective strategy instruction. More than the explanations that may precede this part of instruction, modeling is helpful in "exploring with students the range of possibilities" that each strategy entails (Collins 63). While modeling strategy practices for students, we can discuss with students the ways that strategies could be adapted to fit both individual needs and the needs of different writing tasks. So, for example, when I model the says-does strategy (a way to annotate texts) with my students (Dean, *Strategic* 65–68), I work first as a whole class, guiding students' responses. Then I have students practice in small groups before they try it individually. After students have applied the strategy to their own writing, I ask them how they might use it in other situations, and I share how I have found it useful in my own writing experiences. My explicit modeling—the class activity—and my implicit modeling—sharing my own uses of the strategy—serve as scaffolds for students in acquiring strategies they can use independently.

After teacher explanations and modeling, students need guided practice where we support them in practicing the strategies. Research shows that "progressing directly from adult modeling to independent student performance does not produce general application of strategies" (Pressley, Harris, and Marks 9). In between, students need supported practice. And if students struggle with writing, Sexton, Harris, and Graham assert that this guided practice "appears to be critical to realizing the full potential of writing strategies" (308). To be successful with strategy instruction, then, we can't neglect this element of scaffolding: supported practice. For me, this has meant giving my students time to write and practice strategies in class. When they do this, I can move about the room, making sure they are able to implement the strategies and individualize them to serve their own purposes. Sometimes I have asked students to give me a little piece of their writing, a paragraph to review during the evening, so I can see if they understand the principles. For instance, when my tenth graders were working with explaining symbolism, we practiced writing paragraphs as a class using a simple strategy: identify the symbol, explain how it works in a piece of literature, and then show how the use of the symbol enhances the overall themes or ideas of the literature. After we'd worked as a class, we read another piece of literature that provided content for students to write their own paragraphs in class—drafts I could review that evening to know if students were ready to write more extensively on literary symbols. I found that if I neglected this supported practice, students tended to get home and then not know what to do. Fewer students completed the task, and even fewer completed it successfully.

For some teachers, guided practice also involves conferencing with individual writers as they attempt the strategies and helping each student adapt the strategy to his or her own needs. In this way, we can recognize what Collins calls a writer's "problematic moment" (135) that would allow us to help students find strategic solutions. Obviously, when we have hundreds of students, such individualization—an important element of strategy instruction—is difficult to achieve. But the classroom community can also be used as an element of supported instruction when students work with each other, an idea supported by Englert and colleagues, who assert that "participation in a writing community contributes to the overall success of the strategy instruction" (340). It's important that this sense of community be part of the classroom environment, so that we can use it for scaffolding strategy use. What Wong and colleagues call "interactive dialogues" among students can be a part of the scaffolding needed for effective strategy instruction (197). When teachers and students negotiate meaning and take important roles in classroom talk, strategy instruction is more likely to be effective.

In general, scaffolding means helping students through the process of writing in authentic situations, working on tasks where they are motivated and where they face challenges that encourage strategy use. In such situations, we use our knowledge of students and tasks to help students see how they can achieve their goals in individually meaningful ways. As Collins explains, "strategy instruction is good coaching" (209), and coaching is a good metaphor for the scaffolded help essential to writing strategy instruction.

Reflection

An essential component of strategy instruction must be reflection or *conditional knowledge*, a term coined by Paris, Lipson, and Wixson to represent the "knowledge about *when* and why to apply various strategies" (Collins 52). Other researchers call this kind of knowledge *metacognition*, which Welch defines as "writers' awareness and implementation of their repertoire of cognitive resources to complete a task or solve a problem" (120). So whatever term is used, the concept is a kind of thinking about thinking, and thinking about the choices we make as writers—and how they influence our performance.

Reflection is used to achieve a primary goal of strategy instruction: transfer, or the ability to use a strategy in situations beyond the one where the strategy was learned. Research shows the value of reflection. For example, Pressley and Hilden find that "a learner is more likely to understand and successfully apply a strategy to a new situation if he or she has been encouraged to think about why the strategy works and has received instruction about why it works" (521). Part of this knowledge comes from a teacher who shares with her students her own use of strategies in a variety of situations, and who collaborates with students in their own use of strategies. But some of it also must be developed individually by students. Learning to develop conditional knowledge is important because students will sometimes develop strategies on their own; and reflection will help students determine the effectiveness of these new strategies and their usefulness in other situations, something that students may not consider without practice in reflection.

It's not easy to get students to practice reflection effectively. In some cases, they resist it; some of my students, not seeing any value in it, called it "busy work." In other cases, students just don't understand the kind of thinking we are asking of them; after all, it isn't the kind of thinking they are asked to do very often. Because, as Wong points out, "strategy transfer does not 'pop up' spontaneously from students' instantaneous recognition of superficially similar perceptual cues" (111), we can't just assume that students will transfer strategy use, especially if it involves *far transfer*, or transfer to a situation that is not similar to the one where students learned the strategy. For transfer to be possible, we should ensure that they make reflection a serious and consistent part of the strategic classroom.

To make reflection meaningful, students must understand its purpose: to help them become better writers when they are on their own. Wong asserts that students need to "think or to 'dig at' transfer rather than merely being told to transfer" (112). Reflection is how that digging occurs, but first we have to help students see how this will assist them. I recall being frustrated when students didn't seem to use what they'd learned while writing a previous piece when they were writing the next one—they didn't transfer. Instead, they saw the strategies they used to successfully write in one situation as attached to the product of that situation, not as strategies they could use in other situations. Reflection was the only way to make that transfer happen, and it took some work on my part, first, to convince my students that they *should* transfer, and then, to help them see how they *could* transfer strategies.

To make this transfer happen—or at least more likely to happen—reflection should encourage students to make connections between their strategy use and their successful learning or writing. Beyond that, reflection should also help students consider what other situations might be good places in which to use those strategies again. Such considerations can happen during whole-class discussion, especially when students are first learning to make these connections. Eventually, however, students should reflect in writing so that we can be aware of how they are doing in making these important connections. Some of the questions I have used (and these vary from assignment to assignment and among student groups, depending on where they are developmentally) include the following:

1. What strategies did you use on this writing assignment that worked well for you? Consider strategies of inquiry, drafting, and product in your answer.

2. Why do you think they worked well? In other words, what did the strategy do for you that improved your ability to write or your writing?

3. Under what conditions might you use this strategy again?

4. What aspects of the writing process were particularly helpful to you during the writing of this paper? How did they help you? How might those aspects be beneficial to you in future writing?

5. What aspects of this assignment were challenging to you as a writer? Why? How did you resolve those challenges?

6. What have you learned about writing from writing this paper? What have you learned about the topic from writing this paper? What have you learned about yourself as a writer from writing this paper? How will any of this learning help you in the future?

7. It's time to turn the paper in. One writer has said that a piece of writing is never done—it's just turned in for a deadline. If you had more time, what would you still like to develop in this piece of writing? Why? How would that improve the writing? What strategies would you use that you have not used to this point?

A graduate instructor I worked with conducted an experiment on reflection's influence in a writing class. On one hand, her finding—that if teachers want higher-level reflection, they must teach what that means—seems obvious. What her research shows, on the other hand, is the impact of our work in making reflection effective. For one thing, she found that the kind of talk we conduct in class can impact students' valuing of reflection as well as their quality of reflection. When students were making connections orally, the graduate instructor used questioning to push them to make deeper connections that they might not have made without her questioning. The oral work with reflective practices found its way into students' individual written reflections. Additionally, regular reflection rather than intermittent reflection seems to be important. The graduate instructor used weekly reflections in her experimental class and found statistically significant results. Finally, she found that her comments on students' writing also needed to reinforce the strategies students used, and their quality of reflection, for their reflection to improve (Green). In other words, to achieve higher-quality reflections, we must, as Yancey says, weave reflection not so much through a class as into it, into its very essence (201). For students to truly become strategic writers, then, they must have multiple opportunities and plenty of time to consider their use of strategies and to ponder on the value to them as writers. And they must have a teacher who reinforces what it means to be an effective and reflective writer.

Applications

Expanding Ideas

As they are polishing a piece of writing, inexperienced writers often have trouble with revision because they don't generate enough text to work with effectively. There may not be enough to allow them to cut material, no matter how ineffective it is, and still meet length expectations. Because of this problem, Pritchard and Honeycutt encourage content-generating strategies so that students can "revise from abundance" ("Best Practices" 38). That's the point of expanding strategies: to help extend ideas, or to find hidden ones that could come to light before revision.

The context for this expanding strategy is during the writing process and prior to revision. The ideas in this strategy are common enough; I've just put them in a list that creates a word, so that students are more likely to remember and use the elements for generating text. I call the strategy EXPAND, and students can remember it because that is its purpose: to expand their draft. Students can add to their texts in these ways:

Entertain a new perspective on your point; add it in as a dissenting voice.

EXplain a detail in more depth.

Provide additional examples for points you make.

Add a story, an example, or more facts.

Notice a contradiction someone might raise to your ideas—and then show how it isn't as valid as your own point.

Develop other voices to support your own: add quotes, paraphrases, or summaries.

Each of these elements should be explained and practiced, as a class and individually, prior to asking students to use the entire EXPAND strategy. After revising their writing, have students reflect on this strategy. Specifically, students should consider how the strategy helped them improve their writing and how they can use it in other writing situations.

Writing Graphs

When Graham and Harris discuss self-regulating strategies, they recognize the importance of goal setting and self-assessment of those goals. One method that I've found useful to help teach self-regulation is writing graphs. The writing goal is to develop fluency, which as Graham and Harris acknowledge, "may not be the most important aspect of writing instruction" (*Making* 164). Simply getting words on paper isn't necessarily good writing. But fluency is still important. When students have the ability to get ideas on paper quickly and easily, they are often able to focus on more substantive matters. Their minds are freed from some lower-level concerns to concentrate on others that matter more. I found, as did Graham and Harris, that as students increase their fluency, they also "learn to extend content, elaborate on concepts, provide detail, and reduce anxiety regarding length" (*Making* 164). Graphing can help students with self-regulatory strategies.

This is how graphing works: Each day in class, students write for five minutes. They should try to write without stopping, for the most part. Sometimes I provide a topic, but students also have the option to write on topics of their own choice. When the time is up, students count the number of words they have written and add the data to a graph they keep to monitor their progress in getting more words on paper. If students have regular access to computers, they can both write and graph on the computer (using the word-count feature) and keep the entries and graph in a special folder. If they don't have access to computers, the same thing can be done in class with traditional technology: pencils and spiral notebooks. The graph is kept on a piece of graph paper with the date written in the row at the bottom of the graph and the number of words indicated in the vertical columns. Students attach the graph to the inside cover of the spiral notebook so it's easily accessible and visible. Each quarter, students work toward improvement by writing more words as time goes by. Graham and Harris found that keeping a "visual record of improvement has proven to be highly motivating to the majority of writers" (*Making* 166). The use of the graph provides both a goal (improvement) for students to work toward and a way to monitor progress toward that goal.

Although freewriting can teach students a strategy for generating ideas and for determining what a writer knows, useful to their writing development, the graphing serves as a self-regulatory strategy. We should help writers see how the graph can be useful as a tool for setting goals and monitoring progress toward those goals. Through discussion and student reflection, we can help students discover other goals that they might set for their writing, and other tools that they might employ to monitor those goals, even when they don't use something as visible as the graph. For example, when students are writing something based on research, I often ask them to set a goal of how many facts they are going to collect when we spend a class period in the library. My students write their goal at the top of their note-taking paper, but others might choose a different method for recording the goal. The point is that students don't just think it—they have to write it down. I don't know where he learned this, but my husband always says that a goal is just a dream unless we write it down. I've found that to be true: if students don't write their goals, they're unlikely to monitor or adjust them as needed. After the class time in the library, I take a few minutes to ask students to review their work and to write about their achievement of the goal. If they met the goal, they write about what helped them. If they did not, they reflect on what prevented them from meeting the goal, and they readjust, noting how they will make up what they didn't accomplish, so they can stay on track in their inquiry. Although not all goals are as measurable as the examples I've given here, any way that we can help students set goals and monitor them builds self-regulatory behaviors toward writing.

Annotated Bibliography

Collins, James. *Strategies for Struggling Writers*. New York: Guilford Press, 1998.

> This book was influential in my own understanding of teaching writing. It gives an overview of what is meant by strategic writing instruction, and it provides some examples of specific strategies the author used with students. Collins frames the strategies in examples that read like case studies, focusing on specific students, but his text is clear. This is one of the most effective sources for a good view of what is meant by strategic writing instruction.

Dean, Deborah. *Strategic Writing: The Writing Process and Beyond in the Secondary English Classroom*. Urbana: NCTE, 2006.

> At the risk of being self-serving, I include my own book here. It differs from the other two in that it's more focused on applications than is the Collins book, and it's more about regular classrooms than is the Graham and Harris book. *Strategic Writing* provides an overview of what is meant by strategic writing, but it puts the strategies in the context of specific, varied writing tasks in ways that the other two books do not. In that sense, I think it expands the ideas of this chapter.

Graham, Steve, and Karen R. Harris. *Writing Better: Effective Strategies for Teaching Students with Learning Difficulties*. Baltimore: Paul H. Brookes, 2005.

> Graham and Harris have probably been involved in more research than any other researchers on the topic of writing strategies. Their work, though, as the title of this book indicates, has focused on students with learning disabilities. That said, their work still has application in general classrooms with students of a range of abilities. The strategies collected in *Writing Better* have been validated in multiple studies; here, those strategies are explained clearly, and they are accompanied by extensions and portability discussions. The book has sections for self-regulation strategies, general writing strategies, and genre-specific strategies.

Summarization

I couldn't imagine a more crucial skill than summarizing: we can't manage information, make crisp connections or rebut arguments without it.

—*Mike Rose*

Overview

When a close friend died suddenly, I found myself back in Alaska after an absence of many years. As I met people I'd known but not contacted in the interim, they asked about my life since I "went outside"— Alaskan terminology for leaving the state. What had I been up to? I knew they wanted a short version of the past twenty years—a summary—but I found it difficult to reduce my life in such a manner. What did I say was the main point? What counted as less important? "Keeping busy" was my standard answer, not a very descriptive summary at all. More like the answers my teenaged children used to give when I asked what had happened at school that day: "Nothing." The ability to summarize is a valuable life skill: when we want to tell someone about a book we've read or a movie we've seen, when we want to explain why we support a particular position on an issue, when we want to explain how the window got broken. Even "I love you" is a summary of numerous feelings and experiences blended together. We all use summaries every day of our lives.

In addition to its widespread use outside of school, summary writing is a staple of many classrooms, and in most subjects. Because it links reading and writing and requires higher-level thinking, the ability to summarize is essential to students' development as thinkers and writers. Summarizing helps students learn more and retain information longer, partly because it requires effort and attention to the text. As students determine the main idea from a text and then frame it in their own words, they process it more thoroughly than they might with other reading or note-taking strategies, such as highlighting or underlining. In Guinee and Eagleton's study, a student commented that "you can highlight and not actually be learning anything. Until you have written something and passed [it] through your own brain, you have not necessarily interacted with the text" (51). That's not just true for our students. I know from personal experience that I can use my highlighter pretty effectively, marking up a text to appear as though I've identified the key ideas. When asked to explain my reading, though, I may have trouble if that's all I've done: highlight. Summarizing requires students to understand a text, to make sense of its ideas. As Friend notes, "summarization provides cognitive shopping bags" (322). It allows us to arrange others' ideas into packages that make sense to us.

Although teachers often use summarizing as a way to assess students' understanding of their reading, it has many benefits beyond assessment, benefits that aid students in their writing and learning far beyond what might be apparent—in the kinds of thinking they are able to do for many different tasks. Frey, Fisher, and Hernandez recognize that "the ability to summarize text accurately and efficiently without plagiarizing is a core competency for other genres" such as research papers, persuasive essays, and analysis papers (44). As students move beyond highlighting or copy-and-paste methods of note-taking, they are more likely to avoid issues of plagiarism; they are also more likely to write with clear understanding about the information they've gained from their sources.

Although summarizing is essential and commonly practiced, it isn't simple. Instead, it really is "more complex than it may appear" (Frey, Fisher, and Hernandez 43), partly because of the kinds of thinking it requires. Beyond mere comprehension of the material read, summaries require the reader to make judgments about what is important and what is not—and that importance isn't necessarily easy to ascertain. "The summary writer must decide what to include, what to eliminate, how to reword or reorganize information, and how to ensure that the summary is true to the original's meaning" (Anderson and Hidi 26). Summarizing requires evaluation and synthesis, two higher-level thinking skills.

The ability to summarize a story is generally considered the earliest summarizing ability: What happened? What did you see? What is the story about? The frames of narratives are the earliest understood frames, and understanding structure is an important part of being able to summarize effectively. But summarizing isn't something that students learn in elementary school and then use effectively forever. Instead, as texts change in structure and complexity, students must continue to develop the ability to perform high-level tasks with these more challenging texts. The increasing complexity of texts and their purposes can explain why secondary teachers sometimes wonder why students in their classes seem not to have learned summary writing. Students need to learn how to summarize again and again, as the texts they read change.

As they move through school, students seem to retain the concept of what summarizing is; that is, they know that it means to write a shorter version of a text in their own words. They don't seem to know that there may be different purposes for summarizing, and that those differing purposes may require differing strategies for summarizing. They may also not realize that the strategies they are using for simpler texts may be inadequate for more complex texts. Summarizing for yourself—for notes or for study—requires a different perspective of a text than summarizing to complete an assignment for a teacher or summarizing to write certain genres, such as an abstract or précis. The differing purposes and audiences necessitate different approaches to the texts and different structures and expectations for the actual summary. Issues of correctness and organization matter when students write summaries for teachers or formal summary genres; such issues may not be a factor when students use summarizing for their own purposes.

What may be problematic, as students practice summary writing in school, is that if they use ineffective strategies and have these strategies reinforced, even intermittently, by teachers' positive responses, they will continue to use these ineffective strategies. In fact, Kissner finds that "as long as students have a reasonably functional strategy, one that works at least some of the time, they won't feel any great need to learn how to use the more complex rules that lead to increased comprehension" (16). Two common ineffective summarizing strategies are "copy-delete and knowledge telling" (Brown and Day 13).

Copy-delete means that students copy a passage and delete a few words as they do so. Many students, even into their college years, may use this method of summarizing when they are writing for school. Brown and Day explain that this approach often keeps students from seeing an overall main idea in a text because students move sequentially through the text, attempting to identify important ideas as they go. Students who use this strategy often get more ideas from the beginning of texts than from the end; they know a summary should be shorter than the original, so when they get "enough," they stop engaging with the text.

Another ineffective strategy students sometimes use is telling all they know. When students do this, they rarely shorten the original. When one of my children was little, he would get excited about a story he'd heard at school. When we'd ask about it, he would pretty much tell the whole story—adding in personal or unimportant details ("I really like that part" or "I think the duck was white"). His older siblings would get frustrated at his lengthy retellings and encourage him to "summarize!" It took him a while to learn that summarizing is not just retelling; it involves selecting key details that will give the listener or reader the best overall understanding of the original text. Sometimes our students make the same mistake, thinking that a summary is more of a retelling than it should be. We need to be aware of students' use of these ineffective summarizing strategies, and should help them learn and practice more effective ones, especially as the kinds of texts they summarize change and become progressively more complex.

One way to address both the concern for effective strategies and the concern for adjusting summarizing to purpose is not to see summary writing as an end in itself. Kissner reminds us that "the goal is not to learn about summarizing; the goal is to use summarizing as a tool for learning" (117). If we teach students how to summarize, and then we incorporate summarizing in the service of learning other concepts in our courses, students will develop a more nuanced view of the purposes and procedures associated with summary writing—and we will be helping them develop as writers and learners while they are engaged in authentic work in our classes.

Principles

Discrete Skills

Summarizing is not a single act. Instead, it consists of a series of related steps that we should address separately instead of just telling students, "Summarize!" The steps for summarizing derive from work by a number of researchers, but essentially come down to four processes that Casazza credits to Brown and Day: "*delete* minor and redundant details, *combine* similar details into categories and provide a label, then *select* main idea sentences when the author provides them or *invent* main idea sentences when the author is not explicit" (qtd. in Casazza 203). Effective summary writers see these four processes from a strategic perspective—that is, they know when and how to apply and adapt them for the needs of the situation, text, and task. Essentially, summarizing requires using the basic process to accomplish these three steps:

1. Identify the main idea.
2. Recognize the text structure.
3. Generalize from the details.

Although there is more to summarizing, these key steps should be taught to students.

The first step, identifying a main idea, requires students to differentiate between what Kissner terms *textual importance* (what is important to the author) and *contextual importance* (what is important to the reader) (13). Many inexperienced readers and writers know that they should find important ideas to generalize in order to determine the main idea of a passage. But often, according to Anderson and Hidi, teachers do not clarify "to whom the information should be important" (27), so students tend to select ideas to include in their summaries that are not indicative of the main idea. Instead, students might identify ideas that are important to them personally. Similarly, Winograd found that poor readers often identified sentences as important because they were "full of rich visual detail, detail that perhaps captured poor readers' interest" but weren't pertinent to the main idea (411). Additionally, students' selection of ideas to include as important was "adversely affected by serial position," or where an idea is placed in the passage (421). So students can be distracted by many textual factors when they are asked to identify the main idea.

To help students develop the ability to identify the main idea of a passage, Goodman uses something she calls "Very Important Points" (17). She gives students sticky notes cut into six strips, which they place on a text (like a temporary highlighter) when they find what they think is an important point. Because they have only six strips, students can move them around as they read the text and identify different ideas that might be considered important. When students have individually settled on six, Goodman has them form groups and reduce the number to three, encouraging them to evaluate their selections. In this very interactive way, Goodman helps students work through a practice that will assist them in developing a strategy to find the real main points of a text.

A teacher I know uses oral activities to help students find the main idea. After their reading, students are paired up and given about three minutes to explain the main idea to their partner. Then they are moved to another partner, but now given only two minutes. As they move to the final partner, the teacher tells the students that she's sorry, but time is limited, so now they have only one minute to tell the main idea. As students squeeze their explanations into smaller amounts of time, they are forced to find the primary ideas, to summarize more and more tightly. This wouldn't work, of course, if students knew ahead of time what the teacher was going to do, but as a starter, it can be a productive way to use oral language to teach the concept of identifying the main idea.

The second step in summarizing is recognizing text structures. In some texts, the main idea is stated in a topic sentence or thesis statement; however, when the main ideas are not located in these key positions, "proficient readers make guesses about possible main ideas and check these guesses against future sentences in the paragraph" (Kissner 37). Less proficient readers need to learn how to use the features of texts to help them identify main ideas and supports. Armbruster refers to Kantor's term when she speaks of "inconsiderate texts" (213), ones that hinder a reader's attempt to make meaning. Armbruster identifies ways that texts can help and hinder students' comprehension—and thus, their ability to summarize—through what she terms *textual coherence* (203), a function of both global and local textual characteristics. Context for the content—or where the piece is found—contributes to global coherence. In other words, if I'm reading an article on Abraham Lincoln in *Junior Scholastic*, I will read with certain expectations that may differ if I'm reading the entry about him in Wikipedia. These differences in context contribute to global coherence. Globally, coherence is also achieved through the general organization of a text, what others might identify as types of texts: compare-contrast, problem-solution, chronology, cause-effect. One way to help students see the structures in a text is to teach them to pay attention to the structural signals writers use. Armbruster explains that these types of signals include "(1) explicit statements of the structure or organization; (2) previews or introductory statements, including titles; (3) summary statements; (4) pointer words and phrases such as 'an important point is. . .'; and (5) textual cues such as underlining, italics, and boldface" (204). Rhoder suggests posing questions to identify text structure: What is the relationship of ideas in the text? How do I know? What cue words do I find? (501). Cue words that suggest global structure might also reflect local coherence.

Local coherence, or how ideas relate to those near them in a piece of writing, is achieved through signals such as synonyms, pronouns, and transitions. Students can learn to identify transitional words or phrases that show both how individual ideas relate to each other and how a text is organized overall. Some possible transitional cues that can aid readers are found in Table 2.1.

Having students see these words as cues for how ideas relate can assist them as they identify main ideas and supporting ideas. We should help students recognize that because some of these cue words could possibly signal different kinds of relationships, students also need to look for other cues to confirm their thinking. To help students see other elements of local coherence, I ask them to look for key nouns and then find synonyms for those nouns or pronouns referring to them. Synonyms and pronouns help readers keep track of ideas and identify text structures. For example, in the following paragraph from Giblin's *Secrets of the Sphinx*, I ask students to identify the main noun—*pharaoh*—and then the pronouns and synonyms (underlined in the paragraph) that connect back to him, to show that he is the focus of the paragraph. I put this paragraph on a transparency to work with as a class, so we also notice nontraditional transitional devices, words that by their use show they are intended to make a

TABLE 2.1. Transitions as Cues

To show comparison or contrast	also
	although
	on the other hand
	similarly
	but
	however
	nevertheless
To show cause and effect	as a result
	because
	consequently
	therefore
To show relationships in time	before
	during
	meanwhile
	then
	finally
	subsequently
To show relationships in space	above
	below
	next to
	beyond
	beneath
	inside
	near
To show an example or support	for example
	for instance
	such as
	in addition
	likewise

connection. I then draw lines from those words to what they connect with: *in life* connects with *in death,* which connects with *There*.

> Religion was central to Egyptian life from the beginning, and the **pharaoh** played a key role in its rituals. In life, <u>the ruler</u> was thought to be the son of Ra, the all-powerful sun god. In death, <u>he</u> rejoined his father in the west, the place where the sun set. There, in the Egyptian afterlife, <u>he</u> would enjoy eternal life, but only if <u>his</u> earthly body was still intact. (n.p., emphasis added)

All in all, this is a very coherent paragraph. Helping students see *why* it is coherent can aid them as both readers and writers. When students are aware of linguistic cues such as those mentioned here, they can identify text structures more effectively, which assists them with summarizing.

Generalizing, the third step essential to summarizing, helps students see how details elaborate main points. Instead of seeing the details as points in themselves, students should be taught how details add up to the main point. Although Anderson and Hidi identify the ability to condense or generalize as more difficult for young children (27), when the details of a text are abstract or complex, even older or more experienced readers may find it hard to see how to generalize from specific details in order to identify the main points of a text. Kissner explains that she gives students lists of items (such as the names Washington, Lincoln, Roosevelt, Clinton, and Bush) and then asks them to identify the general category (presidents). I suggest letting students develop lists for other students, or giving them a number of random objects and asking them to come up with a label or category that would encompass all. As students develop this ability, we should give them more abstract lists so that they can see how writers use different kinds of evidence in support of a main idea. For example, in *Walking the Bible*, Feiler uses the following examples (among others) to support a main idea that camels are well equipped for desert life:

- can survive without water for two weeks
- match body temperature to climate to avoid use of water for cooling
- use fat in humps to live without food for long periods
- have broad feet so they can walk on sand and not sink
- can seal off nostrils to keep from inhaling blowing sand
- possess an extra eyelid to wipe eyes, and which can be closed without impeding vision (252–53)

If we give lists of evidence like this to students, they can also practice generalizing from the evidence in paragraphs to the main idea, and seeing how details contribute to, but are not, the main idea.

Direct Instruction

Although Friend cites research showing that "expert readers learn the cognitive processes of summarization gradually through immersion" (322), most students learn how to summarize by following procedures that can be taught through direct instruction and guided practice. In fact, Anderson and Hidi assert that students should receive instruction in summarizing because it is so "different from other kinds of writing" (26). Frey, Fisher, and Hernandez go even further, stating that "improvement in summary writing is particularly resistant to a trial-and-error approach" (43), another reason to use direct instruction to teach students how to summarize.

Direct instruction can have several faces. Although in some summarizing situations, the text is broken up and examined in parts, it's advisable to begin by considering the whole text so that students can look for a main idea. Also, we want students to give as much attention to ideas at the end of the reading as they give to ideas at the beginning. From one or more readings, students should develop a main idea statement, what both Friend and Kissner call the topic plus what the author is saying about it. In other words, referring to the paragraph that contains the details listed earlier, the main idea is not "camels," but that "camels are well equipped for desert life." Next, students should work with the teacher to find supporting ideas, which can sometimes be accomplished by writing a sentence for each paragraph in the passage. When the summary is written, the class checks it against the original text to make sure that it accurately represents the main ideas and tone of the original.

Following the same basic processes, Guinee and Eagleton teach CHoMP, a more structured approach to summarizing that lays out these procedures:

- **C**ross out small words [. . .]
- **H**ighlight important information in the remaining text
- **M**ake notes on the highlighted information by abbreviating, truncating, making lists, using symbols, and drawing [. . .]
- **P**ut the notes in their own words (48)

Through direct instruction, teachers model these steps, putting a text on a screen for students to use as they all contribute to the process. As the teacher works through the steps with the students, she is able to help them understand what is meant by "small words" and "important information." She can also help students understand what it means to write something in their own words—and how writers go about doing that. If students work through the CHoMP process effectively, they can develop a strategy for summarizing chunks of text.

Kissner also uses a direct instruction approach, but hers is more spread out. In other words, she teaches discrete skills that contribute to the ability to summarize before working with students to actually write summaries. She works on the subskills of identifying a main idea, interpreting a text structure, and creating a good topic sentence or statement of main idea. Each subskill is taught through direct instruction and practiced in activities prior to the work of writing complete summaries independently. Kissner also advocates continuing to practice these discrete skills even after students are writing whole summaries, as a way to improve their summary writing.

As a part of direct instruction and as a way to reinforce the qualities of good summary writing, Kissner advocates having students compare differing qualities of summaries. She does this by creating her own summaries of varying qualities, and then asking students to evaluate these and give reasons for their evaluations. Through discussion about specific summaries she has generated, Kissner reinforces the qualities she has been teaching about writing summaries: the ability to identify accurately the main idea and state it in your own words, and the ability to eliminate unimportant or redundant information. When students are taught the important pieces of summaries and encouraged to practice them and then evaluate them, they are more likely to write effective summaries than if left to their own devices.

Scaffolding

Even when we use direct instruction to teach summarizing, we should still scaffold that instruction and incorporate a gradual release approach for students to gain the most they can from the process. The whole class should work through summarizing practices together first, with the students giving input to the teacher, who writes the summary using that input. Next, students should work in small groups or partnerships to practice the same skills before they are eventually asked to write summaries on their own.

Discussion is an important part of the scaffolding that should occur during summary instruction. As students work in small groups and as individuals, they benefit from articulating the choices they make during the process, and from comparing and contrasting the resulting products. Rhoder suggests that teachers "have the students work in groups, let them have fun, and make sure the activity is non-threatening" in the early stages of summary instruction (502). If students can share ideas orally, either in whole-class or small-group discussions, they are more likely to take the risks that will help them develop the kind of thinking that summarizing requires. In addition, Wormelli asserts that summarizing can occur through drama and other physical activities, as well as visually and artistically. These other activities can function as scaffolds to develop summarizing skills.

Teacher feedback is also an element of scaffolding. Without it, students might produce writing but not really learn the skills of summarizing—and they might persist in ineffective strategies because they are getting credit for them. They need feedback as part of the learning process. The problem: how to give that feedback? As Bushman asks, "Who wants to read the same paper 150 times?" (138). And I add: even if I did read the same paper 150 times, would I want to comment on each one? No! To solve the problem, both Bushman and Kissner suggest that students can be helpful in giving some of the feedback needed for learning. By not leaving the peer feedback open, by guiding it to a certain extent, the teacher is still providing scaffolding for students' summarizing. Kissner offers the following suggestions to show how to combine teacher input with student feedback:

- Consider what aspect of summary writing you want students to focus on for the peer evaluation. This might mean that students should focus on succinctly stating the main idea, or generalizing the supporting details thoroughly. The "target criteria" depends on what each teacher notices about students' summary writing at that point. Put the "target criteria" on the top of a handout or transparency with directions for the peer evaluation and then teach a short mini-lesson on it to refresh students' understanding before they evaluate it in another's summary. (138)

- On each peer response, require the students to sign their name and write one positive aspect of the summary. (139)

- As part of the peer evaluation, create some criteria that are unique to the particular summary. So, if students are summarizing from a novel, one task for the peer might be to identify a place in the summary that could benefit from the use of a character's name or to underline a place that could use character details more effectively. With other types of summaries, peers might be asked to highlight details that are extraneous to the summary or to circle words or ideas that are repeated unnecessarily. (138–40)

- For special problems in student summaries, ask students to do something more. So, for example, if students are not including many main ideas, peers could be instructed to "put a star above every main idea from the text." If students receive their summaries back with only one star, they know immediately that they need to add main ideas. Likewise, they could be instructed to "highlight phrases that come directly from the text" as a way to identify that they are not putting enough of the summary into their own words. (140)

These and similar visual prompts linked to specific problems can provide the effective feedback that students need as they develop their summarizing skills.

Besides using classroom procedures as scaffolds, texts can also be part of the scaffolding. Anderson and Hidi offer this for us to consider:

> The characteristics of the text are important. It is easier to select important ideas from certain types of text, such as narratives, than from others, such as expositions. Also, the longer the text, the more judgments are needed to decide which ideas are important. (26)

Learning to summarize with familiar material or familiar genres first can be crucial to developing more effective summarization skills. When students summarize, they identify and restate main ideas, select important supporting details, decide what is unnecessary and therefore can be left out, and generalize from examples. All of this takes a lot of thought. If students are also working with unfamiliar genres or unfamiliar content, the task becomes huge. Students might be subject to cognitive overload. But if they can practice summarizing, or skills related to summarizing, on familiar material or known texts, they are more likely to develop competence with those skills. That competence means that as they move on to unfamiliar or challenging texts, they are able to focus more on the texts and less on the skills required for summarizing.

Kissner suggests following an order of increasing difficulty in selecting the texts used to teach summarizing. She begins with "single paragraphs with [an] explicit main idea at the beginning" before moving to "single paragraphs with [an] explicit main idea in another location" (41). When students are adept at summarizing these texts, Kissner moves to "multiparagraph pieces with an explicit main idea" before finally using "poorly written pieces" (41). With this progression, students are able to accomplish the tasks of summarizing without facing too-difficult texts too early in their learning.

Teachers should also consider the clarity of structure available in any text we choose. Casazza urges selection from "content textbooks or periodicals," authentic texts instead of artificial ones such as those written specifically to teach students summary writing (203). Textbooks and periodicals are written with structures and textual features that guide the reader. These structures encourage students in the skills essential for summarizing. Teacher-developed exercises can be either too hard to too simple to provide the scaffolding that students need. In addition, if students see summarizing as an exercise, they may lose motivation or interest. Authentic texts can provide real-life purposes for summarizing. For example, students might enjoy collecting reviews of familiar movies or video games and then summarizing three or four reviews to reach a general conclusion: what do most reviewers say about the quality of this movie or game? In this way, students are working with texts that are generally clearly written about content that is somewhat familiar.

It's also useful to consider the presence or absence of texts during summary writing. Research has shown that early in the process of learning to summarize, it's important for students to have the text they are summarizing with them as they do the work of summary writing. Certainly there are times when we use summaries as a way to assess students' understanding of the material they've read. However, during instruction in summary writing, this is not optimal. Again, the cognitive load of working through the steps of summarizing, and at the same time having to recall information that is no longer available, can be overwhelming. While students are learning to summarize, they should have access to the texts they are summarizing (Anderson and Hidi; Kissner).

Applications

Finding Main Ideas

One way I've helped my students learn to identify the main idea is by using a pattern found in Brown's *The Important Book*. In her book, Brown identifies several objects common to a child's life—grass, rain, apples, spoons—and then explains them following a repeated frame. Each page begins with "The most important thing about [. . .] is [. . .]" followed by a list of other important characteristics of the item being explained. Each explanation ends with a repetition of the first sentence: "But the most important thing about [. . .] is [. . .]" (qtd. in Dean, *Bringing* 124–25). I read Brown's book to students and ask them to identify the pattern. When I know they understand it, I ask them to write, following the same pattern, about whatever topic we have been studying or reading. Although not all students identify the same aspects as the most important, their writing shows that they understand main ideas—and this short writing is much more interesting than traditional summaries because it is so individualized.

Another activity, this time with a computer program, allows students to identify the main idea visually. With Wordle, it's possible to see—literally—the main idea of a passage. The site first identifies the words in a given passage by word count. Then, in the resulting image it creates, the words appearing with the most frequency are the largest—and words that show up less often are smaller. It's possible to identify the main idea in many texts from the largest words. To show how this works, I pasted a paragraph about camels from Feiler's *Walking the Bible* and requested a twenty-five-word limit (see Figure 2.1). The largest words signal a main idea of CAMEL and LOOKING—in other words, the appearance

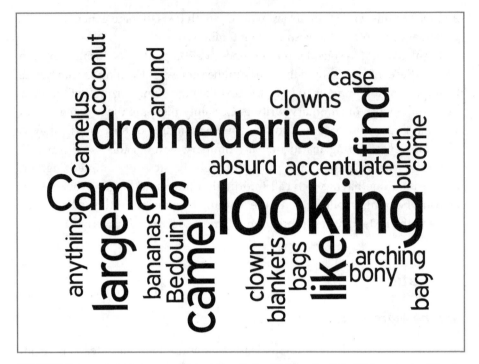

FIGURE 2.1. I created this image with text from Feiler, *Walking the Bible* (252), and using Wordle.

of a camel. Several other words in the image—absurd, bony, clown—suggest the camel's odd appearance as the main idea of the passage. Wordle isn't a foolproof method for identifying a main idea, but it works more often than not, and students find it interesting to use because they can play around with fonts, colors, number of words, and designs. I have them print their Wordle images and then write down the main idea and how they know it. This tool can help students begin to notice how key words and repeated words often signal main ideas. And students can use it for their own writing by pasting in their own texts and making sure that the resulting Wordle shows the main ideas they had intended.

Finally, if students post on class blogs, deciding on tags can help them practice finding a main idea as well. Tags allow blog users to search for all posts related to the same topic, so choosing an appropriate tag is an important task— and a valuable summarizing skill: if I must choose only one or two key words to say what a blog post is about, what would they be? Chris Sloan gives his students this prompt to help them decide on tags: underline all the nouns in the post and consider them as possible tag options. Certainly that suggestion could teach students a lot about how main ideas should be reflected in writing—and something about language, too.

Making Transformations

The idea of generalizing, or condensing ideas into one general one, is a key element of summarizing. *Not Quite What I Was Planning*, edited by Fershleiser and Smith, provides a model for transforming ideas into condensed statements. In this book, people have written about their lives in six words, without being vague or general. Here are several examples:

"Over fifty, still a Boy Scout." Jerry Richstein (57)

"I still secretly read wedding magazines." Lestlie Berryhill (157)

"Still lost on road less traveled." Joe Quesada (56)

"Country girl seeks, finds, abandons city." Jenny Rose Ryan (129)

"Outcast. Picked last. Surprised them all." Rachel Pine (129)

"Poet locked in body of contractor." Marilyn Hencklen (114)

I suggest selecting examples from the book rather than giving the book to students because some memoirs may not be appropriate for all students.

To begin, I think it helps students to choose an example from the ones you provide, and then elaborate on it (this is creative work, of course) to come up with what might have been the original statement that was condensed into the six words. Once we have modeled the process and students have tried it for themselves, they can try the reverse: writing six-word memoirs of their own lives. Beyond asking them to write about their own lives, though, I recommend having students write a six-word memoir for a character in a novel or story they have read. They can write it on a notecard, and we can post all the cards around the room. Then students can try to identify the characters from the memoirs their peers have summarized on the cards. An effective summary will be one that students can connect to the character.

With the advent of Twitter, students are becoming more adept at short communications. Why not use that to our advantage when teaching summary? David Greene, a host on National Public Radio, challenged "Song of the Day" editor Stephen Thompson to meet the 140-character limit imposed by Twitter in his music reviews. Thompson decided that he would also make sure his words were spelled correctly and that his sentences were complete—and he could. As he explains, "I don't think anything should necessarily replace an extremely well-thought-out long-form opinion from somebody who listens to thousands and thousands of records. [. . .] But, at the same time, I want to know what my friends think, as well" ("Twitter"). We can ask students to do the same thing: condense an opinion into exactly 140 characters but keep traditional spelling and punctuation. I've tried this—and I suggest having students work in groups at first. The kind of thinking I had to do was challenging, but working with a group made it doable.

Annotated Bibliography

Frey, Nancy, Douglas Fisher, and Ted Hernandez. "'What's the Gist?' Summary Writing for Struggling Adolescent Writers." *Voices from the Middle* 11.2 (2003): 43–49.

>This article offers some valuable practical advice for teaching summarization to writers who may have difficulty with the concepts associated with it. The authors discuss different types of summaries, provide a sequence of steps for teaching summarizing, name some possible texts for beginning, and present a rubric that teachers might use for assessing the summaries that students write.

Kissner, Emily. *Summarizing, Paraphrasing, and Retelling: Skills for Better Reading, Writing, and Test Taking*. Portsmouth: Heinemann, 2006.

>This very beneficial book is written with examples from junior high school, but the ideas are practical and applicable to a wide range of grade levels. Because Kissner provides so many examples of the worksheets she uses, teachers can adapt the concepts to their own classrooms and grade levels. After making a case for why we should teach summarizing, Kissner presents chapters on each skill related to summary writing: finding a main idea, identifying text structures, and collapsing lists. All in all, a very useful book.

Wormelli, Rick. *Summarization in Any Subject: 50 Techniques to Improve Student Learning*. Alexandria: ASCD, 2005.

>This book begins with a short overview of summarizing and then gives directions for fifty activities that encourage the skills involved in summarizing. The activities are varied to reflect Wormelli's view that students can summarize in many modalities—graphically, orally, and physically, individually and in groups.

Collaborative Writing

3

For excellence, the presence of others is always required.

—*Hannah Arendt*

Overview

I recently conferenced with a student after his paper had failed to meet the expectations of an assignment. I had not only assigned but also taught the process and defined the expectations for the paper: a reversal of a commonly held view on a topic that the student writer knew a lot about but had also researched. This student had written a radio play about aliens. In our conversation, he kept repeating, "But my peers liked the story." Even though they wrote their own papers, students were going to post them to the class wiki, so they had collaborated with peers at several points during the writing process. I asked this student about some of those collaborative conversations. It turned out that his peers *had* somewhat encouraged him to pursue this topic and this format—apparently because they didn't know what else to say. All of his original topic choices had been unsuitable for development in this kind of writing, and when he had completely written a very entertaining radio play—what were they to say? This isn't the kind of thing we were supposed to write? Start over? Although this experience might not represent total collaboration in writing, it probably represents the most common way for collaboration to be used in writing classes. It also represents some of the challenges that arise when peers work together on writing.

Collaboration has a wide range of interpretations in published writing. At one end of a continuum, some suggest that collaboration should refer only to tasks that involve students working together to create coauthored pieces of writing, writing that is created by all the contributors participating in all aspects of that writing. Others consider collaboration to be writing in which students divide the tasks to complete the final product. Still others suggest that collaboration can include processes such as those I described earlier—students working in small groups at several points during the process of writing individually constructed papers. And, at the opposite end of the continuum, regarding what some might consider totally individual writing, are those who say that because we never write in a vacuum, any piece of writing (even if it seems to be written by a single person working alone) is collaborative. This kind of intertextuality is seen by some as a kind of collaboration, even though there is not, physically at least, more than one writer involved in the actual production of the text. In their *Writing Next* report, Graham and Perin assert that collaboration occurs when "students help each other with one or more aspects of their writing" (16), a definition that encompasses most of the range of possibilities for collaborative writing.

Because of this range of possibilities, we don't have to think of collaborative writing as a singular practice, with only one right way to conduct it. What we do need to consider in our teaching, though, is what outcomes we intend to derive from collaboration; the answer to that can create a big difference in the kinds of decisions we make, and in the kinds of tasks we ask students to collaborate on. Although some teachers hope that the outcome of collaboration is better writing (and research suggests that as a possible outcome), some researchers see this as a short-sighted goal: they believe that we should see social goals, including shifts in power, as more valuable. My own students always mention the social interactions in their reflections of collaborative writing, usually more than they mention the quality of the writing they produced together. They recognize the roles they take and that they sometimes feel empowered or silenced, depending on the group and the task. So both writing and social skills are influenced by writing collaboratively.

As goals vary between quality writing and developed social skills, classroom practices of collaborative writing also vary; from all practices, however, students benefit. Writing as a citizen (often online) or as a professional is becoming increasingly collaborative, which suggests that using collaboration in the classroom will help students as they leave school. Research indicates that besides enriching students' future lives by teaching them how to work with others, collaborative writing produces a variety of other benefits, including helping writers generate ideas (Storch 153), develop a sense of audience (Dale 68), recognize the social nature of writing (Gere 3), and learn to take risks (Bishop "Helping" 15). With these advantages available to students, it's no wonder that teachers and researchers are interested in using collaboration to teach writing. But making it work is something else.

Researchers and theorists assert that one reason collaborative writing may not always work is related to the instructor's experience and knowledge. Gere explains that teachers are usually better at using collaborative writing in their classrooms when they have experienced writing collaboratively themselves. With that experience, she notes, these teachers are better able to "anticipate problems and offer more useful guidance" (106). Bishop found that claim to be true in her experience. She explains that she had tried collaborative writing occasionally in her classroom, but didn't get the results she wanted "until I experienced the benefits of coauthoring poetry myself with a fellow poet" ("Co-authoring" 54). After that experience, Bishop felt that she had a better understanding of not only the structures and outward appearances of collaboration, but also the processes and the potential pitfalls—important issues to take into consideration when implementing collaboration in a writing classroom.

Not all of us have personal experience with writing groups, but we may still want our students to benefit from collaborative writing. One point that we need to understand, then, is that the shift to collaboration can shift potential outcomes, too. As Weiner explains, "[M]any teachers who attempt collaborative learning but abandon it are frequently trying to achieve the same ends in groups that they tried to achieve in the more familiar lecture-recitation session" (59). We might anticipate that traditional classroom practice would lead to students' understanding of the course content, yet collaboration might lead to more questions, fewer answers, and unsettled conclusions. It's possible that collaborative efforts might even undermine the concepts that we have instructed, and that students might discover questions that challenge what they've heard from us or what they've read in their text. According to Bruffee (among others), failure to change the ends to match the means suggests that teachers do not understand the theory underlying collaboration, and that they need to learn more about it in order to find success in a collaborative classroom ("Sharing Our Toys" 17).

One way in which a knowledge of theory may affect classroom practice involves the difference between cooperative and collaborative learning. Reither and Vipond, differentiating between these two types of learning, note that using collaboration requires "wholly reconceived and redesigned courses" (855), suggesting that cooperative learning does not disturb the regular structures of classrooms in significant ways. Yancey and Spooner create a continuum with collaboration at one end, individuality at the other, and cooperation in the middle. What these researchers suggest is that compared to collaborative work, cooperative learning is more structured and aligned with traditional classroom structures, and less concerned with changing social relations or creating new knowledge.

Bruffee probably makes the sharpest distinction in his explanation of the two. First, he sees cooperative learning as appropriate to primary or elementary school because it can dissolve competition among students in gaining foundational knowledge. For Bruffee, cooperative learning "guarantee[s] accountability," which he considers important for the kind of learning that occurs in the early grades ("Sharing" 18). When groups are structured by the teacher, when students are assigned roles or at least given roles to choose from, when the teacher can intervene in the working of the group, when the group's processes may be evaluated, and when students are accountable for their work in the group—for Bruffee, that is cooperative learning, not collaboration.

Collaborative learning, on the other hand, is appropriate for secondary or college students because its purpose is to create knowledge that challenges "authority relations" (Bruffee, "Sharing" 18). Collaborative learning, by Bruffee's definition, requires the teacher to leave the learning up to the groups, even if the groups are not functional or even if they are in disagreement. Collaborative learning, for him, challenges authority and structure, and it is appropriate for older students because it's most useful for "questions with dubious or ambiguous answers" (15).

We can see the point made by several of these writers: simply putting students into groups does not make an activity collaborative. Though some feel that true collaboration requires a philosophical stance that isn't always at the core of assigning group work, teachers who implement collaboration should at least be willing to give some authority to students to make decisions for the goals and outcomes of their writing together. Understanding these issues is crucial for teachers to make informed decisions about collaborative writing in their classrooms.

Beyond the teacher's experience with collaborative writing and her understanding of collaborative learning theory, students' feelings also can be a challenge in making collaboration work effectively in a writing classroom. Although they are writing about students' resistance to collaborative writing specifically with wikis, researchers' findings reported by Beach and colleagues reflect the same issues that have always been problematic for teachers implementing any kind of collaborative writing in the classroom (even with pencil and paper):

- Students do not believe that knowledge is socially constructed.
- They dislike groups in which there is a leader and followers.
- They distrust their peers as having less knowledge or writing ability than their teacher.
- They believe that they are not capable of helping their peers.

- They perceive little value in shared talk to improve their writing.

- They disagree with their peers' beliefs, leading to struggles in sharing ideas.

- They respond negatively to poorly designed collaborative groups and assignments.

- They become frustrated with peers who do not contribute. (72)

This list delineates major challenges in implementing collaborative writing. Issues of group construction and functioning, issues of consensus, and issues of expertise and ownership are addressed here. I will discuss other issues later.

Grouping writers—no matter what method teachers choose, assigned or self-selected—can be problematic. Grouping issues include size (of groups), ability, gender, personality, and culture. Some of the decisions for grouping seem like common sense to most teachers: groups shouldn't be so small that one person's absence might be too problematic, or so large that an individual could easily fade into the background. From experience, most of us know that the larger the group, the more complex the issues and the more possibility for ineffective social interactions. Most teachers prefer groups ranging from two to six members; I like groups of three to four generally, but sometimes the task determines the best group size. In terms of creating groups, teachers may consider ability or personality if they know their students well enough. Topping and colleagues generally recommend against putting friends together, and they also don't consider gender an issue in grouping, except when topic choice might make mixed-gender groups uncomfortable. However, Styslinger's study of her students' work in groups caused her to add gender as a consideration in creating groups. Although she explains that she watches to make sure that students are not "subjected to verbally and/or sexually charged battles for dominance," she urges students to have mixed-gender groups to help compensate for gender inclinations (boys having limited interactions and girls getting off task) (55). A key seems to be knowing our students well enough to make wise choices.

Beyond issues of group construction are issues of group functioning. Dale's study of ninth graders functioning in collaborative groups found that high-functioning groups tended to avoid issues of personality, while low-functioning groups spent some of their time together making negative comments (12). As teachers, we should be aware of social concerns within groups, concerns such as students jockeying for leadership roles or even dominating others in the groups. Some teachers assign a "group leader" role, but students don't often like that arrangement—and in some ways it violates the spirit of collaboration and respect for groups' autonomy. On the other hand, younger students may need some structure and, therefore, some roles assigned. We should be aware of issues of interaction (including leadership roles) in groups, and we should help students learn skills for negotiating conflicts that are bound to arise.

Finally, some issues of expertise and ownership among group members may be difficult for us to address. Members of groups often have varying levels of writing abilities, as well as varying abilities in other skills useful to groups: content knowledge, access to information, and social interaction, among others. Because of these inequities, participants in collaborative writing in schools sometimes worry that they "will get a bad grade" because of the writing of others in their group; as a result, they tend to do the work themselves, and the weaker members of the group allow this. Howard suggests one solution to this problem: at the start of the collaborative project, have groups discuss these potential problems and agree (as much as possible) on the consequences that should follow the problematic behaviors if they occur (64). This allows the collaboration to impact not only the writing but also the group dynamics.

Some writers working in groups also worry that their writing will be credited to someone else, that they will lose ownership of their contributions, a conflict that goes back several centuries to when copyright laws took form (Gere). Some teachers try to address these inequities by assigning roles (which may not match the individual strengths, and which Bruffee would argue makes the project cooperative instead of collaborative) in order to avoid having some more adept students do all the work of the group (a real problem for many students assigned to work collaboratively). Other teachers name roles and allow students to select the role they want; this method might create a better match between roles and group members' strengths, but also might allow some students to dominate (so that less dominant students, usually with the fewest strengths of value to the group, are assigned tasks that don't really allow their strengths to be used in the group's task). Some teachers give individual grades based on each student's contribution (a solution that encourages students to divide up the writing task and fail to collaborate effectively—or risk one part of the project being incomplete). There isn't really an easy answer. As with most of the concerns mentioned already, the keys are to (1) consider the task and the needs of the situation (both school goals and the students involved), (2) know the range of problems that can arise, and (3) monitor groups closely so that we can provide strategies at appropriate times to help students overcome problems that do arise. No matter how much we might want to in some stressful situations, we cannot give up on having students collaborate in writing. The benefits to them are just too important.

One current possibility—using computers for collaboration—helps solve some problems that come up in group interactions. For one thing, using digital technologies allows more room for individual strengths to be useful to the group: students who may not be adept at writing might be very good at finding resources online or formatting documents, for instance. Also, research shows that, with computer interactions, "the group solidifies and formulates its document earlier than do groups which collaborate face-to-face by pen and paper writing" (Passig and Schwartz 398). These findings suggest that something about online collaboration smoothes some of the concerns that arise with in-person groups.

It's possible that students' familiarity with online communities may help them in these collaborative writing situations. Using free tools like Google Docs allows writers to work collaboratively away from the classroom at times convenient for them—my students find this appealing when they have trouble getting schedules to mesh. The ease of meeting online might encourage some writers to participate more substantively than they would in other situations. At the same time, Google Docs allows teachers to see both the quality and quantity of individual contributions by checking the revision histories of all documents. Other programs and online sites (such as fan fiction) also encourage writing and collaboration with other writers. All in all, Web 2.0 is providing more ease and opportunity for collaborative writing.

Principles

Preparation

Although there is no one single right way of using collaboration in the classroom, Gere explains that "there are, however, some clear ways for writing groups to go wrong" (102–03). When researchers explain effective collaborative writing—of any kind—in the classroom, they all agree that lack of preparation is probably the most important reason for the failure of the practice. In fact, Gere continues, "[S]chool-sponsored writing groups require months of preparation" (103). Months. And in his research on peer review, Simmons found that it took years for students to develop good peer evaluation skills. Years. That didn't mean that teachers gave up; it simply meant that it was crucial to get started helping students develop the appropriate skills. One of the problems I think most of us might have is that we begin too soon. We need to prepare. Preparation falls into two main areas: first, planning for collaborative work in the classroom, and second, instructing and training groups to function in collaborative situations.

Weiner reminds us that, even though it might appear to be so from outward appearances, "collaborative learning is not unstructured learning" (61). The kind of structure we need to plan for is more than just making sure the physical arrangement of the classroom allows for collaboration, although that is a critical part of planning. It can be discouraging to plan for students to work collaboratively, only to find that the setting doesn't allow students to move into groups that allow for face-to-face conversations while maintaining enough distance to keep conversations from interrupting the work of other groups. Once, when my classroom was flooded after a storm, my classes were temporarily moved to another room with fixed seats arranged in rows. My lesson plan, which involved students collaborating on writing projects, didn't go as well in this new room because it was so difficult to get into groups, not just to talk but to see each other's writing. Still, this kind of planning is surface; the more significant planning involves larger questions of classroom environment.

Collaborative work involves trust—not only student-to-student, but also teacher-to-student and student-to-teacher. So the classroom environment must be prepared from the first day of class. Students need to know that they can feel secure when taking risks in the classroom, that their class is also a community. The classroom should be a place where "put-downs are disallowed," where "people are encouraged to express their ideas without fear of recrimination," and where "diversity is appreciated" (Gere 103). Students should be given opportunities to take responsibility so that they can learn that this, too, is an expectation of the classroom. Flower and Higgins suggest that "the way teachers present or students perceive the 'rules of the game' can make a visible difference in the social interactions" exhibited in groups (46). This means that many subtle aspects of relationships and teacher attitudes might affect the success of collaborative activities in the classroom. Because there is risk involved, I suggest building up to more involved collaborative activities. I try to build trust with students by ceding authority to them in small ways first, so I know that when (or if) I give them more, I won't be sorry about it. I give them choices about who to partner with on in-class, short-term collaborations. I give them choices on topics with some guidance first, and then later give them more autonomy.

Students also need to be able to develop the skills that allow them to be accountable for their own choices, and that allow them to help other students—and this leads to the training that is part of preparation. Simmons's research on peer review groups led him to conclude that "students must be taught to respond helpfully to the writing of their peers. Simple academic ability does not ensure that seniors will know how to read like writers" (689). Students need instruction in working together. Bishop's observation of collaborative work in her classes led her to name five characteristics of successful peer writing groups that can help us direct our instruction:

1. Group successfully involves all members [. . .]

2. Group works to clarify goals and assignments [. . .]

3. Group develops a common vocabulary for discussing writing [. . .]

4. Group learns to identify major writing problems [. . .] as well as minor writing problems [. . .]

5. Group learns to value group work and to see the instructor as a resource [. . .]. ("Helping" 19)

It's interesting to me that three of these characteristics (numbers 2–4) are ones that we can develop as part of whole-class instruction prior to having students work in groups or partnerships. The first and last characteristics, then, could develop from well-structured collaborative projects that would allow students to practice working together.

Whole-class training should involve engaging the class in evaluating writing together. In doing this, though, the writing examples should be the same kind of writing that students are currently working on: memoirs, for example, or letters to the editor. Not generic writing, although that has a place, too, in beginning to consider general writing qualities. Most of the time, however, the characteristics we want students to learn to identify in preparation for their work with others are specific to the writing situation at hand. Although students certainly can learn about general writing qualities, they are more likely to be helpful to their peers if they are attuned to the specifics of the kind of writing under consideration. Otherwise, everything defaults to spelling and grammar.

It's usually better if the piece of writing being evaluated isn't from a current student, because knowing the writer can inhibit the kind of questioning and evaluation we want students to engage in during the whole-class practice. At some distance from the writer, students can learn how to talk about writing before they have to learn how to do it with a real person. I have tried to use my own writing in training my students, but it hasn't always worked as well as I would like. Because of the inherent authority issue, some students are less willing to engage in critiquing a teacher's writing (even if it needs it and I invite it), while others want to belittle it just because it is mine. Graner found that training with anonymous student essays "seemed to free students from their reluctance to make critical comments" (43). I've found the same thing.

I also recommend using the six traits of writing (Education Northwest) as the common vocabulary. The traits—ideas, organization, voice, sentence fluency, word choice, and conventions—apply to all kinds of writing and are concrete enough to give students something real to talk about in the sample essays. They work better than the static abstractions of coherence, unity, and emphasis that have been used for years and that might describe good writing, but don't help students understand how to create good writing. By using the six traits, my students and I can discuss the effectiveness of an introduction for the specific kind of writing we are critiquing (an organizational element), or the effectiveness of detail or evidence (an aspect of ideas). In applying this vocabulary and the inherent concepts, students not only develop a common vocabulary and an ability to talk about writing and its effectiveness, but they also learn characteristics of effective writing that could apply to their own writing.

While training students as a whole class, we can also model the kind of questioning that students should engage in when they are working in collaborative writing groups. Our modeling of questions about writing can help students who otherwise are inclined to give their peers the benefit of the doubt. Speck found that "students will fill in gaps of information" instead of asking for more information from the writer. He argues that a teacher's modeling of good questioning can help students "enlarge their storehouse of peer review questioning techniques" (90). So our training needs to show students the way to discuss and question another's writing choices.

As part of the training, though, we also need to give students opportunities to work collaboratively on low-stakes projects so that they can learn how to share ideas, give feedback, and work together toward common goals. The tasks should still be meaningful (not busy work!), but they don't have to be full-blown, high-stakes projects. I often use small collaborative tasks, such as having small groups list the supporting evidence in an essay or prepare reading quiz questions for other groups, as a way to help students learn to work collaboratively and a way for me to see how they are doing. As we monitor how groups are doing on these smaller collaborative tasks, we will know if it's time to move ahead with more complex collaborations, or if students need more training as a whole class.

Obviously, some aspects of collaboration require students to be mature and responsible. These characteristics can be nurtured in class, through counseling and small-group work that is monitored by the teacher. When we hear a group not functioning as it should, we can refer the students to group guidelines established prior to the group work and ask what students could do to get back on track. By training in this fashion, with the whole class first, then doing collaborative work, and then counseling and practicing with small groups on lower-stakes tasks, we can prepare students for effective collaboration.

Structure

Related to preparation, part of the success of collaborative writing involves making sure that the collaborative situations are well structured. This has two parts: structure in the kinds of tasks assigned for collaboration, and structure in the roles that students can assume to complete those tasks.

As a way to begin to consider effective collaborative tasks, Ede and Lunsford delineate characteristics of *poor* collaborative writing assignments: one person could really do them alone, and they don't provide enough structure for students to successfully complete the task (66). Although collaborative tasks should be work that students couldn't do alone, collaborative writing assignments should not require individual group members to do more than they would if they were writing an individual assignment. Instead, the best collaborative writing assignments take advantage of the group structure: they should need more than one person to come up with ideas, to find information, or to construct a document that will carry the group's meaning to others.

Ede and Lunsford identify three types of tasks that invite collaboration: "'labor intensive' tasks that need to be divided into small subtasks in order to be accomplished effectively and efficiently; 'specialization' tasks that call for multiple areas of expertise; and 'synthesis' tasks that demand that divergent perspectives be brought together into a solution acceptable to the whole group or an outside group" (66–67). With this framework and the previous guidelines, we can begin to consider the kinds of projects that would make effective collaborative writing assignments.

Beginning with short assignments before moving on to longer ones can become part of the training that will help students develop their collaborative skills. Although short collaborations tend to be more specialization or synthesis types of assignments, they can still help students learn how to work together, learn to ask task-specific questions and listen to the answers, and learn to use time well. As an example of one of these short assignments, Speck suggests a synthesis project that asks students to write summaries of their reading, then get into small groups and read each others' summaries, and finally coauthor a summary representing the ideas of the group (24). This task could also take place online, in a wiki or with Google Docs. Gere suggests another short collaborative task that provides a synthesis type of collaboration. After teachers present a writing assignment, they put students into small groups and have them generate ways to approach the writing task. Then, as a class, students share their ideas and consider "the potential and pitfalls of the various possibilities" (61–62). In this small way, students can begin to see that writing isn't only an individual venture, and they can see how collaboration—even verbal collaboration prior to writing alone—can be beneficial to writers.

Trentin explains a collaborative writing assignment that is a little more involved, and could be considered to include all three types of tasks: labor intensive, specialization, and synthesis. Students create a wiki on a topic they all agree on. They individually conduct research, but then work together to plan "the hypertext's general structure and division of work" (46). Once those decisions have been made, students write individual pages on aspects of the topic, but within each of their pages they must show links to pages written by other students in the class. This requirement for links encourages students to consider how their own writing fits with that of others, and how it extends some ideas or relies on ideas established by others. So, even though students write their own pages, both in the planning of the overall document and in the topic decisions, they collaborate with the rest of the class. They also learn to consider how their own ideas relate to others'—and they can negotiate when they find duplication or gaps.

As an example of a collaborative project on a synthesis task, Bishop describes a brief poetry writing activity that "loosely introduces students to co-authoring" ("Co-authoring" 60). She begins by having students "list single words that are important to them in a variety of categories—favorite colors, smells, sounds, months, types of weather, etc. [. . .] primarily concrete nouns" (59). When students have forty to fifty words each, they write their most interesting words on notecards, which they then share in small groups. In groups, they negotiate until they have a common list of ten words, with some from each group member. Next, each group decides on its own composing rules: whether words can change in form, how many words from the list need to be included, and so on. Then each student composes a poem according to the rules before getting back into a group to compare the results.

As collaborative writing tasks become more complex, especially when they involve coauthoring, the need for roles for individual group members and guidance in possible ways to accomplish the task become a vital part of the structure of the assignment. Instead of assigning a leader to a group, a practice Gere discourages (65), we can allow groups to choose a leader. More effective, perhaps, is suggesting a role of manager, someone who ensures that all the other roles or tasks are accomplished on time. The roles for group members should be as task specific as possible, so roles and their names may change from assignment to assignment. It's also important to make sure that the tasks associated with each role should be of value, not just nominal—and as equivalent as possible in terms of what that role contributes to the group task. Finally, the roles suggested by the instructor should not be so encompassing as to take all decision making away from groups.

Young describes a helpful example of balancing assigned roles in the sequence and roles she uses to help students generate a contemporary American poem. Students in groups of four have the following roles: image weaver, who provides two concrete images to the group's poem; language keeper, who brings in five exotic words for the poem; metaphor generator, who supplies two original metaphors or similes; and music maker, who has responsibility for ensuring a sense of music in the poem through the use of alliteration, assonance, or other poetic devices (52). The teacher has students write a series of four poems together, so that individuals in the group can have a turn with each role, and the group learns negotiation skills as well as poetic ones from their work together. Students choose the topic for the poems within a broad category—family relationships, myths, or incorporating a book title, for example—so they make group decisions almost from the beginning. In this case, students aren't generating particularly long texts, so the task isn't labor intensive, but the emphasis on specialization and synthesis helps students learn how collaborative writing can work. Practice with teacher-generated roles can help students consider possible structures for establishing their own roles when they work collaboratively on longer, more complex collaborative writing tasks.

Purposefulness

For collaborative writing activities to be effective, we must make sure that the activities are purposeful, that they are not just gimmicks designed to (as I've heard some teachers give as a reason for "group work") produce fewer papers to grade or give students a chance to do something "fun." Students generally like writing in well-designed collaborative projects, and their enjoyment should not be disparaged. When they enjoy writing, they are more likely to engage in it. But if fun is the only reason—or if our reason is only to end up with fewer papers—then we are less likely to achieve the benefits that research shows for collaboration. Students recognize when we have a valid purpose for our instructional choices; something about our manner suggests our purposefulness. Yes, we will end up with fewer papers to assess, and yes, students should enjoy the writing. But we should make sure that our collaborative writing tasks also reflect the theoretical goals of collaborative writing, and that we evaluate the activities to ensure that those goals are actually being met.

Whether we want to use collaborative writing to shift social and power structures or to help students improve as writers, we need to remember that collaborative learning reflects Bahktin's theories on the social construction of knowledge and it works on Vygotskian principles. Assignments, as Dale explains, should "target teaching to the skills just beyond what a student is presently capable of achieving alone" (2). If that is the case, then students will see how their work with other students enables them to move beyond previous learning and abilities. Additionally, students should reflect on the processes in order to understand how the group's functioning facilitated the learning, and what learning (beyond a specific task or project) they can take with them as they move beyond the classroom.

We should also reflect on the collaborative processes in our classrooms to evaluate the effectiveness of our practices. We could consider these questions:

- Does the activity achieve the intended goals?
- Do students benefit more than they would by doing the work individually?
- Do they gain skills in writing and in working together with others?

This reflection is a crucial part of making sure that our uses of collaboration in our writing classrooms actually achieve the desired benefits and purposes.

Part of ensuring that students see the collaborative work as purposeful often means that we must evaluate that work in some ways, but assigning a grade or evaluative score to a collaborative writing project can be problematic. It's difficult, partly, because of ownership issues mentioned earlier: some students want to be recognized for their individual contributions, and they don't want to get the "same grade" as others in the group. But Howard makes the valid point that assigning individual grades "undermines the purposes of collaboration" in coauthored projects (66). Speck suggests connecting the group's interaction to the assessment, a natural connection, he asserts, because "the quality of group interaction and the quality of the document the group produces are inextricably bound together" (59). I've found this difficult as well. Perhaps a combination of individual and group grades that also reflect group interaction is best, if it fits the nature of the assignment. Whatever method of assessment teachers choose, students should know at the start of the project the criteria by which they'll be evaluated.

Applications

Wikis

A wiki is a website that allows participants to create and modify content. Both teachers and students can post items on the site, creating, as Beach and colleagues explain, "a one-stop site for students to acquire and share information" (79). Once students understand its purpose, they see the wiki as a place to help them in all aspects of their learning and work for class.

According to Beach and colleagues, Ward Cunningham invented wikis in 1995 because he wanted "Web pages that would be readily revised by a number of different users" (75). Numerous wiki platforms are open for teachers today, many without cost. I like PBworks, but I've also used Wetpaint. Both provide "training" through follow-up emails, and both are easy to set up in the basic form, even without the tutorials that are available. Some schools have access to Moodle, which has a wiki built into it. Beach and colleagues also recommend Wikispaces and Jotspot. If parents are concerned with privacy issues, I suggest making sure that the highest level of privacy is engaged. With those settings, teachers don't have to worry about outsiders accessing a site or posting on it.

The benefits of using wikis to establish a collaborative classroom and to promote collaborative writing are plentiful. First, because students have access to everyone else's work through the wiki, they tend to care more about their writing. They want to make sure that other students will enjoy (and understand) their writing. Beach and colleagues suggest that besides benefitting students' thinking and writing, "wikis can be used to improve students' reading ability" because students know that the text is participatory. In that way, writing for a wiki often seems more engaging, and students approach it differently (81).

Wikis can also contribute to collaborative writing and learning in our classrooms in a variety of ways. Deciding how to use them requires remembering their purpose: "The actual purpose of a Wiki is not to simply communicate information, but to invite participation at the level of input that will contribute to the understanding and application of the information shared" (Reynard par. 6). The point is to make a shared space for knowledge making; understanding this is key to deciding which of the possible uses will be most effective for an individual class or situation. That said, here are some possibilities for teachers:

- Have students create wikis based on the course content, with links to other sites that could contribute information to the course material. So if they are studying Dickens's *A Tale of Two Cities*, for example, students might create a wiki with pages on the French revolution or the guillotine that include links to other informational sites.

- Use wikis to create course texts. I have found this beneficial. Students' individual writing is posted to the wiki and then referenced in class and on tests, with the expectation that students will read and respond to their peers' work just as they might to more traditional (published) texts. Again, the content comes from the course, and students can contribute how-to pages, such as ways to prewrite for a personal narrative or revision strategies for letters to the editor.

- Use wikis as publication sites. Students can have access to everyone's writing, either before polishing or after. My students like to see how other students respond to an assignment or interpret a particular prompt. This helps them generate ways to revise and refine their own responses.

- Have students work together to create study guides that are posted on the wiki to help other students study. For instance, have different groups make study guides for various assigned chapters of a novel; or assign each student group to be responsible for the study guide for one novel over the year.

- Have students post drafts of writing on the wiki, and then ask other students to go online to make comments and suggestions for revision. This is especially effective if students have been prepared, in some of the ways described in this chapter, to be effective responders to others' writing.

- Use some wiki spaces as a place for collaborative writing in the more traditional sense: groups of students working together on a single piece of writing. The wiki keeps track of who contributes what in the process.

It's evident that wikis allow for a range of collaborative processes, from coauthoring to peer reviewing to simply sharing writing through "publication." For more ideas about using wikis, visit the "Wiki Walk-Through" on the Teachers-First website.

Peer Review

Peers can be used for a variety of purposes during revision. Providing an audience for students' writing is one key purpose because it helps students learn to consider other perspectives. Speck also believes that peer review of writing can "strengthen students' critical-thinking skills" and motivate them to improve their writing (89). Storch adds that peer review can give students "an opportunity to compare ideas and to learn from each other different ways of expressing their ideas" (166). Styslinger notes "an increased sense of community" (50). But beyond those worthy goals—or maybe as a consequence of them—is the primary purpose of helping students improve their writing: peer feedback should give students ideas about how their writing communicates its meaning, and how that communication could be improved.

This goal isn't often realized, however, when students give feedback on others' writing. The reasons for the lack of success often reside in one significant factor: students' trust in other students' abilities to provide effective feedback, or what Graner refers to as "the blind leading the blind" (40). Additionally, though, students don't often know how to talk about writing, or they don't want to make negative comments about a peer's work. As Speck notes, students "tend to prize friendship and goodwill among their classmates, so they are unwilling to risk making their peers angry with them" (87). As part of preparing for peer review writing, teachers must help students develop trust in their peers' abilities, gain the ability to talk effectively about writing, and know what elements of writing they can talk about. I addressed some of these issues in my discussions of whole-class instruction, but some of the preparation for peer review happens as a result of the ways that we practice peer reviews in the classroom.

What follows are some suggestions for improving peer reviews of writing. These ideas build on the principles associated with collaborative writing that I explained earlier: preparation, structure, and purposefulness.

- Require students to read their writing aloud. This can be noisy, but it's good for students to read aloud to an audience what they have written. First, it helps them hear problems that they might not notice during a silent reading. Second, it helps them consider what their writing sounds like to an audience—this is even more immediate than just thinking about audience while writing. Howard explains that reading aloud is also a good way to develop audience roles: "If group members silently read the paper themselves, marking on it, they inevitably assume teacherly roles, becoming doubters and critics. If, however, they listen while the writer reads aloud, they more readily assume audience roles and can better focus on their responses" (60).

- If possible, let students have a printed copy of the paper being read aloud. DiPardo and Freedman report on Nystrand's research, which suggests that the combination is most effective: when students can both see and hear a text, they are "more likely to attend to higher order considerations [. . .] whereas merely listening results in more attention to lower order problems" (138). With technology, the possibility of multiple copies is easier now than in the past, but teachers still must consider how many students have access to printers; if that number is low, teachers would need to print copies, which could be problematic. Still, given the potential benefits, I recommend doing this if possible.

- After students have read their writing, ask them to listen to comments from group members without responding to the comments or defending the paper. This silence prevents students from explaining what they "meant to say," which happens often in my students' interactions in peer evaluation groups. It's important to emphasize that the writer's silence in this stage of peer evaluation does not mean that the writer agrees with the comments or will follow all the suggestions; instead, it's just a time to listen to others respond. I suggest writing down the comments or jotting notes. When I have worked in such groups, my notes remind me of what impressed me in the feedback.

- Train students in how to talk about writing by first making a distinction between response and evaluation. I've had some trouble with this because asking for *response* often results in general "I liked it" statements that do no one any good, or what Simmons terms *cheerleading* (685). He explains that a response should "assure the writer of what to do next" (691), not simply state how it made the reader *feel* (or think she should feel). Instead, Simmons notes that "one early sign of progress in writing workshops occurs when students begin to demand more from their peers than 'I liked your story'" (685). If students want to say that they liked the writing, I encourage them to follow that statement with an explanation, or with a reference to a specific passage they liked and why. This specificity forces the student to make a thoughtful response and offers good feedback to the writer: if something works well in one spot, it could work in others.

- Make sure students know that commenting is substantive, not cosmetic. Simmons suggests making sure that "students think of writing as something other than getting the words right" (689). Sometimes this is challenging because it seems that the easiest elements to teach—and the most noticeable in student writing—are issues of editing: spelling, grammar, punctuation. But students don't develop as writers without getting past the idea that the only response is to local-level concerns. If they learn to consider global concerns, they are more likely to look at ideas, organization, voice—the areas we hope they will respond to in each other's writing. Simmons recommends a strategy he terms *text playback*, asking the reader to summarize the ideas of the text, thus "focus[ing] on the ideas or organization of the text" (686). Strategies like this can help students move away from surface-level concerns in their responses.

- Although there is some disagreement on this, consider providing students with printed prompts to guide their reviews of others' writing. DiPardo and Freedman are reluctant to use what they call "editing sheets" because they fear that these diminish student interaction, and in extreme cases, put students in the role of teacher (127). I believe that much of this fear is related to poorly developed peer-response prompts. Weiner urges the use of prompts because, in his experience, "without clear guidelines, students will just pat each other on the back, attack each other counterproductively, or fall silent" (57). Graner uses a checklist that he notes "was tailored to the particular assignment" and which, for each item on the checklist, "called for some kind of action, either underlining, circling, or bracketing some section or rating an aspect of the essay on a four-point scale (no middle point for the uncommitted)" (42). I agree that prompts should be specific to the particular writing task at hand. Checklists, though, should be carefully constructed to avoid being reduced to a point of the presence or absence of an element in the writing: *Is there a topic sentence for each paragraph? Underline the thesis statement.* These can be appropriate exercises if students are also asked, as a follow-up, to consider the quality or effectiveness of the element. I prefer more open-ended prompts that are linked to students' work during their writing process, and that reflect their understanding of the product goals for the type of writing they are doing and reviewing. So, for instance, if a product goal for a persuasive letter to the editor is to acknowledge potential opposing views, then a prompt for the peer evaluation should not be, *Does the writer acknowledge opposing views?* but instead, *Highlight where the author acknowledges opposing views. What other opposing views might the writer consider? How might the writer more adequately counter the opposing view that is included?*

- Allow time for the peer review process. Time, first, for training and learning to work together. But also, time for discussion. Nystrand and Brandt's research showed that they could predict the kinds of revision that students would engage in based on their talk in their groups: "In a very basic way, the *extent* of the discussion predicted the extent of revision. If a discussion was short, perfunctory, or focused on surface correctness, subsequent revisions were typically perfunctory and limited to surface changes. On the other hand, extended talk typically led to more revisions, and talk that focused on clarifying and elaborating specific points in a draft more predictably yielded revisions at the level of genre, topic, or commentary (and sometimes all three) (219–20). Certainly, the time allotted for discussion of writing can't just be a free-for-all. Students need to be trained—and they can be—and should be guided effectively to understand that these substantive elements are the kinds of things they discuss in their groups. But if we hurry them along, it's possible that we are, inadvertently perhaps, also suggesting that they don't have substantive comments to make to each other. We might, then, undermine our own efforts. As Nystrand and Brandt state, "Functional revisions seem to depend on functional discussions" (220). Our work in preparing assignments, classrooms, and students can go a long way toward ensuring these kinds of functional discussions.

Annotated Bibliography

Beach, Richard, Chris Anson, Lee-Ann Kastman Breuch, and Thom Swiss. *Teaching Writing Using Blogs, Wikis, and Other Digital Tools*. Norwood: Christopher-Gordon, 2009.

> This book provides valuable information about collaboration because of the nature of digital tools: they are almost all based on collaboration. Students understand the participatory nature of most digital technologies. Our job as teachers is to help them use digital technology for learning and writing more effectively; this book can help us do that. And it's useful at times when a teacher feels that the tide has swept past her, leaving her stranded, with too much to learn to catch up. With its accompanying wiki (yes, a wiki that readers can add to!), this is a rich resource written for digital immigrants.

Speck, Bruce. *Facilitating Students' Collaborative Writing*. San Francisco: Jossey-Bass, 2002.

> In very readable style, this book explains briefly some of the theory behind collaborative writing. Beyond explaining the benefits, Speck also addresses the challenges, and gives practical advice for dealing with those challenges. He explains a range of collaborative assignments, from short, in-class work to longer, out-of-class projects that address these primary issues: creating effective assignments, forming and training groups to work well, using computers in collaboration, and assessing collaborative writing.

Specific Product Goals

4

"Cheshire-Puss," she began, rather timidly [...] "Would you tell me, please, which way I ought to go from here?"

"That depends a good deal on where you want to get to," said the Cat.

"I don't much care where—" said Alice.

"Then it doesn't matter which way you go," said the Cat.

—Alice's Adventures in Wonderland, *Lewis Carroll*

Overview

I have a *Peanuts* comic strip that shows Sally writing a paper. It's vague, wandering writing about Memorial Day. In the final frame, Sally turns to Charlie Brown and explains, "This is the sort of theme where you either get an 'A' or an 'F'!" When a student feels that way about a piece of writing, the situation is probably typical of what Soven calls the "contract of vagueness" (135). The essence of this contract is that teachers give vague writing assignments and students don't ask questions beyond the basic "How long does it have to be?" Soven gives the example of a teacher telling students to write about snow. With that vague prompt, what should students write? A poem describing the emotion associated with snow or a description of it? A story about an experience with snow? A report on what creates snow? An argument asserting that snow sports are more dangerous than water sports? (I don't know if they are—I'm just making a point here.)

When the contract of vagueness is in effect, what happens mostly is that students write something (if they care about their grades or what the teacher thinks) and hope for the best, but, like Sally, they have no idea if they're close to the target expectations. With this kind of vague writing assignment, teachers are often disappointed that what they must read is not what they had hoped for. Even though the teacher is really at fault for not having communicated more specific expectations, it often seems that students are blamed for not figuring out what they were supposed to do.

How *do* writers know what to do in different writing situations? How do they figure out the expectations, not just in school, but in a variety of situations in and out of school? Bawarshi suggests that genre theory can help writers understand the anticipated expectations—product goals—of a particular situation, and can help writers determine how best to achieve success in a specific writing task. Genre theory explains that these expectations arise out of the social situation in which the writing occurs; expectations of genre help writers understand how to go about the writing, even where to begin generating ideas.

Just think how, as writers, we limit our thinking in specific directions when we know what we are going to be writing: if it's a grocery list, we don't worry about paragraphs, but we do think about what we're planning for dinner; if it's a memo to employees about a new department policy, we think about conventions, but we also think about how to explain change that some might not understand or appreciate and the appropriate tone to use. Understanding genre can help establish product goals. And product goals can help shape writing, from our earliest inclination to write until we've completed the writing task.

I understand the potential problem that some teachers might have with product goals. For one thing, if the product goals are too constrained ("In the first sentence, tell . . ."), students don't get to make the writing choices vital to their development as writers. If goals are too vague ("Write about friendship"), students have no idea what to do. Hillocks, in commenting that state tests often encourage formulaic writing, suggests that ineffective product goals (along with the specific situation) are partly to blame (*Testing*). In those testing situations where product goals (such as "developed ideas") are so general as to be meaningless, we can see the potential problems associated with some teachers' idea of what *product goals* mean. From these same testing situations, we might also begin to see how product goals need to be framed (both in terms of what they are, and in how they are integrated into the writing process) to help avoid the potential pitfalls that interrupt students' writing development. These situations help us realize why it's so important that the product goals we provide or negotiate with students are specific enough to move them toward success, but not so limiting that students' writing abilities can't develop.

Because students sometimes have trouble setting appropriate product goals for their writing, some researchers suggest that teachers set goals for students

(Ferretti, MacArthur, and Dowdy). This may be an appropriate choice when the genre is unfamiliar enough that students wouldn't know what kinds of product goals to make. Another situation in which teachers might set goals for students could be when students are still learning how to develop effective product goals—for instance, if students are inclined to look at goals as formulas, or in such general terms that the goals have little value. However, with other students or in other situations, it may be more appropriate to work with students in selecting and setting specific product goals, as Graham and Harris suggest (*Making*). We can conference with students and assist them in setting appropriate product goals, providing scaffolding to help them move toward independent goal setting. The decision about who sets goals may depend on each situation and what students need in that situation.

Students can learn to develop product goals independently by first learning how to use writing models to do what others have called *reading like a writer*. For this, I have used an excerpt from Cisneros's *The House on Mango Street* titled "My Name" (Dean, *Strategic* 65–68). When I read the excerpt with my students, I ask them to notice the ways Cisneros talks about her name. We list examples like these: not telling her name until the third or fourth paragraph; talking about the person for whom she was named; comparing her name to colors or sounds; explaining how she feels about her name; and identifying other names she wishes she had. Then I ask students to select one or two of the options we have listed and use them as a guide when they write about their own names. Essentially, students use the model to establish individual product goals for their writing. So, although the writing is all their own, they now have some ideas for drafting that they didn't have before. The product goals give them a plan and, for some students, a glimmer that they might do something they hadn't considered before. They can, therefore, create more effective writing. Overmeyer observes that "in classrooms full of product-oriented talk [. . .] students can set meaningful goals for themselves" (59). I agree. If we surround students with talk about effective writing, they can learn to set goals independently, advancing their development as writers.

Product goals are most effective either before drafting (as in the Cisneros example) or during revision. Experienced writers, who understand how genre and situation interact, are more likely to set product goals prior to drafting, and then adjust those goals as they write. Teachers know from experience what Page-Voth and Graham found in their research: novice writers pay little attention to goals before writing. They usually just begin, with no plan to consider their writing situation or to guide development of content or structure. Instead, they use the practice that Scardamalia and Bereiter call knowledge telling: they simply begin writing, and what they generate in one sentence prompts the idea for the next sentence—and so on, until they exhaust the chain of thought. As can be expected, this process is not very useful for producing successful writing.

In contrast, Youth Voices, an online student writing site, provides "guides" (similar to product goals) for many of the types of writing that students post there. Although some students may follow the guides exactly, many don't. But it's obvious that the guides offer help for most of the writers. When I compare posts on this site with those on other sites, Youth Voices shows much better, more substantive writing. It's clear that the guides—product goals—help to improve writing, and that's probably because they help students avoid simple knowledge telling.

In addition to using product goals prior to writing, experienced writers are more likely than novices to use product goals to help them during revision. At that time, they compare their writing to the product goals associated with the genre, noting places where these fail to match up, and then revise according-ly. Page-Voth and Graham review several studies to show that setting product goals that direct attention to "substantive concerns" enhances poor writers' revi-sions (230). Graham, McArthur, and Schwartz support those conclusions and note specifically that shifting students' focus away from surface concerns during revision could be influenced by the goals set during revision (237). De La Paz, Swanson, and Graham found that even "very young children can make sub-stantive revisions when teachers provide [. . .] support for revising through the questions they ask during writing conferences" (448). In other words, questions or directions that guide students to consider product goals during revision can benefit even the youngest or most inexperienced writers and can help all writers consider more than surface features during revision.

Many product goals made both before writing and during revision are relat-ed to genre. Prior to writing, a writer's knowledge of genre influences the writ-ing by providing "an organized schema" for that writing (McCutchen, Teske, and Bankston 460). Research shows that "even skilled writers may resort to less mature strategies" when they lack genre knowledge to provide the product goals that could help them write (461). We often see this behavior when students are asked to write literary analysis but turn in plot summaries. Unfamiliar with the characteristics of analysis (its product goals, if you will), students resort to a simpler task, retelling.

Because current genre theory asserts that genre is more than form, prod-uct goals related to genre should consist of more than formatting characteristics such as placing a thesis statement at the end of the introductory paragraph in an essay, or formatting margins for an inside address on a business letter. Donovan and Smolkin report that how much teachers know about genre is key, suggesting that a teacher's understanding of genre as more than its formal characteristics will benefit students as they develop product goals (140). When teachers know that genres entail more than form, they can help students consider issues of content, tone, and language, which are also potential product goals for the genres that students are writing.

This deeper understanding of genre is reflected in an example Kittle recalls. When he asked his college students to write a multimodal literacy narrative, they didn't know what to do. Even though these were experienced writers, they had little idea of how to approach the writing because the genre (telling a story through words, pictures, and sound) was unfamiliar to them. As he had with traditional print versions of the assignment, Peter Kittle found that he needed to provide models of the assignment so that students "could inductively determine the genre features of a multimodal document" (168). In other words, prior to drafting, his students needed some product goals. After viewing a sample multimodal literacy narrative several times, his students developed the following product goals:

- Include a compelling narration of a story;
- Provide a meaningful context for understanding the story being told;
- Use images to capture and/or expand upon emotions found in the narrative;
- Employ music and other sound effects to reinforce ideas;
- Invite thoughtful reflection from their audience(s). (169)

As is evident from this list, these product goals—as all effective ones should—do not shut down writing or writers' choices. Instead, they provide writers with options for all aspects of the genre—form, tone, content, and so on—that will lead them to successful completion of the task. And these product goals can be used again during revision to consider avenues to improve the writing.

What are the benefits of setting these goals? Schunk and Swartz find that setting goals is one of the most influential behaviors related to task performance because goals help us plan—and therefore, write. Other researchers find that goal setting provides additional benefits for writing: increasing writing output (Page-Voth and Graham 230); improving "writing performance and behavior" (230); helping students "see the possible consequences of their writing decisions" (Boehnlein 4); and enhancing motivation (Ferretti, MacArthur, and Dowdy). As is evident, setting product goals can aid developing writers in many ways. And they benefit me as I work with developing writers, too, because product goals suggest elements of writing that I can consider for class instruction.

Some teachers are concerned with the explicitness of considering product goals. Despite research showing that direct teaching of genres and structural patterns benefits writers (Donovan and Smolkin), some teachers feel more comfortable with what's sometimes called a "natural" approach to writing instruction that leaves much to students' intuition and experience. Williams and Colomb, in response to Freedman's claims against explicit teaching of writing, argue instead that "writing is not rendered immune to explicit teaching simply because it is a social action that requires tacit knowledge" (254). They continue that "the question is not whether students get by without explicit teaching, but whether explicit teaching improves their performance" (255). As teachers, we shouldn't be afraid to provide the guidance that knowledgeable mentors should provide. Only when instruction is so explicit as to shut down writing options should we be concerned.

When I mentioned the aspect of product goals from Graham and Perin's *Writing Next* to another teacher at a professional development experience, he referred to Hillocks's 1986 study of writing instruction. Explaining that Hillocks found the environmental method to be most beneficial, this teacher took exception to the concept of product goals as part of effective writing instruction. To him, product goals reflected models-based or scales-focused instructional methods, both of which Hillocks found less effective. Williams and Colomb note that what Hillocks describes as the environmental approach actually involves the teacher using "specific criteria in the context of active problem solving" (256). In fact, the inquiry approach to instruction, supported by Hillocks, involves instruction of specific strategies of writing (Hillocks, *Research* 181). In other words, what this teacher interpreted as a natural approach—with teachers keeping hands off—was not really what Hillocks intended. Instead, a certain amount of explicit instruction may actually be more effective. What I wanted to tell this teacher is that we don't have to be afraid to be the "Teacher with a capital *T*," as Atwell calls it (*In the Middle* 25). We don't have to fear giving some instruction along the way as students learn to write. It's true that we can all learn many things without instruction; but we should consider how much better we might learn them—how much faster and more effectively—if we have a little guidance during our learning process. That's the point of product goals: to provide guidance.

Principles

Effective Goals

To benefit writing, product goals should be good ones. That is, effective goals should be specific, not too distant, and attainable.

Specific goals help writers know how to plan, and help ensure that "the writer knows what he or she is striving to accomplish, providing additional structure to the writing task by making it better defined and directing attention to important aspects or features of the composition" (Page-Voth and Graham 230). Because writing is what Ferretti, MacArthur, and Dowdy refer to as an "ill-defined" task (694), writers need to have specific goals to know how to proceed with it. In a study comparing specific and general goals, Graham, MacArthur, and Schwartz found that students given specific goals "made greater improvements in the quality of their compositions than did students assigned a general revising goal" (237). Peck found that telling students to make their papers "better" was less effective in getting them to engage revising strategies beyond simple correction of surface concerns. On the other hand, a more specific prompt (to interpret the purpose differently) helped "elicit more instances of problem-solving behavior than" the more general prompt (10). Concerns arise when a goal is too specific: a topic sentence is the first sentence of every paragraph or the essay must start with a rhetorical question. Such statements are not really goals. They are formulas. And they don't allow writers to decide what's best for the writing. Goals need to be specific enough to guide writing without closing off writing options.

When goals are too far in the future, students are less likely to be able to meet them—and in fact, distant goals may actually discourage students from working toward them because students are unsure what to do with such goals. Ferretti, MacArthur, and Dowdy suggest that teachers should help student writers break long-term goals into feasible chunks. Instead of setting a goal to write a good persuasive essay—a goal that is both vague and distant—setting subgoals such as writing two good reasons in support of an opinion or writing an effective counter-argument would be more likely to help students develop as writers. When goals are related to what writers are doing at the moment, or what researchers call *proximal goals*, students are more likely to be able to meet them and feel good about their work because they see progress toward the overall goal.

Realistic, attainable goals can't be too hard *or* too easy. Schunk and Swartz note that "goals viewed as challenging but attainable increase motivation and learning better than goals perceived as very easy or too difficult" (225). Most of us understand how goals that are too difficult can shut down student motivation. But goals that are too easily attained may be as problematic as goals that are too hard. For one thing, Page-Voth and Graham found that when students find a goal "well within [their] grasp," they tend to avoid using a strategy, and they complete the work without learning anything new (231). A goal that is too easy just doesn't help students develop as writers. Either they think they are doing fine, or they fail to engage any new strategies of process or product. At the same time, beginning writers are often unable to set reasonable goals, either in specificity, in proximity, or in appropriateness.

Supported Goals

An important aspect of making product goals effective in a writing class and with students is the teacher's support of students in the goal setting and goal application process. Ferretti, MacArthur, and Dowdy conducted research suggesting that goals, by themselves, may not be enough to get the best results in writing. They found that "the provision of explicit goals, along with intensive, scaffolded instruction" was the most effective in students' development as writers (700). In other words, we need to teach product goals *and* support students as they develop and implement their own goals. De La Paz, Swanson, and Graham suggest that this support can come through holding writing conferences, teaching students how to develop their own goals, and modeling the use of goals in our writing.

As teachers, we also need to help students see the difference between product goals and the actions that writers take to achieve those goals. "If I make a goal to eat healthier food, my plan for this is often just a restatement of the goal: I will eat more healthy food. My plan for getting more exercise is to—surprise, surprise—get more exercise" (Overmeyer 59). Instead of only making goals with students, we should also help them differentiate between the goal and the steps to accomplish it. For example, a goal may be to write a more effective introduction. The plan of action is what I need to do to be able to achieve that goal. This is where writing strategies come in. If I have strategies, I will use one—reading models as examples—until I notice a series of traits that I can use to write my own interesting introduction. For instance, I might see that I can pose a problem but put off resolving it, or tell a story but delay its conclusion, thus engaging the reader. Now I can reach my goal of writing an effective introduction—but my plan of action, my strategy, helped me. It wasn't the goal itself. When students set goals, we must help them also plan ways to reach those goals, and some of that help might involve teaching them strategies to achieve goals.

Teacher support will be particularly important when product goals are related to unfamiliar genres. We may need to facilitate multiple experiences with a genre so that students can begin to see the possible product goals for the genre. Even when we provide the genre's characteristics as product goals—for example, "statement of premise or belief, supporting reasons, refutation of claims that can be made against the initial premise, and conclusion" as product goals for argument writing (Perin 251)—students benefit from seeing these characteristics as they occur in the genre. Without seeing these product goals in actual writing, students are unlikely to implement the goals in their own writing. When students read a new genre, we may need to guide them to notice the characteristics that could constitute product goals as students eventually write their own versions of a genre.

One aspect of support relates to the place of goals in the curriculum. As Graham, MacArthur, and Schwartz point out, "[D]espite its considerable potential, goal setting will have little impact on writing instruction if it cannot be integrated into existing programs" (239). In other words, goal setting needs to be woven into the fabric of a class, made a part of all the writing work of a class, and not just considered at the last minute, or with only one writing assignment, or only with revision. Overmeyer's observations of classes caused him to conclude that the "ongoing talk in the writing classroom" was essential to students' goal setting (59). Goal setting derives from the overall work with writing in the classroom. As students come to see product goals as an integral part of writing and the work in our classes, they will more likely use them to improve their writing.

Task-Appropriate Goals

In addition to being specific, goals need to be relevant to the task. As research by Williams and Colomb shows, it's probable that even experienced writers need to understand the specific features of a kind of writing in order to produce effective products of that type. Supporting that finding, Nystrand and Brandt report that "genre appears deeply implicated in both the motivations and effects" of students' revisions (223). So, if writers need to know the features of the texts they are producing, the product goals that help them do that will be related to specific genres.

To formulate task-specific goals, we must consider the ways that goals can be adapted to fit different genres. For example, students might work on introductions or conclusions, making product goals to create more engaging introductions or more effective conclusions. But even though most genres have both introductions and conclusions, the shape and style of these vary from genre to genre. The introduction to a story is very different from the introduction to an informative essay, so a product goal for an effective introduction, although fairly specific, isn't task appropriate enough to provide the kind of benefit that the best product goals could.

What this means is that we must consider the genres we ask students to write—and we need to know the characteristics that will make strong product goals. At the same time, we don't want to suggest product goals that close down student writers' choices. All genres allow for flexible responses to the situation that the genre addresses. Because of that, task-appropriate product goals should be specifically related to the genre, but not so narrow that they become formulaic or restrictive.

I've been scoring Advanced Placement English language exams for seven years. After a recent experience doing this, I was thinking about the responses to the rhetorical analysis question that I had been reading for several days. I had just read an excellent response that happened to be written using the five-paragraph structure. It wasn't obvious; it was subtle. And it was thoughtful. I had also read many ineffective five-paragraph essays; they had been plentiful. What I realized from this experience is that if we think too narrowly about writing, we might be inclined to suggest product goals that not only stop students from making choices that generate effective writing, but we also might create different problems. For example, if we tell students to organize their writing in a specific way, we may prevent them from expressing their ideas in a better way, perhaps even one that we might initially reject. Instead, if we consider the genre, we could consider product goals like this for a rhetorical analysis: *Include examples from the text to show the tools being used in the text, and then be sure to explain HOW the tools achieve their effect, instead of simply stating that they do*. With this product goal, students would be more likely to write an effective response that still allows them to make choices about which kind of structure would best help them do that.

Applications

Analyzing a Writing Prompt and Rubric for Prewriting Goals

One way that students can benefit from setting product goals is to set them prior to writing—and this can often occur when students learn to analyze a writing prompt or rubric to understand what is being asked of them.

First, students need to consider the genre: what are they being asked to write? A problem occurs when the task is general: *paper* or *essay* or *response*, for example. Any of these words can mean different things to different teachers, so students may not know from our terminology what they are being asked to write. If we use these terms, students will probably need some additional guidance with product goals, and the question they're likely to ask first—"How long should it be?"—may not be the most helpful in establishing those goals, although length can be one goal. To establish some product goals, we can help students analyze a variety of samples of the target product. Additionally, we might ask students to write a variety of genres—memos, case studies, lab reports, blog posts, and so on—that inherently provide some element of product goals.

Have students begin their analysis of the prompt by reading it at least twice to assess the general task they are being asked to complete. Through these readings, students should determine the overall purpose expected from the writing: to persuade, to inform, to entertain, to analyze, to enlighten, to assert an opinion, to reflect, or to accomplish some combination of these purposes. The purpose can help establish an initial product goal. For the following prompt, typical of one from a state exam, the purpose would be to "assert an opinion" or "to persuade," depending on how a writer interpreted the prompt:

> Recent funding cuts have been made to the school district. To cope with the problem, your school board has plans to eliminate all sports and music programs. Some members of the community have questioned the board's controversial proposal.
>
> Write a letter to the editor arguing your point of view on the proposal. Be sure to support your position with reasons, examples, facts, and/or other evidence. Readers should feel convinced to take your position seriously. (Gere, Christenbury, and Sassi 73)

Students should know that they will need to agree, disagree, or take some nuanced stance that still asserts a clear opinion about the school board's plans that would be taken seriously by the readers. Gere, Christenbury, and Sassi suggest asking questions beyond determining the purpose to help set deeper product goals: asking about the role the writer is to take, the genre (if one is mentioned), and the audience. They also suggest considering what strategies would help achieve the purposes and address other constraints established by the prompt (73–74). In this writing prompt, the audience is identified—newspaper readers and members of the community—and the genre is a letter to the editor. What product goals should these elements of the prompt indicate for writers? Ask students what they think, and set some possible goals with them. For instance, one goal might be to anticipate community members' feelings and, if the writer disagrees, to rebut them instead of just asserting her own opinion. Other goals might relate to the genre, letters to the editor, and the kinds of evidence and tone associated with that genre.

Next, have students examine the prompt for any specific requirements it indicates. In this case, the requirement for support should be noted. Of course, students might say that a product goal would therefore be to "support your position with reasons, examples, facts, and/or other evidence," but that is too vague. Instead, if they consider the prompt as a whole, students will establish more precise goals: assert a position regarding the elimination of sports and music programs in your school; provide an example (personal or from someone you know) that supports your assertion. Although students would need more goals than these two, this process of working from prompt to goals should benefit them as writers.

Once students anticipate the kind of writing the prompt requires—that is, the product goals indicated through its language—ask them to write responses in groups and then exchange the responses with other groups to see if the writing has met the expectations. Some states provide sample responses that students can review to see how well they address the product goals.

Teachers can find examples of test prompts on most state education websites (I haven't looked at all fifty, but I've found them on all state sites I've checked so far). I like practicing with test prompts first because we can criticize them without offending anyone. Eventually, though, it's good for students to analyze the writing tasks we give them for class. Such analysis will show that students understand the assignment, and by generating the product goals the prompt suggests and then comparing them to the grading criteria, students learn how to be more successful as writers on those assignments—and they build their ability to use situations to set product goals.

Beyond using the prompt to establish product goals, students should also consider a rubric as a potential source for goals. In a testing situation, these are not always given, but most states provide them for state tests. Although the sample rubric refers to Florida state standards, it is similar to those in many states and works well as a source for teaching students how to set product goals from a rubric.

Begin this practice by reading the rubric together as a class and making sure that students understand its language. Then, ask them to work in small groups to review the rubric and generate goals related to it. Eventually groups should share their goals with the whole class to build a class list. During this sharing, we can help students refine goals to become more effective, modeling for them how to make sure that a goal will benefit them as writers, and that it is task-specific and clear, rather than formulaic or vague. Here are some possible product goals that students might generate from this rubric:

- Make sure each example is fully explained.
- Use transitional devices to appropriately signal text structure.
- Create both short sentences for emphasis and long sentences for flow.
- Use words and examples that tie closely to the main point.

Focus. Focus refers to how clearly the paper presents and maintains a main idea, theme, or unifying point.

- Papers receiving lower and middle scores may contain information that is loosely related, extraneous, or both.
- Papers receiving higher scores demonstrate a consistent awareness of the topic and avoid loosely related or extraneous information.

Organization. Organization refers to the structure or plan of development (beginning, middle, and end) and the relationship of one point to another. Organization refers to the use of transitional devices (terms, phrases, and variations in sentence structure) to signal (1) the relations of the supporting ideas to the main idea, theme, or unifying point and (2) the connections between and among sentences.

- Papers receiving lower scores may lack transitional devices and summary or concluding statements.
- Papers receiving higher scores use transitional devices (signals of the text plan or structure) and developed conclusions.

Support. Support refers to the quality of details used to explain, clarify, or define. The quality of the support depends on word choice, specificity, depth, credibility, and thoroughness.

- Papers receiving lower and middle scores may contain support that is a bare list of events or reasons, support that is extended by a detail, or both.
- Papers receiving higher scores provide elaborated examples and fully developed illustrations, and the relationship between the supporting ideas and the topic is clear.

Conventions. Conventions refer to the punctuation, capitalization, spelling, and sentence structure. These conventions are basic writing skills included in Florida's *Sunshine State Standards*.

- Papers receiving lower and middle scores may contain some or many errors in punctuation, capitalization, spelling, and sentence structure and may have little variation in sentence structure.
- Papers receiving higher scores follow, with few exceptions, the conventions of punctuation, capitalization, and spelling and use a variety of sentence structures to present ideas. (Gere, Christenbury, and Sassi 105–106)

This practice in analyzing prompts and rubrics to help establish product goals can help students see how effective writing responds to something—a prompt, a situation, a need. Granted, outside of school our writing prompts aren't spelled out like these, but we still have prompts for our writing. I recently had a bad experience with an airline employee. When I went to the airline's website to find a phone number to complain about my experience, all I found listed for customer service was a mailing address: the company apparently thought that fewer complaints would come in if customers had to write a letter and mail it. I wrote my letter. The prompt was my experience and my understanding of the situation and audience. I made my product goals based on my analysis of those factors in the same way that we train our students to work with state test prompts and rubrics and with the assignments we give them to build product goals.

Revising with Product Goals

One way to help students build independence in developing and using product goals is to help them consider how evaluative criteria could be reinterpreted as product goals and then used as guides for revision, much as we did in the previous application with analyzing the rubric to develop product goals for drafting. In this application, students work through a similar process but reinterpret the evaluative criteria—and use the goals—at a different stage in the process. This means that the product goals become immediately useful in evaluating writing, not in starting it.

Some concerns are associated with product goals and revision. One involves the nature of the goals. For example, a goal to "make my writing better" leads most students to correct spelling or punctuation. A goal to "add more information" encourages more substantive revisions. Graham, MacArthur, and Schwartz also note that some product goals may inadvertently direct students' attention to particular areas while ignoring other potential problems. For instance, although the goal to "add more information" might lead writers to make needed substantive revisions, student writers may think that's all they need to do and fail to consider issues of coherence or comprehensibility (239). This is something that we must consider: the goals that we or our students set should be specific enough to provoke effective revision without creating new or additional problems. In order to be effective, then, teachers should consider exactly what the goals encourage students to address.

Frost, Myatt, and Smith have their students write multimodal essays, similar to literacy narratives but allowing multiple modalities beyond just written text: sound, art, technology, and so on. In their work with multimodal essays, these teachers provide the following evaluative criteria for their students:
Satisfactory projects will

- Include only those details relevant to a discussion of the person's experiences as a literate person;
- Effectively incorporate field research (observation and interview) and synthesize information rather than present a straight reporting of facts;
- Reveal the writer's attitude toward the subject, offering an interpretation of it;
- Effectively employ the affordances the selected mediums offer;
- Contain evidence of careful planning and an attempt to present information vividly. (194).

Each of these evaluative criteria—and any that individual teachers devise for their own writing assignments—has the potential to become a product goal. Although some writers might see each one as a checklist item (Yes, I've done that or No, I don't have that yet), teaching students to break down the criteria will benefit them more as writers than simply giving them the list of criteria.

At first, model this process for students. Then work with them collaboratively as they move through the process themselves, ultimately leading them to be independent in their ability to translate expectations into product goals for revision. Work on one element of the criteria at a time, asking students to offer their ideas about what a particular element implies. In the case of the criteria just listed, let's just look at the second item, concerning field research. What might students say is expected from this item? They might note the following expectations:

- I should have observations and interviews as part of my research.
- I should connect this research to my own experiences.
- I should report all of this not in a simple listing of information, but in a way that shows how the ideas and information fit together to make a point.

Modeling for students, I use this list (or the product goals associated with the writing we are working on) and review my own piece of writing. I compare my writing to the product goals. In this case, I could ask these questions: Am I including the necessary elements? What do I not include? In this self-evaluative process, I see that I have all the elements—my own experiences as well as observations and interviews. But I also notice that these are reported separately in my paper: first, my own experience, and then the other two elements. As a result of using the evaluative criteria, I make a product goal to find common threads among the three, and to reorder the information so that the next draft shows the connections among the three elements more clearly instead of just reporting the information.

Certainly the process of moving from evaluative criteria to product goals is more meaningful when students know and are invested in the criteria and the product, but the process should be similar to what I've described here: break down the criteria, match them against the writing, and make a product goal for revision based on areas of discrepancy.

Annotated Bibliography

Burke, Jim. *Writing Reminders: Tools, Tips, and Techniques.* Portsmouth: Heinemann, 2003.

>The first part of this book is about teaching writing in general: reminders about what we should be doing. The second part, "Write in Many Genres," contains a section for each of twenty-two genres and explains how to teach them. As part of the instruction, Burke sometimes lists what I consider to be product goals, such as these for writing a review: "knows and anticipates the questions and needs of the intended audience" and "identifies and applies the criteria by which the subject is being evaluated" (350). Though I believe that genres are situated and responsive to social situations, this book can offer teachers a place to start devising product goals. And this is a good reference if teachers want a quick tutorial for a genre.

Lattimer, Heather. *Thinking through Genre: Units of Study in Reading and Writing Workshops, 4–12.* Portland: Stenhouse, 2003.

>This book doesn't provide product goals, but it does include chapters on a variety of genres, with explanations of how to teach students to read the genres and develop their own set of product goals. Some of these product goals are explicitly stated in the book, as in the chapter on memoir, where readers find a list of that genre's characteristics (45). Mostly, however, the book describes how to help students work through determining their own product goals (as a class) through reading workshops and interaction with a teacher and other students. The questions and overviews of each unit will be helpful to many teachers beginning this kind of work with students.

Word Processing

....

5

Electronic writing is changing the way we read, write, and think, so it is also changing our writing classroom.

—*Edward Klonoski*

Overview

When my students and I discuss the writing process, I ask them some questions about how they use computers: Do they prefer to compose on the computer or on paper? If they draft on computer, what planning do they do prior to writing on the computer—or do they also do some planning (notes, outlines, brainstorming) on the computer? Do they print a hard copy to revise with a pencil, or do they revise on the computer? What features of the word-processing program do they use during their writing? The responses I get to these questions are interesting. They show me that the use of computers for writing varies—sometimes greatly—among student writers. And the uses are not always effective for high-quality writing or the strategic application of the writing process. Research shows that students are more likely to compose on the computer with increased computer experience, and to do more revising than they would writing by hand (Eklundh). Yet research also shows that students who compose on the computer often fail to plan as much before writing (Goldfine), and are more likely to revise at the local level than at a deeper, global level (Parr). In other words, when students write with computers, they gain some benefits as writers but also face unique challenges that our teaching practices should address.

In working on this chapter, I've been more conscious of how *I* use word processing in my own writing, and how this has changed for me in the recent past.

I still write an outline of sorts by hand, but I now draft online more than I did before. I revise as I write—sometimes more drastically than might be expected during drafting—by moving large sections of text around to see how the flow of my writing changes. Even though I revise onscreen during drafting, at some point I also print a hard copy to check for development of ideas and to gain a good sense of overall organization. I write, by hand, ideas for revision on the paper copy, and then transfer those changes to the document on the computer. I generally make most of my local revisions—sentence fluency, word choice, editing—on the computer, reading aloud from the screen. More recently, I've started moving some of my planning to the computer document before I begin, creating a kind of outline on the screen that I flesh out as I draft. Even with the structure set up by headings in the document, I still sometimes "draft myself" into another section, developing an idea in one part of the paper that really belongs to another section. Then I have to move it, which is relatively easy with word processing, but I am aware of the challenges of planning and drafting on the screen—and their limitations for giving a global perspective of my writing.

When they read the eleven elements of Graham and Perin's *Writing Next* report, some teachers question the inclusion of word processing. In some ways, this is surprising: a tool as an element of instruction? It's so unlike the other elements. On the other hand, it makes sense that the tool we use for composing would have some effect on our writing. As I just showed with my own writing processes, using a computer changes how we write. If it changes our writing, then it also probably requires changes in the way we teach writing.

Research has found many positive results from using word processing for writing instruction. One of the most consistent findings shows that the use of word processing creates positive attitudes toward writing, attitudes that contribute to motivating student writers. This doesn't mean that we can just tell students to use computers to write, and then think that all motivation issues will be resolved; however, the findings about increased motivation can be put to good use. A key aspect of students' underdevelopment as writers is the fact that they don't write: they don't like to, and they don't do it. If a tool can aid in motivation, teachers can hope for even greater benefits if they add to the use of word processing other motivational elements, such as interesting, authentic assignments and opportunities to work with others. These elements can combine to further improve students' attitudes about writing. And, as Bangert-Drowns reports, "As the attitude becomes more positive, the writing quality improves" (83). That's what we're working for, right?

Partly because they are more motivated to write, writers who work on a computer spend more time writing, and they create longer pieces than they do with pen and paper. Time spent writing generally leads to better writing: most teachers know that practice with writing usually helps develop writing skills. If students are willing to spend the time writing onscreen, that's a good thing: they won't become better writers unless they spend time practicing.

Word processing also encourages collaboration among writers, and helps them see writing as a social activity. Snyder explains that, when students use computers, "writing is seen not so much as a personal and private means of creative expression but rather as a social act that helps define an individual's place within a given culture or subculture" (147). Interestingly, students use writing on computers outside of school to participate in a variety of social situations, but they don't see their writing in these situations as "real" writing (Lenhart et al.). By using computers and word processing in classrooms, we can encourage the sense of the social nature of writing common to students' lives outside of school. Another consideration researchers have found: the neatness that accompanies word processed writing encourages students to read others' writing, and to make suggestions. Many of the elements of word processing foster collaboration, and, as we know from a previous chapter, collaboration is beneficial to student writers.

Finally, many aspects of word processing encourage revision: making changes to existing text is easy, moving large sections of text is easy, and the neatness of the writing makes rereading easy, too. Because of these characteristics, students revise more between drafts and overall (Goldberg, Russell, and Cook). Students increasingly see the writing process as recursive because of their ability to revise at any point in their writing. The ease of creating text on a computer encourages writers to take risks, to try out ideas that are easy to undo if they don't work, and to abandon ideas in the middle of writing. Goldberg, Russell, and Cook discovered that students who revised using word processing produced better-quality writing than did students who used paper and pencils (16). Not only more revisions, but more effective writing because of those revisions? Pretty important finding.

Despite the benefits of using word processing that I've noted, some research has not found improved quality in the written products. What we can learn from these conflicting reports is that word processing, by itself, isn't the only factor at play in the results; some of the improved quality of writing that can result from word processing depends on other variables. One of those variables may be typing ability. Research with younger students doesn't always show the positive correlation between word processing and quality of writing found in studies with older students. This may be because young or inexperienced keyboarders need to focus so much on the act of typing (which fingers go with which keys), and might be so distracted by the red lines under misspelled words, that they don't have the ability to attend simultaneously to issues related to quality of writing, such as content and organization.

Research also shows complex interactions between word processing and several other factors, including

- the kind of technology students are using, and how familiar they are with it (think about when you have to use a new or unfamiliar program!);
- the social context of the writing situation (are students writing for a test?);
- the genre being written (research shows that the connection to quality writing is stronger for arguments than for narrative writing);
- the quality and quantity of instruction (teaching students about writing differs from just assigning writing);
- and even the individual.

Because we don't all use the same tools to the same advantage, the use of word processing varies from person to person, and may even vary for the same person from task to task. But even with this contradictory research, as *Writing Next* shows, word processing has the potential for positive effects on the quality of students' writing.

As I've mentioned, though, some of the benefits of word processing can create new concerns that we should consider when working with students writing on computers. A major concern is that word processing can allow students to create nice-looking products to hand in or to share with others without concerning themselves with the quality of the writing. That "finished" look may give students a false sense of quality: if it looks good, it must *be* good, right? Related to appearance, a similar problem occurs when students get so focused on the formatting that they worry only about the look of the product and not the content. Another problem is that the product can look good very early in the process: students just start "writing" instead of planning before they write. Especially if they don't value the task and see it as "only for school," students might feel that they can create a piece of writing that looks like it does the job, without doing any real thinking or planning about the writing ahead of time.

Even if they do revise, students face some challenges because of the limitation of the screen: writers are less able to get a global perspective of a text when they can see only a small segment of it at a time. Some research has examined the benefits of having students look at documents in different views on the screen, but ultimately, many writers find that scrolling challenges their internal view of the structure of a piece of writing. Instead, many writers combine paper and screen writing, printing copies at some stage (as I do) to get the global perspective of their writing that they need for revision. Eklundh found that this happens more when writers are working on long or difficult texts (76), and that experienced writers combine print with electronic versions more often than do novice writers (77). It's something to remember when we are helping students improve as writers: we can encourage them to combine print and screen versions in their processes.

Writing on computers may also give students a false sense of audience—a feeling that they are writing to themselves or to the computer (Dowling). Online writing that students do outside of school might contribute to this lack of a sense of true audience, even if students know the writing will be given to a teacher. When students write on Facebook, for instance, they often forget about audience altogether. I don't seek out my students, but they often ask me to be their "friend" on the site. If I do, I'm able to see them describe all of their social activities—even though they've told *me* they are working too many hours to do the assignment for my class. One student wrote about being "schooled out" just after the start of the year. When I asked him about this in class, he seemed surprised. He asked me how I knew; I replied that he'd written it on Facebook. Then he said, "I guess I'd better start remembering who might see what I write." True. Writing on a computer for class can result in a reduced sense of audience for many students because it's so similar to their other online writing experiences.

This situation isn't helped when students use automated scoring programs for writing, or when they write for standardized tests. Both can encourage a decreased sense of audience. Standardized test writing is so often without a true audience and with an artificial purpose. Even when a test instructs students to write their responses to a specific audience, students aren't fooled. They know that some test grader will read the test, not the city council or school principal, or whoever the supposed audience is. So the concept of audience is diminished. When students write on programs that give scores or evaluations of the writing, the lack of audience is further reinforced. Students must know that getting a score in thirty seconds means that no real person reads the writing they submit. Even though the feedback suggests that an audience exists, none does. Herrington and Moran report a response that tells a student, "You have put together a convincing argument" and goes on to note as a specific strength that the essay "responds thoughtfully and insightfully to the issues in the topic" (12). All of this suggests a human reader when the computer is unable to evaluate the true thoughtfulness or insight of the ideas. Students must be aware of these discrepancies. These aggregate experiences with writing on computers might encourage them to neglect audience considerations when they write in other situations where audience is important.

Finally, another challenge with using word processing is that it can make teaching more difficult. I'm reminded of a time when I was observing a teacher who had handed out laptops so that students could work on their writing. Prior to their writing, however, she wanted to give a short mini-lesson. She kept asking for students' attention, repeatedly and more loudly each time, but the students were online, checking email, Facebook, even their grades on the school's website. Finally, she told everyone to close the computers. She even had to physically close some, as students insisted on continuing their varied online tasks. With the computers in front of them, students wouldn't pay attention to her lesson. In my own experience, even college students say that if the computer is open in front of them, they can't help themselves—they have to be checking multiple sites while I am trying to provide instruction or lead a discussion.

Computers can challenge instruction in other ways, too. Snyder reports a teacher's experience teaching writing in both a computer lab and a pen-and-paper classroom. The teacher felt that she had fewer spontaneous instructional moments in the computer classroom (154). Part of this, I believe, is that it's so hard to get students' attention. Part of it may be that students are certain they can do multiple things at once when in front of a computer, so they might believe they are listening as they would in a class not held in the computer lab. And happily, part of it may also be that students are more engaged in their writing and less inclined to stop writing for a mini-lesson than when they write in class.

Despite these challenges, it's still important to remember that research shows that word processing can improve student writing. The key is to be aware of the drawbacks and consider how they can be avoided or minimized. We must reinforce the benefits of revision, encourage students to write for authentic purposes, and help them learn the characteristics of quality writing in a variety of genres (including that appearance and correct spelling are not the most crucial elements of quality). Additionally, we should remember that our jobs as writing teachers do not include teaching students how to use computer programs. We aren't software teachers, so we should consider how to focus on teaching writing and avoid focusing on technological instruction. If we do need to provide some instruction on software or computers, we should determine whether the benefits to our students' writing development are worth the time we give to that instruction.

Principles

Purposeful

To be effective, word processing should contribute to the writing goals and support the writing instruction of the class, rather than direct the teacher's pedagogical choices. It should serve purposes that it is uniquely designed to serve, not just fill in for old methods. Kajder refers to a "treacherous assumption" that "because technology is made available, it must be used" (7). This idea often leads to classroom practices in which word processing (or some other form of technology) determines writing instruction rather than serves it. To be effective users of technology, teachers should think first of what students need for their writing, and then consider how specific aspects of word processing can help them gain what they need. So, for example, if we want students to consider ways to improve introductions, we can have them write three or four different introductions for a piece of writing they are working on. They can then copy and paste each version into the document to see how each works with the rest of the writing. This is much more difficult to do with pen and paper. In such a way, the word processing contributes to the goals of instruction rather than drives the teaching.

Although computers can aid writing instruction, they should not supplant the teacher or instruction. To do so might lead to another assumption that Kajder notes, the belief that the technology can do the teaching for us. Some writing programs, such as MyAccess, provide students with steps along the process, including prewriting strategies and revision feedback. These aspects of the program can benefit writers. But because these features are available, some teachers wrongly think they can count on the program to *teach* writing. That's not the way that word processing should contribute to good writing or writing instruction. Just sending students to the computer lab or giving them laptops will not help them improve as writers. As Patterson reminds us, technology is not a "magic pill" to solve all the problems of teaching writing (66). It does not take away a teacher's responsibility for teaching writing.

Part of that responsibility involves suiting instruction to the tool. Snyder points out that teachers need to design new strategies for teaching writing that are suited to computers, "start[ing] with what they know about writing and teaching rather than what they know about technology" (159). This is the best way to approach these challenges: instead of trying to adapt older practices to new conditions and tools, consider how we might create new pedagogical strategies to meet the new demands of using computers. How can computers meet needs that traditional tools do not? In research that reports teens' thinking about computers and writing, of those who felt that their writing had changed (for better or worse), a majority thought that instruction was a major factor of that change, while only 39 percent thought that technology contributed to change. (Lenhart et al. 43). Students want teachers to teach them; they want the use of computers to be purposeful.

Young and Bush assert that teachers should not use technology for the same reasons that mountain climbers climb mountains: "Because it's there" (12). Instead, we should remember what Owston, Murphy, and Wideman emphasize: "It's what students know that makes the difference in the effectiveness of the tool" (252). Our purposeful use of technology can help students use word processing in ways that benefit their development as writers. If technology is woven into a well-planned curriculum that integrates it effectively with writing instruction, then word processing can reach the potential its supporters claim in benefits for our students.

Supported

The use of word processing, if it is to aid students' writing development, needs to be supported by a general pedagogical philosophy that encourages writing and the aspects of writing that are enhanced with word processing, especially risk-taking and collaboration. The benefits of word processing, according to Snyder, are intricately connected to the classroom context. We should particularly consider the role of talk, the roles that students play, and our own role in supporting word processing if it is to benefit student writers.

Moeller finds that "in most current theory, computer-assisted writing instruction and constructivism are wedded in inseparable bliss" (4). Constructivism includes student-centered instruction, with collaboration and student knowledge valued. Word processing both encourages and is supported by classrooms that value these same things. In constructivist classrooms, students do a lot of talking—with the teacher and with each other. Classrooms with traditional lecture styles often do not produce the environment conducive to the democratic atmosphere that word processing encourages. When students work on writing with pen and paper, researchers find that they talk less than they do when they write with computers. Something about the tool encourages talk, so we should be prepared for that and consider how to use it to assist student writers. My own experience reflects what research shows—that initially, the talk while students work on computers might seem off task. Eventually, though, students' talk is more about the writing—and that's the kind of talk we always hope to encourage in classrooms without computers. Now that we can get it, we need to be prepared for it.

In classrooms that use word processing, students' roles shift from passive to active. Students are experts in some ways, but they are also producers in ways that writing on paper doesn't seem to suggest. Because they are producers, students work more collaboratively, giving advice on sites that might be helpful or a word that someone seeks. They often move around to look at what other students are writing and to comment on it. All of this means that they don't see themselves in the same way in a computer classroom—and we should expect this shift in roles. Expect students to feel more like they have a contribution to make, and encourage it.

When students are using word processing for writing, they also must be supported by a shift in the teacher's role. This isn't something that we necessarily choose. In fact, Kajder asserts that "integrating technology into the classroom absolutely *requires* change in the role of the English teacher" (10; emphasis added). She does not mean that we need to become experts in technology. Instead, she refers to different roles we play in these more democratic classroom spaces created by the use of technology. We give up some expertise to students, allowing them to make decisions for their writing and to work with other students more frequently. We train students to work collaboratively, to give feedback on writing to their peers, and to help other writers meet their writing challenges. In that way, we hand some of our authority over to them. Additionally, the use of word processing tends to remove us from the center of the classroom, sometimes diminishing the idea of the teacher as the "expert" in the class. We should be aware of this potential shift and support it by teaching from a more constructivist position—creating the situations that encourage students to learn for themselves, much as the computer encourages. In these ways, we support the use of word processing in the classroom and can help to lay the foundation for the best possible outcomes from its use. Word processing isn't just something we add into our courses; it's something that we support through our choices in changing pedagogy.

Applications

Revision Strategies

Revision is one aspect of the writing process that particularly benefits from word processing. Although computers make it easier to create writing, seeing them as what Lee calls "expensive typewriters" (G. Lee 25) undermines the real value that word processing can bring to the writing process. Some researchers who find students focusing on local concerns instead of substantive revisions (Parr, for example) wonder if the reason these students stay away from more effective, global revision is their lack of awareness of how to use the word processor to better effect. Also, some researchers find that the features to help with spelling and grammar allow some writers to feel less worried about conventions and thus more free to focus on ideas; yet Moeller argues that spell check and grammar check may also diminish creativity because they allow students to focus more on appearance than on substance. To have students focus early on global concerns such as ideas and organization, some teachers suggest turning off the spelling and grammar checking features until later in the writing process (G. Lee). To help students learn to exploit word processing features for more effective revision, I include the following suggestions that involve limited instruction on the program, but that could greatly benefit student writers.

1. **Find**

   Even students who have spent a lot of time on computers may be unaware of the find feature in their word processing programs. It allows writers to input a word or phrase that the program will find in the text it is searching. I often use it to find key words in a text to make sure that I stay focused on certain topics in a section of my writing. So, for example, I could search this chapter for the word *revision* to make sure that it appears in certain parts of the chapter where I'm discussing revision, and is not spread throughout—which might create difficulties for my readers. Have students do the same thing with their writing: search for key words and make sure they group together, or if they don't, that there's a good reason for the spread. What about other ways to use the find feature?

   Klonoski recommends using it to help writers make more effective word choices or to improve sentence fluency (75). For example, if students search for the word *very*, they are likely to find a weak adjective following it: *He felt very happy.* If, as this example shows, the word choice is vague, they can find more effective phrasing for that place in the writing: *He felt ecstatic* or *He shouted, "Yes!" and pumped his fist into the air.* By using the find feature, students are also encouraged to use the synonym or thesaurus feature in word processing. To help students effectively use these features, teach about connotations. For example, when I request synonyms for *recommend*, the program offers these choices: *advise, advocate, urge, propose, commend.* Obviously, these words all have slight nuances in meanings that may or may not meet my needs. Students should be aware of this aspect of selecting, but the synonym feature can help them clarify what they really mean.

Another way to use the find feature is to have students search for pronouns that novice writers often use in ineffective ways, pronouns such as *it* and *this* (Klonoski 76). When students find these words, have them review their sentences to determine if the referent is clear. If it is not, or if it is too far distant, they can change the wording for clarity. In *The Brief Penguin Handbook*, Faigley suggests that when writers find these pronouns, they should ask themselves, *this* what? or what is *it*? If the answer isn't clear, they should add the noun to which the pronoun is referring (457). The same process can be followed with *there*, a sentence beginning that novice writers often use ineffectively: *There are many reasons for this problem* could be revised to *Many factors contribute to this problem*.

2. **Copy-and-Paste**

An element of word processing that some students may not know about or use effectively is the copy-and-paste feature. In fact, Parr found that many students, even after several months of working with word processing, still did not "perceive a need for a function which would help them revise their text at other than a word or phrase level" (3). With the copy-and-paste feature, writers select a section of text, use the copy function, then move the cursor to another place in the text, and use the paste function. I recommend that students not delete the copied portion until the paste is complete; after the paste is in place, they can go back to the original position and delete the moved text. This may seem like an unnecessary extra step—returning to reselect text so that it can be deleted—but sometimes the copy or paste function doesn't work, and students may lose their writing. Although it's usually possible to use the undo feature to retrieve an earlier version, it's safer to move the text before deleting.

Students should not only be taught the simple process of copying and moving parts of their writing, but more important, they should also be taught why they are using this process. The point of moving text is to see how writing works when it is rearranged or regrouped. This knowledge of the paste feature is especially valuable because a global perspective is so much more challenging when we write on the computer (Goldfine; Eklundh). When we move a paragraph or a piece of a paragraph to another place, we can see if the flow is improved or weakened. Students should try out various placements of phrases, sentences, and paragraphs in their writing. Ask students to try a different move, perhaps suggested by a peer, and then to write a short reflection about the difference made by the move. Students might decide to move the text back to the original position, but they should be able to articulate why they decided to do what they did.

As students learn to use the copy-and-paste feature, they become more attuned to revision, especially to the ease of moving text, and they are more likely to see their writing as fluid, developing, instead of set when it is on the screen. They are more likely to see their writing as something that can be changed—and therefore get a better sense of what revision can mean.

3. **Highlighting**

Two simple word processing functions—selection and highlighting—can also benefit students in their revising efforts. Warshauer recommends highlighting to color code sections of writing (68). What students select to highlight can vary from class to class, but also from genre to genre. I recommend using product goals to decide what to highlight. So, for example, if students are writing a movie review, have them highlight the general statement of evaluation in one color, the summary elements in another, and the analysis in a third. In this way, students can determine (by comparison to published movie reviews) if these elements are adequately represented in their own reviews and if they are in the most effective places; color coding model texts can reveal to students the options for organizing these elements (Dean, *Strategic* 60). When they write arguments or persuasive essays, students might highlight the thesis in one color, the evidence supporting the thesis in another, and concessions or acknowledgments of opposing views in a third color. In this way, they can visually represent elements of text that connect to product goals, and then make decisions about developing elements that may seem undeveloped or moving elements that might be more effective in other places. The highlighting should lead to decision making on the part of the writer, not be merely a way to "color" the writing.

4. **Graphing Sentence Lengths**

Although different genres have differing characteristics with regard to sentence expectations, many kinds of student writing can benefit from more attention to sentence-level flow. I suggest having students first graph sentence lengths for sentences of model texts in the genre they are writing, so they can make some generalizations about the sentence variety typical of a genre. Then have them graph their own sentence lengths to see if they are in the range of sentence-length variety they find in the models. These graphs are also a good visual way for students to consider the similarity or variety of sentence lengths, because most genres value some level of variation, and much student writing is typified by similarity in length. Also, make sure that students don't think that varying sentence length is done just for variety's sake. That isn't the goal of such attention. Instead, students should consider how the kinds of sentence lengths in the model texts reflect the purposes and situation of the genre, and how their own sentences might reflect those same purposes and their own situations. With this in mind, word processing, along with a simple graphing tool, can make the graphing process much easier.

To create the graphs, have students highlight each sentence, one at a time, using the select function they would use to copy a section of text. Then, have them use the word count feature to get a word count of the selected text, and write it down. When they have the word counts of their sentences, have them use an online graphing program, such as Kids' Zone Create a Graph (National Center), to create graphs by following simple directions. I counted the words in the first seven sentences of a draft of Chapter 12 of this book to create the following graph in Figure 5.1:

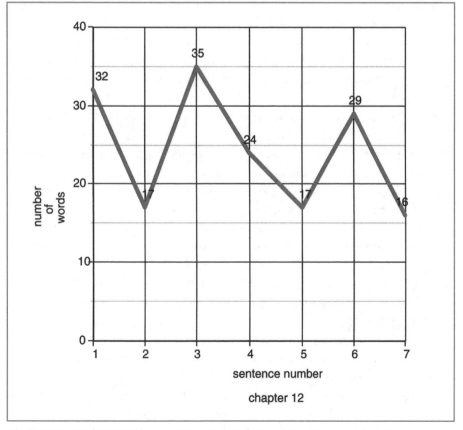

FIGURE 5.1. Graph created by counting words in first seven sentences of draft chapter.

Students could do the same, and then compare their own to the graphs of the model texts to direct their revision of local concerns—sentences—in their writing.

Peer Response

Peer response is an effective use of both the ease of writing and the increased socialization that occurs when students write onscreen. Despite these obvious connections, though, Moeller asserts that the use of peer response groups with computers needs to "mesh with the larger classroom strategy of collaborative activities" (7). In other words, teachers can't use peer responses only when students are on computers and expect it to work as well as it could. Instead, peer response to writing on computers needs to be part of an overall classroom philosophy that values collaboration and student input.

The ease of reading a word-processed draft might contribute to the increased social aspect of using computers to write. When students write by hand, peer review is often limited because simply reading the text can be difficult, or because poor handwriting may lead to misreading. Warshauer notes that laptops, in particular, encourage revising because of "alternate mechanisms for provision of feedback" and "the students' ease at making changes to papers" (68). Students can pass laptops around to other readers to review their writing, though in a computer lab, students can also move from one computer station to another to review others' writing.

Word processing allows students to provide feedback to peers in a variety of ways. First, they can write directly in the document—changing the color or style of font to differentiate it from the author's original words. Students can also use the comment feature to give feedback. The comment feature allows comments to be identified with a specific portion of the writing without interrupting it. With the ease of typing, as opposed to handwriting, many students are more likely to provide abundant feedback that they would resist giving in other situations. Although it doesn't happen often, one limitation of inserting comments is that if the text contains many comments—or lengthy ones—the writing can be somewhat interrupted.

Despite the advantages I've described, my own students reported mixed responses when comparing computer peer feedback to face-to-face feedback. Those who favored computer feedback saw the ease in timing—they could do it when they liked and take as long as they needed, and were not bound by the class period's time constraints. They also found electronic feedback to be less personal, but not always a bad thing. As one student noted, "I think it can be a little less uncomfortable" to tell a writer about something that needs work, and "a little more honest." Students found that they could easily read the comments from peers (because they didn't have to deal with poor handwriting) and that they received more feedback with computers than during face-to-face evaluations. Still, students encountered problems when the technology wasn't compatible or when they had trouble getting access. And some students simply like to have a *person* talk to them about their writing, and to ask questions for clarification; they still want that personal connection. My preference is to combine the two practices—face-to-face and electronic peer feedback—so that the benefits of both are available to students.

Annotated Bibliography

Hicks, Troy. *The Digital Writing Workshop*. Portsmouth: Heinemann, 2009.

> This book shows how to use elements of the writing workshop in digital environments. I especially like that it includes important instructional aspects of writing and assessment. Hicks presents a responsible way to approach writing with computers—not just for the gimmicks, or because students are enthusiastic, but with learning in mind.

Kajder, Sara B. *The Tech-Savvy English Classroom*. Portland: Stenhouse, 2003.

> Although this book goes well beyond the use of word processing, to using the Internet and additional technology, it offers lots of ideas on how to get students writing with computers. In the chapter "Going Beyond Word Processing," Kajder shares some noteworthy ideas for using computers throughout the writing process, including creating tables in documents to serve as graphic organizers for planning writing and for keeping track of information about that writing. She also encourages teachers to take advantage of images from the Internet that can become writing prompts for students. Kajder's suggestions extend to communication tools (emails, listservs, chat rooms), virtual field trips, and WebQuests. Throughout, she integrates students' learning to write with the technology available to them for that purpose.

6

Sentence Combining

I have pulled threads from magic tapestries already woven and used them to weave my own cloth.

—*Jane Yolen*

Overview

Once, when my students asked me why I had them work so much on constructing sentences, I responded with a question of my own: "If you wanted to get a job and put me as a reference, which would you rather I say?

Although he's a hard worker, he usually turns his work in late.

Although he usually turns his work in late, he is a hard worker."

The students all chose the second option. When I asked why, they said that it sounded better. Right. Option two puts the positive in the independent clause instead of minimizing it by placing it in the subordinate clause. At this point, the students made snoring noises; they didn't care about my grammatical explanation. I went on to explain, though, that working with sentences could help them make those kinds of shifts that direct a reader's attention to what the writer wants to emphasize. Then one student said, "Oh. It gives you power." Yes. Although all of our writing work can't be done at the sentence level, some work there can be valuable for writers. Sentence combining is one way we can work with writing at the sentence level.

At its most basic, sentence combining has students join two or more short sentences into one longer one. But sentence combining is more than that. Sometimes a set of short sentences contains cues to help the writer combine them; at other times, students are asked to combine any way they can. In some cases, sets of sentences are designed in groups that are meant to help students create a series of sentences to form a longer text (a paragraph or more), so that students see not only how to create more effective sentences, but also how those sentences might fit together. Some sentence-combining exercises consist simply of ideas, which students are supposed to select from and organize, or paragraphs that students revise "in order to achieve differing emphasis and tone" (Faigley, "Performative" 175). Sometimes students create their own kernel sentences, and then combine them. In whatever form, sentence combining is meant to help students learn about the syntactical options available to them for writing sentences. As Strong asserts, "The intent of sentence combining is to make good sentences, not long ones" ("How" 336). Good writing. That is at the heart of sentence combining.

In research conducted during the mid-1970s to mid-1980s, study after study showed that sentence combining not only helped students improve their syntactic abilities, but also improved their general writing quality. But the whole idea died away—and quickly. In fact, Connors, writing in 2000, asked colleagues about sentence combining: "At least half of them replied that it had lost currency because it had been shown *not to* work, *not to* help students to write better" (119; emphasis added). Yet Connors disagrees with these colleagues: "So far as I can determine, this is simply not true" (119). Studies conducted in the United States (Graham and Perin, *Writing Next*) and in England (Andrews et al.) reestablished Connors's claim: sentence combining is an effective way to help students improve their writing.

What had happened to create this wrong notion about the failure of sentence combining? Many teachers believed the lore that developed in the 1980s, which argued that sentence combining didn't work. That belief has hung around, and some teachers still hold it. Part of the reason for the belief was that at the time, no one really knew why sentence combining *did* work; they only knew that it did. Crowley notes that a lack of theoretical explanation "does not, of course, invalidate the positive results it [sentence combining] has been able to demonstrate in the improvement of student writing" (491). But without a theoretical foundation, questions arose. Instead of theory, we had lots of suppositions about why sentence combining works.

Myers supposes that its success has to do with vocabulary. She stresses that vocabulary is key to good writing, and, because words don't exist in isolation, sentence combining teaches how words work together (collocation), thus helping students learn patterns of words that offer ways to use vocabulary to improve communication: "Sentence-combining exercises not only present students with words for writing [. . .] but with contextual information about their collocations" (615). Thus, sentence combining helps students learn words and, more important, learn how words work together. Myers acknowledges that this learning about words "is an inadvertent result of sentence combining, not one of its stated goals," but she believes it addresses at least part of the reason that sentence combining improves overall writing quality. And she adds that "if students are called on to read their sentence(s) aloud, the words are processed again. [. . .] Words, lots of words, words in the right contextual register, alternative words, and combinations of words are the raw material of composition" (616). So writing and then talking about the writing work together to help develop this facility with language that benefits student writers.

Strong offers another possible reason for the success found through sentence combining: automaticity. He argues that building automaticity helps writers deal with the complexities of writing. When writers compose, they have to hold in mind many issues: content, form, language, genre, purpose, audience, and so on. Strong refers to the "inner game" and the "outer game" of writing; that is, the issues related to what goes on inside our heads (decisions about content and structure and so on) and what is visible outside (the physical act of transcribing) (*Coaching* 22–23). Sentence combining provides practice and develops facility with the outer game, so that student writers can focus on more important issues related to content and overall structure. With automaticity, then, overall writing quality improves.

Additionally, through sentence combining students get enough practice with the rhythms of sentences that they "internalize images of the sound, feel, and shape of successful writing" (Strong, "How" 340). They have a way to practice, and subsequently apply in their own writing, sentence constructions that they may not have used in speech or prior writing. Some researchers even suppose that improved writing is a result of learning sentence patterns that encourage more thoughtful content: "If syntax provides categories for expressing one's thinking, widening the range of syntactical structure available may extend one's capacity to express one's thinking" (Freedman 21). Further, because of their practice with sentences in low-stakes situations (classroom practice and discussion), students may build confidence that can extend beyond sentence-level work to their sense of themselves as writers in other situations. Of course, none of these suppositions is supported by research; they are simply assumptions made by those who observe how sentence combining helps students develop as writers. This lack of theoretical foundation may be one factor that led to the decline of sentence combining—but it wasn't the only one. Almost like a perfect storm, several influences came together at the same time, all with negative effect on the use of sentence combining in the classroom.

One of these influences leading to the decline of sentence combining was what Connors titles "The Erasure of the Sentence," a dismissive attitude about any work that focused at the sentence level. Even though much composition pedagogy prior to the 1980s worked on a parts-to-whole basis, theorists of the period (like Moffett, Elbow, and Graves) began more and more to consider writing not as made up of parts, but as holistic and related to self-expression. Sentences weren't as important for those concerns; in fact, sentence pedagogies were often seen as antithetical to self-expression, despite assertions by sentence-combining advocates like Strong and Christensen that understanding sentences (forms) could help writers generate meaningful, even personal, content. As interest in the writing process developed, teachers and researchers began to see sentence combining as detrimental to the writing process and its (often expressive) interests.

Supporters of sentence combining tried to assert what we know today: that sentence combining can work within the process model. Morenberg argued that, "though it is concerned with matters of form, there is nothing in sentence-combining instruction that should be anathema to writing-process instruction" (8). Strong acknowledged that "SC is not real writing." He knew that "[h]owever cleverly devised they may be, exercises are no substitute for naturalistic (real writing) experiences in which students create personal meanings" (*Creative* 22). But Strong also felt that sentence combining could help writers write for personal meaning. Supporters like Strong and Morenberg tried to show a place for sentence combining within the writing process, but ultimately, they couldn't hold back the momentum. Eventually a variety of factors and attitudes undermined sentence combining, leading Connors to conclude, "The degree to which the attacks succeeded can be seen in the curious growth of the truly lore-oriented conception that 'research has shown that sentence-combining doesn't work'" (119). And the power of this belief in lore is evident: decades later, teachers are surprised at the Graham and Perin findings that sentence combining is a research-proven practice, useful in helping students develop as writers.

So how, exactly, does sentence combining work? Sentence combining consists of two primary forms—open and cued exercises—each with value. Open-ended sentence combining asks students to combine sentences in any way they think will be effective, so it offers plenty of choices. However, students may be limited to what they already know how to do with sentences. To minimize that problem, Strong suggests posting options such as these on the board during open-ended combining: "(1) *add* connecting words, (2) *take out* unnecessary words, (3) *move* words around, and (4) *change* word endings" (*Creative* 26). These general directions can help students consider their options, but students might still need more guidance.

Cued exercises give students more specific directions for combining sentences. Such exercises are sometimes very scripted, but they give students practice creating structures that they might not otherwise know how to create (appositives or participial phrases or absolutes, for example). I recommend alternating open and cued exercises. Open exercises give students the opportunity to show what they know and to get used to the concept of sentence combining. Then, cued exercises that focus on a specific construction (subordination, for instance) build an additional skill with new syntactical structures that can be used when students go back to open-ended constructions. And so on.

Open exercises can be created from any texts that students are reading, or from any sentences that have interesting structures. Here's a sentence from Steinbeck's *The Pearl* that I thought would be interesting for students to work with: "The dawn came quickly now, a wash, a glow, a lightness, and then an explosion of fire as the sun arose out of the Gulf" (3). By *de-combining*, that is, breaking the sentence into its constituent kernel sentences, I can create a sentence-combining exercise. An open-ended combining exercise based on this sentence could look like this:

> The dawn came.
> It came quickly now.
> It was a wash.
> It was a glow.
> It was a lightness.
> Then it was an explosion.
> The explosion was of fire.
> The fire came as the sun arose.
> It arose out of the Gulf.

Because this exercise is open, students can combine these sentences in multiple ways. Although the original sentence from the novel contains a series of appositives, students might not combine to create them without directions to do so. If I want to ensure that students create appositives, I can make the sentence set cued by adding codes. Here are basic cueing directions: beginning with the base clause, underline items that should be added or kept, and put punctuation or added words or word endings in parentheses after the sentence in which they should be placed, as follows.

The dawn came.
It came <u>quickly now</u>. (,)
It was <u>a wash</u>. (,)
It was <u>a glow</u>. (,)
It was <u>a lightness</u>. (,)
<u>Then</u> it was <u>an explosion</u>.
The explosion was <u>of fire</u>.
The fire came <u>as the sun arose</u>.
It arose <u>out of the Gulf</u>.

With these cues, students will probably create the same sentence as the sample sentence, thus creating a series of appositives. Although Strong provides guidelines for constructing cued exercises, he also suggests that "studying cued SC exercises is the best way to learn their conventions" (*Creative* 25). That has been more effective for me—looking at examples and figuring out the process.

It might seem that creating sentence-combining exercises for individual classrooms could take some time, but I usually find it goes relatively fast—and it gets faster the more I do it. I don't make extensive lists. Instead, I select a couple of sentences from our readings and de-combine those. Because students are expected to combine in multiple ways (with the open-ended groups), they get practice writing several sentences from just two sets of kernel sentences.

Another way we can create exercises is to have students de-combine sentences. My students enjoy the puzzle of doing this—and some say they are better at it than I am! I have them select a sentence from a passage of our reading to de-combine, so they can choose a level they're comfortable with. Then, they put their sets of kernel sentences on transparencies to be used in upcoming lessons. I believe that having students do some de-combining also teaches them about the nature of sentences—and how many ideas can be contained within each one. It encourages students to pay attention to sentences.

Principles

Context

In one of his books on sentence combining, Strong states that "to talk about 'good sentences' out of context is nonsense. A sentence is effective only if it works; and sentences only work in the context of other sentences" (*Sentence Combining* 40). This statement is at the heart of an important principle related to effective sentence combining: work with sentences by themselves has limited effectiveness. Practice with individual sentences doesn't always translate into larger pieces—so, although students might be able to combine kernel sentences to create appositives or participial phrases, they don't always know how to link these sentences to appropriate sentences that come before and after. Although we can work for a while with individual sentences—and this has merit—eventually students should consider how sentences work together to create meaning, and how their work with sentences can influence the larger piece of writing.

According to Strong, sentence combining "is an adjunct to writing instruction, not an escape from it" (*Creative* 23). Students still need to write their own extended pieces of writing and use that writing for authentic purposes. Comprone argues that "real" writing possesses a tension between the writer's intent and her ability to use sentences effectively. Sentence combining might help students with the second part of that—sentence effectiveness—but it does not address a writer's intention: "choices made on the whole-discourse level" (227). Comprone's argument clarifies the need for sentence combining as part of a writing curriculum that asks students to do a lot more than simply combine other people's sentences—or even their own. We should teach sentence combining as part of our writing curriculum and then expect students to use their developing skills with sentences in longer compositions.

As students work with sentence combining, then, in connection with writing "whole" compositions, we should consider that different genres use different kinds of sentences. Context changes sentences. When I have my students combine sentences taken from political speeches, the resulting constructions may be inappropriate for them to use in personal narratives. We should be aware of this issue and make sure we provide sentences that create structures typical of the genres that students are writing. In arguments, for example, research shows that writers use many adverbial clauses (Nippold, Ward-Lonergan, and Fanning), so helping students focus on sentence combining that creates effective adverbial clauses when writing arguments would be a good move. Similarly, movie and book reviews often use appositives, so combining sentences to create appositives when students are writing reviews would benefit them as writers. Teaching sentence structures that will fit the genres that students are writing is one way to create an effective context for sentence combining.

Supportive Environment

For sentence combining to improve student writing, an environment that encourages risk-taking is fundamental. As we learn any new skill, we are likely to make mistakes. That's the nature of learning. So, as students practice with sentence combinations, they need to know that it's okay if all their sentences aren't the most effective—and that no one will judge them harshly for their mistakes. In fact, I felt that my class was successful when a student began her sharing with this statement: "I don't know if this works or not, but . . ." This meant that my students were willing to take risks in our class—and that willingness is important for any writing class, especially for the trial and error that accompanies sentence combining. It's important for students to know that other students are joined in the learning effort, and that they won't be belittled for sharing an example that might not be as effective as someone else's.

Effective teaching in this aspect means that we must do groundwork in establishing a classroom that supports developing writers by expecting a lot from them, but allowing them to make mistakes without fear of disparaging remarks or punishing grades. One way I worked toward this was to have students do their sentence combining practice in a spiral notebook that was collected periodically and just given points if students had tried the combining exercises. Eventually, they were expected to use their developing skills in polished writing, but the work we did daily with sentences was risk free, in terms of grades. Also, when students read their sentences aloud, we would acknowledge something that worked, even if the sentence wasn't the greatest. We'd compare the effects of different combining choices to develop a sense of how syntax affects meaning. My responses helped establish an atmosphere where students felt comfortable trying out ideas.

Our response is essential in creating the environment necessary for sentence combining to work well. Time spent on sentence combining should be time to experiment, without concern for a single, correct answer. When he was reviewing studies on sentence combining, Hillocks noted that in one report that showed negative findings, the researcher later "rescinded" the findings, claiming that "poor teaching was probably the cause of negative attitudes and results" (*Research* 144). The way we handle the whole process is key in using sentence combining to help writers develop. Even good teaching approaches may fail to improve student writing if teachers don't implement the approach as intended. For example, Strong tells of a teacher he met who told him, "It [sentence combining] doesn't work in *my* class." When he questioned her on her practices, he found these: she used sentence combining at the end of class to keep students occupied; students worked on sentences alone; and "answers" were marked right or wrong by the teacher or when students exchanged papers to correct them. No wonder she didn't see positive results (*Coaching* 43). The supportive environment that nourishes experimentation and sharing is essential to reaping the benefits of sentence combining.

Talk

I might have included talk as part of the principle of supportive environment, but it's so important that I've made it a separate principle. A lot of talk needs to occur in conjunction with sentence-combining work—talk among students, and talk with the teacher. During discussions, it's singularly important for students to know that combining sentences is not a right or wrong activity, with only one correct answer. As Strong asserts, sentence combining is "not an approach for people who need an answer key. Indeed, its real aim is to make students the answer key" (*Creative* 23). Instead of looking at sentence combining as a kind of "worksheet activity," we should use the students' work with sentences as the basis for discussions that explore the *effects* of the combinations that students have created. In fact, I ask my students to provide two options for every sentence combination—and then star the one they like better and be ready to explain why. As Strong notes, it's important for us to emphasize "that audience and writing purpose affect one's decisions about sentence length and complexity" (27). The audience aspect of sentence combining is hard to achieve without classroom talk about sentences.

In my experience, teachers who implement sentence combining without classroom discussions, and without attending to how sentences work in patterns in different kinds of discourse, are not using sentence combining to achieve its desired effects. By itself, the written work can take students only so far. But discussion about the sentences can provide the oral reinforcement and focus on their reading to move students much further along in their development as writers.

An additional aspect of talk is reflection on the use of sentences in writing. Although reflection can be written, it should also be an integral part of classroom talk that reinforces the learning derived from sentence-combining practices. Frequently during sentence-combining work, we should ask students to consider how the moves they are practicing could be useful to them in more authentic writing situations—and how they will remember to consider them in those situations. Reflecting on their practice increases the likelihood that students' practice will translate into effective writing in other situations. When students discuss how they applied their learning from sentence combining—not necessarily a particular construction, but a conceptual application—that reflection can be powerful instruction for other students. Even articulating the concept can benefit student writers. So some classroom talk needs to be reflective.

Applications

Writing Starters

Part of our work with sentence combining is also the extension of writing into longer pieces. The writing starters application helps us do that. Provide a series of sentences that, when combined, explain an idea or tell the first part of a story. Then ask students to combine those sentences and complete the story or idea on their own. For example, students could combine the following sets of kernel sentences that begin the topic of cell phones in school:

- o Cell phones are banned.
- o They are banned in our school.
- o Cell phones cause distractions.
- o The distractions are to learning.

- o Some students use cell phones to text.
- o They text during class.
- o They don't pay attention to the lesson.

- o Sometimes students use texting to share answers.
- o The answers are for a test.
- o Sharing answers isn't fair to other students.

- o Cell phones allow students to take pictures.
- o Sometimes students take pictures in locker rooms.
- o These pictures can embarrass other students.

After students have combined the sets of sentences into four, ask them to complete the paragraph with their own perspective about banning cell phones in schools. Teachers can make sets of kernel sentences—or have students create them—on a variety of topics to double as sentence-combining activities and writing prompts.

Paragraphs

Strong suggests an activity that blends sentence combining with paragraph writing. To begin, teachers cut a sentence-combining exercise (like the one in the previous section) into strips, each strip containing one set of sentences meant to be combined into a single sentence—but with all the sentences part of one paragraph or excerpt. Students work in groups to combine the set of sentences they are given, and then collaborate with other groups to arrange the combined sentences in a logical, coherent order, adding transitions as needed (*Creative* 30). So, for example, the following sentence sets (created from the first paragraph of Spinelli's *Stargirl*) could be the basis of an exercise of this type.

I was a little girl.
I had an uncle.
My uncle was Pete.
Pete had a necktie.
The tie had a porcupine on it.
The porcupine was painted.

I thought about the necktie.
I thought it was just about the neatest thing.
It was the neatest thing in the world.

Uncle Pete would stand.
He would stand patiently.
I ran my fingers over the tie.
The tie had a silky surface.
I half expected to be struck.
I thought the quills would strike me.

Uncle Pete let me wear the tie.
He let me wear it one time.

I kept looking.
I wanted one of my own.
I could never find one.

After students have combined their set of sentences into one sentence and then put them together with other groups' sentences in a logical order, introduce the passage where the sentences originated, and see what students think about their work. Mine often claim to like their own combinations better than the source structures, which is fine. The activity isn't about trying to get as close to the original as possible; instead, I discuss how different structures create different effects. That is at the heart of what students should learn from sentence combining.

Sentence Play

Another way that students can practice sentence combining is to combine their own sentences. This helps them play around with ideas, and it also better prepares them to combine sentences in their own writing; of course, these are the sentences that we most want them to consider combining for effective writing. What follows are some ways that we can get students creating and combining sentences.

Ask students to pair up with a partner. Have students interview their partners and write several (ten? fifteen?) positive statements about the other person. Then have each pair exchange their lists so another partnership can combine the short sentences into two or three sentences. If students understand cuing, they can include cues with their sentences, or they can allow them to be combined in any way the writers prefer. Strong also recommends challenging students to write sentences with a specific number of words, "six, nine, twelve, fifteen, and eighteen" (*Creative* 24), so that students get some practice striving for target lengths.

Work with student-generated sentences can also occur with the literature students are reading. For example, after reading a chapter or section of literature, ask students to write several short sentences about the plot to that point. Then, have them exchange the sets of sentences and have another student combine them effectively—thus providing sentence-combining work with summarizing practice. The following set of sentences might be generated after reading the first act of Shakespeare's *Romeo and Juliet*.

1. Romeo is sad.
2. He likes a girl.
3. She doesn't like him back.
4. His friends convince him to go out with them that night.
5. The Capulets are planning a party.
6. They send a servant to deliver invitations.
7. The servant can't read.
8. The servant asks Romeo and his friends to read him the names on the list.
9. Romeo and his friends find out about the party.

10. They decide to go to the party in costumes.

11. Juliet's parents ask her to consider Paris as a husband.

12. Juliet agrees to check him out at the party.

13. At the party, Romeo and Juliet meet.

14. They fall in love and kiss.

15. Romeo finds out that Juliet is a Capulet.

16. The Capulet and Montague families are having a feud.

This combination of sentences might be the summary:

> Even though he's sad because he likes a girl who doesn't like him back, Romeo allows his friends to lure him to go out with them that evening. Meanwhile, the Capulets are planning a party and send a servant who can't read to deliver the invitations. When he asks for help from them, Romeo and his friends find out about the party and decide to go in costumes. While this is going on, Juliet's parents ask her to consider Paris as a husband, and she agrees to check him out at the party. Instead, at the party Romeo and Juliet meet, fall in love, and kiss—before Romeo finds out that Juliet is a Capulet, the daughter of a family having a feud with his own.

Annotated Bibliography

Killgallon, Don. *Sentence Composing for Middle School: A Worktext on Sentence Variety and Maturity*. Portsmouth: Boynton/Cook, 1997.

> Although this book has some additional sentence work (imitating and expanding), it provides a nice set of initial work with sentence combining, and the imitating and expanding work well as an extension. One of the exercises works with sentences in paragraphs, offering an example that teachers can use to create similar exercises on their own.

Strong, William. *Coaching Writing: The Power of Guided Practice*. Portsmouth: Heinemann, 2001.

> This book discusses sentence combining in only one chapter, but the examples provide teachers with a foundation for creating their own sentence work for students, which I think Strong would say is best anyway. In these exercises, students are encouraged to move into playing with language, creating puns, and learning definitions.

Prewriting

7

All acts of composing begin as explorations of new ways to understand experience; the urge to write begins in the hope of discovery.

—*David Foster*

Overview

In a Calvin and Hobbes book I own, a sequence of comic strips shows Calvin trying to write a report on bats. He postpones the writing because he doesn't know anything about his topic—and because he's Calvin. When time is running out, he tries to enlist a classmate to do some of his research for him. When he finally runs out of time and sits down to write something, he doesn't know where to begin. Hobbes prompts him to begin by writing what he knows. Good idea. So Calvin writes that bats are bugs—and then moves on to his final draft, convinced he's spent enough time preparing to write (Watterson). In his own way, Calvin is like many students in our classes: they have limited knowledge about their topics, they have limited strategies by which to access more knowledge (either in their own heads or outside of themselves), and they are reluctant to spend time on these processes that they don't consider valuable for their writing.

In the mid-1960s, early in the writing process movement, Rohman explored prewriting in depth. He considered prewriting to be everything before the "point where the 'writing idea' is ready for the words and the page." Rohman was adamant in asserting a claim that still exists, namely that prewriting "is crucial to the success of any writing that occurs later, and it is seldom given the attention it consequently deserves" (41). In fact, Murray claims that good writers actually spend about 85 percent of their composing time in prewriting (*Learning* 15), adding weight to Rohman's argument for its importance.

Not all writing, however, requires a writer to work through the entire writing process. Prewriting is generally considered to be the part of the writing process that precedes drafting when writing *does* require the writer to move through at least some of the writing process. Clark contends that, although activities to "search for, discover, create, or 'invent' material for a piece of writing"—what she calls *invention*—can occur at any time during the writing process, only those aspects that "happen before a writer has produced any actual piece of text" are called prewriting (71). Some of my students have a similar idea. They have told me that they think prewriting means what they do *before* they write anything. But in many cases, writers use writing to conduct the activities that Graham and Perin describe in *Writing Next* as meeting the purposes of prewriting: generating ideas for possible writing topics, exploring the chosen topics, and organizing the ideas generated. So writing itself may be considered prewriting.

Other writers suggest that prewriting can be not only the actual activities (such as writing or talking or researching) but also the thinking that occurs. In fact, for many writers, much of prewriting is invisible (which makes it tricky in schools: students tell teachers they *did* prewrite, yet there's nothing visible). But prewriting can and should be viewed broadly. Johnson considers prewriting to be "that entire period of time, and such activity as may be involved, between knowing that one is going to write on something [. . .] and knowing (at least hoping) that one has found something specific and substantial to say about it" (233). And Ray goes even further:

> Writers prewrite all the time, even before they are actually engaged in a draft for a specific purpose. Because they know written products (drafts) will be a part of their future (they are writers after all), they are always on the lookout for ideas. They *live* their lives prewriting, imagining possibilities and seeing potential for writing in the world around them. (*Wondrous* 97)

With these ideas as a guide, we can define prewriting as a wide variety of activities, visible and invisible, that move a writer toward the goal of creating a draft.

When I mention prewriting to students, they often name brainstorming and webbing as the only prewriting strategies they know. And those strategies can be effective for several purposes. They can help writers generate ideas and see connections among those ideas, accomplishing two primary goals of prewriting. But prewriting should accomplish more than finding a topic or focusing it. Prewriting also involves learning more about the topic under consideration, and it involves planning for the shape of the future piece of writing. It should "push students' thinking beyond the most obvious and accessible ideas about their topics" (Irwin and Knodle 42). All of these are valuable parts of the writing process that students don't often consider when they think of prewriting. Because it involves everything prior to writing a draft, prewriting should include activities that (at least) do the following:

- help a writer find a topic or focus
- investigate the ideas or questions buried within the chosen topic
- gather more information (through reading and researching)
- keep track of new information (through note-taking and summarizing)
- analyze audience, situation, and genre
- create plans for organizing
- develop appropriate vocabulary for the writing task

To begin considering prewriting, we must first recognize that writing grows out of some need or some place. We write because we are asked to do so, or because writing will help us do something that we want done. So prewriting begins in a situation; or, as Kent notes, "[W]riters always write from some position or some place; writers are never nowhere" (3). Part of finding a topic or focus, an initial element of prewriting, comes from the place or position Kent mentions. Bawarshi calls that place *genre*. When we write a résumé, for instance, we don't have to search through all of our memories for topics to select. We know that some aspects of our personal experience are more relevant than others. Some experiences—how to prepare soil for a garden, or how to tweak the oatmeal cookie recipe to get it just right—aren't likely to be eligible as topic choices, as they might be for other genres. Genres limit our options to some degree. So one aspect of prewriting can be a consideration of the genre and its situation. Traditional rhetorical ideas also suggest that a writer might consider audience when making some initial decisions about topic, an aspect that contemporary genre theory subsumes in *situation*. So before writers begin to do anything, even choose a topic, they orient themselves to the writing situation.

Interestingly, this orienting kind of prewriting probably occurs in some instances without our even realizing it, especially when we know the situation well. Without even being aware of it, we consider genre as part of our prewriting, generating only certain kinds of ideas because we understand the range allowed by the genre. What we need to contemplate, then, is how to help students use this same kind of positioning with genres and audiences so that they don't follow unproductive avenues of ideas. Bawarshi stresses that, as valuable as the work on prewriting has been, if we neglect to consider genre as part of prewriting, if we think only of "the writer as the point of departure for writing," we are left with "a partial understanding of the agency at work when writers write" (51). That partial understanding is inadequate for students to develop fully as writers.

Once writers have oriented themselves within a situation, they need to decide on a topic. If one has been assigned, as is often the case both in school and out of it, writers must then decide on what aspect of the topic they will write. Prewriting that helps writers select or focus a topic is probably the most frequent use of prewriting I've observed in schools. Most textbooks suggest the following strategies as ways to generate or focus ideas: freewriting (write on a topic to see what comes to mind), listing (consider elements or characteristics), clustering (find connections between ideas), and brainstorming (start with an idea and see where it leads).

Once students have selected a topic and focused it, they then need to develop that topic, to decide what's possible to say about it and what the writer deems important to say. In other words, the writer must consider how to find out more about the topic. In traditional rhetoric, this kind of coming to know, of exploring the topic, was called invention, and it involved using heuristics to probe the topic under deliberation. Classical rhetoricians developed the topoi, questions which were used to probe the memory and help the speaker determine the most effective proofs for the topic and situation. Notice that the topoi were questions that writers were meant to ask of *themselves*, based on an assumption that all the information was at hand, in the mind of the writer. The topoi do not necessarily move outside the knowledge of the writer to help writers *learn more* content. Invention, from this classical position, wouldn't help twelve-year-olds (who certainly don't have at their fingertips all the information they would need for every possible topic). It wouldn't help anyone much in today's world, for that matter, when there is so much to know that it would be almost impossible to be able to speak or write knowledgeably about a topic without some knowledge-building procedures. In other words, before writers can consider drafting, they need enough information to write. Or, as Louis L'Amour said, "A writer's brain is like a magician's hat. If you're going to get anything out of it, you have to put something in first" (qtd. in Graham and Harris, "Best" 121). Somehow, students need to gather information before they can begin to write.

I recently read a book of personal essays by Anne Fadiman titled *At Large and At Small*. As I read some of the essays, all of which were based on Fadiman's personal experiences, I couldn't help but realize how much information I was learning: according to an Italian doctor who wrote in 1775, flavored ice (ice cream) had medicinal benefits (different flavors achieved different cures); if your ice cream is too cold, it numbs the taste buds that detect sweetness (46); out of every ten people, one will be a night owl and one will be an early riser (62); London in the 1600s had hourly mail service (113); contrary to visual depictions suggesting that Washington crossed the Delaware with a U.S. flag in his hand, the flag was not designed until later (153). As I read the essays, and then the list of sources in the back of the book, I became more certain than ever that all writing, even personal essays, can benefit from research into the topic. The final essay—a moving piece about watching a fellow boater drown in flood-high waters on the Colorado River when Fadiman was a teenager—contains less information than the other essays. But what did Fadiman do as a writer? She still researched the facts of the water runoff for that particular year, not trusting her memory with such a crucial detail. Research—coming to know more—made all the difference for her writing, as it does for our students'.

Prewriting, then, should involve some ways of learning more about the topic that could involve traditional research (looking online or in books, taking notes, and writing summaries) as well as talking (to knowledgeable others and to other writers) and other types of activities: watching videos or documentaries, looking at photographs, listening to speakers, and so on. In fact, Johnson reminds us that "each of us knows full well that all effective writers on the prowl for inspiration use any, every, means to find it with absolutely no scruples about compatibility between one means and another" (237). From this perspective, then, many ways of gaining information can constitute prewriting.

When writers are gathering new knowledge, they need a way to keep track of that information. Students often see note-taking as a purposeless activity, something that teachers make them do to pay attention in class. They rarely see the value in the practice. When I ask my students about their negative attitudes toward recording notes during research, they give a variety of reasons for their feelings. First, they see note-taking as boring: they have to write before they can write. They also comment that they don't use everything they write down in notes, so they consider it a waste of time. They don't mind highlighting, but we know from research (see Chapter 11) that if they don't do something with the information—put it in their own words, summarize it, connect it to something else—they really don't know it well enough to use it effectively in their own writing. Instead, they end up stringing quotes together from sources they don't understand, and they produce ineffective writing. Somehow, as part of prewriting, students must find appropriate ways of keeping track of information, and of working with it, not just writing it down, so that they make it their own, so that they really *do* know it.

With information, students should be ready to start planning, finding some strategies to determine how to shape a text. That isn't as easy as it might seem for most students. In fact, I recently loaned a chapter on planning to several preservice teachers. They passed it around, and, when it was returned, one of them had written this comment in the margin: "I recognize the importance of planning, but I'm not sure I know how to effectively do this." I found the comment insightful. If a person almost certified to teach English doesn't understand planning, how will her students? How do we decide to shape texts? Genre helps to a degree. Different genres have differing ways of presenting information. But beyond that, even when I know the genre, what strategies of planning are useful?

Outlining is one. It may not be one that students appreciate, but research has shown that outlining has a positive influence on the quality of the final product in both style and content (Kellogg 339). Outlining can benefit writers by helping them avoid overload—trying to consider too many things at once. For me, it can mean thinking of my writing in smaller chunks, and thus being able to focus more completely on those pieces instead of on the whole thing at once. My own experience also suggests that the form of the outline is not as significant as the fact that there is some sort of structural framework. If I, as a teacher, focused excessively on Roman numerals, followed by capital letters, followed by . . . my students would worry too much about that structure and not enough about the point of outlining in the first place: to find a way to order their ideas.

Other strategies for planning are more challenging. Graphic organizers can help, but they are most effective when students decide on the shape of a piece of writing and then use the organizer to fill in information, as a structural form they can follow while they move through drafting. Working from the other direction—giving students the graphic organizer and having everyone use the same one—suggests that all kinds of content can be shoved into the same shape. And although it's sometimes helpful to write in that direction, this approach doesn't help students with one of the more difficult aspects of prewriting: figuring out an organization for their ideas.

Prezi, an online tool for creating presentations, is an alternative that might help with planning. The program allows writers to put information or key words on a grid in any order they want. They can add information as it occurs to them, and then group similar ideas or put the information in different sizes or fonts to show its relative importance or relationship to other ideas. When all the ideas are on the grid, users draw lines from one group of writing or one idea to the next in a sequence that seems to make sense. Then they can look at what they've created and see clearly how well they have ordered their ideas. If writers are concerned about the order, ideas can be rearranged and replayed to test out various organizational choices. In this way, a tool designed for making interesting presentations can become a good prewriting tool, helping writers plan organization before creating the text.

In my experience as a teacher, prewriting to plan organization often returns to an analysis of the options available, meaning that my students and I look at examples of the kinds of writing we want to do (the genre) and then make mental notes of the ways those texts are shaped:

- What kinds of ideas are in the introduction? How long is it?

- How do authors determine the order for the information? Is the most important idea discussed first or last? Are all the similarities between two ideas discussed before all differences? Is the topic described from the outside in, the general before the specific—or vice versa? Or is the order something else entirely, a kind of logic related to the ideas at hand?

- What possible ways are there to conclude this kind of writing? Summarize? Project possible outcomes? Leave the reader wondering? Return to my beginning idea?

Once we have some possibilities, students can use a graphic organizer that matches their choice—or create a map of their own.

Graham and Harris note that students "are more likely to plan if they value the writing task" ("Best" 124). That is my experience as well. When what they are writing matters, students pay more attention to all aspects of the writing process, but particularly the prewriting aspects, those parts that otherwise get skipped or get done after the fact. When my eighth graders wrote letters of complaint or compliment to businesses—and they knew they were going to send them—they spent much more time on prewriting (getting the details of the point they were writing about and shaping how to tell it effectively) and revision (especially polishing their writing) than they did on writing that they were simply going to turn in to me. Further, Graham and Harris suggest that teachers can encourage students' future planning by "praising noteworthy planning behavior" ("Best" 124). In other words, when we see students planning, we ought to acknowledge it as something that good writers do.

Principles

Valued Prewriting

Challenges abound to prewriting practices in the classroom. To begin, I imagine that most teachers have had my experience of seeing students create outlines, webs, freewrites, or some other recommended prewriting tool *after* they have written the assignment. In such situations, I've wondered where I went wrong. At least some students saw prewriting simply as *more* writing, unrelated to the quality of the product they eventually turned in. Blackburn-Brockman, teaching preservice English teachers, found similar patterns of behavior: "Only as an afterthought and because it was required, my students would spend literally minutes writing a quick freewrite or a perfunctory web and then staple it to their already completed drafts before submitting to unsuspecting teachers" (51). Rodrigues and Rodrigues report a similar finding: students "often dismiss invention strategies as useless gimmicks" (79). One of the challenges, then, of incorporating prewriting as an effective part of a writing curriculum is to help students see the value of prewriting activities in improving their writing—to help them see the practice as purposeful.

Lindemann suggests that as teachers, part of that responsibility lies with us: we must ensure that the prewriting activities we ask students to practice can produce quality details that *will* be useful in their writing. For instance, in brainstorming, students may just toss out ideas that will be more or less helpful to them. Lindemann asserts that "at least initially, students need guidance in generating *useful* details." When they make lists, she suggests reminding students "that list making serves a larger purpose, to explore the subject thoroughly and discover what makes it interesting or important" (112). In other words, the work of prewriting isn't as simple as I might have made it seem to students in my early years as a teacher, when I encouraged them to just toss out ideas, as though thinking weren't necessary. Perhaps, in endeavoring to make the activities appealing to students, I didn't adequately represent the kind of *thinking* that should occur in activities such as brainstorming and listing. When I reread Rohman, I notice hints of this need for quality thinking. He discusses the level of thinking that prewriting should encourage—active, instead of the passive, whatever-comes-to-mind thinking that I sometimes allowed my students to count as prewriting.

In response to the argument that prewriting activities help writers get started, Blackburn-Brockman counters, "They aren't start-up rituals designed to 'prime the pump' in order to avoid writer's block" (52). In fact, Kellogg claims that "blocked writers may use prewriting activities as a way to procrastinate beginning a first draft" (340). Foster reports that some students (as many of us have observed) see the prewriting activities as ends in themselves, unrelated to the writing task for which these activities should have helped them prepare (27). In all of these cases, students are unable to see the purpose behind the practices we encourage.

As teachers, then, we have to help students see the value and applicability of the prewriting practices we employ in our classrooms. Unless students see these practices as useful in creating a more meaningful writing product, it's unlikely that they will use them in purposeful ways in their own writing processes. If we assign a prewriting task that doesn't match the purposes of the writing or the needs of the students, they will probably see prewriting as something that teachers make them do, another piece of paper to turn in, rather than as meaningful to their work as writers. That said, I have taught students who would use any excuse to avoid planning or gathering information, so *not* assigning prewriting may also fail to help students see its value. What I have found more effective is asking students to select from options that should help with the particular task at hand (more on that in the next principle). The choice seems to help them take some ownership of the purposeful use of the strategy.

We can encourage students to see their prewriting practices as important aspects of their individual writing processes. One suggestion is to "establish a predictable classroom writing routine, where students plan as well as draft, revise, edit and publish their work" (Graham and Harris, "Best" 123). Because students need repeated, valid use of these practices in order to recognize that the practices work, asking them to use prewriting routinely in class will benefit them by helping them see prewriting practices as a regular part of writing. In addition to using prewriting strategies regularly, students should be encouraged to reflect on the way these strategies have helped them in their writing. Reflection can be a key part of helping students recognize the value of prewriting, as they see how it helps them in each writing project.

Another way to help students understand the value of prewriting involves the classroom climate. As Graham and Harris explain, students "are less likely to exert the effort needed to plan if they view the classroom as an unfriendly, chaotic, or punitive place" ("Best" 124–25). This finding suggests that we need to create a comfortable place where students feel able to take risks with their writing. Prewriting means trying out ideas that might not make it through a critical revision process—and this has to be okay. Prewriting also means playing around with ideas that might seem incomplete or even silly to others—and this has to be okay. Prewriting brings order to a jumble of ideas, but this isn't easy if the environment itself is disorganized. We show the importance of prewriting by establishing places and practices in the classroom that reflect the value we see in unfinished thinking.

Finally, it's a good idea to model prewriting for students. In other words, we should be working through some of the strategies ourselves, and in front of our students, for students to really grasp the kind of divergent, critical thinking that is often needed during the early stages of the writing process. Even good direction might be inadequate. Instead, we can and should understand not only how it feels to work through selected prewriting strategies, but also how to model for students where effective thinking can lead and how to avoid ineffective thinking. As we talk aloud during our modeling of prewriting—"I could add another point about my favorite German food to my reversal, but I didn't bring that up in my common-view part. So should I bring up something about food in the common-view part? Or should I leave out the favorite food from my reversal? What would be the effect of each?"—we show students the kind of thinking we hope they will be doing as they develop ideas and plan how to shape them for their writing.

Appropriate Strategies

Part of the challenge of helping students see prewriting as a valuable part of the writing process means that we also have to select appropriate strategies to match the kind of writing that students will be producing. For example, the kind of memory-probing activities that Rohman researched are applicable primarily to personal writing, but not particularly effective for informative writing. As teachers, if we don't consider these concerns—if we use memory-probing strategies intended for a memoir when students are going to write a report on a historical figure, for example—then we not only don't help students with the particular task, but we don't teach the value of prewriting strategies in general. The prompts for developing and planning should address the purposes of the intended writing, the expectations for the intended genre, and the structures appropriate to the genre. What follows are some suggestions for prewriting strategies and the kinds of tasks they might support.

Prewriting to Get Ideas for Writing

- Timelines. Students can make a timeline of their lives, noting highlights at the appropriate times. When they've completed the timeline, they then have a list of possible topics on which to write about their lives, in memoirs, poems, or personal narratives.

- Questioning Heuristics. To get students thinking about their topics in broader ways, I use *synectics*, a strategy that employs analogies to explore ideas (Joyce and Weil 236). When students have a topic, I ask them to number their papers from 1 to 8. Then I ask them to compare their topic to objects. So, for example, I say, "Number one. If your topic were a car, what kind of car would it be?" Students write a response. I then go through a list of items: color, weather pattern, food, television show or movie, famous person, country, animal, or tool. When we've gone through the list, I ask students to choose the most interesting comparison they listed, and for five minutes, to write about how the two are alike. In this way, students often uncover a hidden aspect of their topic that they hadn't considered.

- Visual Prompts. I have an old Mary Engelbreit calendar themed around everyday events. I have used that to help students generate possible topics for personal narratives or memoirs from their own lives. Any set of photos could also be adapted in this way. For instance, one of the calendar pictures shows a first kiss. I tell students to consider other important firsts in their lives and list them: first ride in an airplane, first time they cooked food on their own, first haircut, and so on. Another picture shows a girl and a rainbow; I prompt students to think of significant interactions with nature: experiences with storms or earthquakes, camping on the beach, and so on.

Prewriting to See What You Already Know or Remember

- Freewriting. This is the most common prewriting strategy that students undertake. Once students have a topic, they write about it for a set period of time (ten minutes or so) without stopping. They don't worry about spelling or grammar, just about getting significant ideas on paper. Usually students find that the unstructured nature of freewriting helps them put on paper what they already know. This strategy works for many kinds of writing, even informational. When my students do research, they are frustrated if they take notes on what they already know. Once they've done some freewriting, I tell them they don't have to take notes on what they know—it's already written down.

- Debates. Debates are oral rehearsals of what students know or think they know. Certainly students can be encouraged to conduct debates after they have conducted some research on their topics, but debates in early stages of the writing process can also help students find other avenues of thought or opposing views they might not have considered. In this way, the debate serves to uncover directions to investigate during subsequent inquiry into the topic.

Prewriting to Develop Ideas

- Taking Notes. Students need a place where they can keep track of and make sense of the ideas they gather as they prewrite. Many note-taking strategies exist, and they should also be connected to the kind of writing that students are doing. For example, using index cards is a good strategy for lengthy inquiry projects and for writers who can keep track of them. They are not such a good strategy for junior high students or for writing shorter, inquiry-based writing. When my students write brochures, for example, they use a table with a row for each point on the brochure so that whenever they find information, they can immediately put it with other information on the same point. Regardless of the note-taking strategy that students use, if the ideas they read are to become their own and to inform their writing effectively, students should do more than highlight or copy the words of others. Some teachers ask students to write summaries periodically during their note-taking process, to help make the ideas their own. I use a form that gives students a place to write the source, then record some facts or quotes from that source. Immediately below that area is a place for students to respond to the information: that is, they note how the information will be useful to them or how they still wonder about something related to that information. Other prompts on the form ask students to list the questions they now have because of the ideas they've just noted; and to list connections they can make between the information they've just acquired and other information they've already learned. In these ways, students are prompted to do more than simply write down other people's words during prewriting—and they learn more about their topic because of this. An online tool that writers can use to keep track of information is a Web Scrapbook (Center for History). It allows writers to collect information in one place, but also allows them to comment on and annotate these items. This tool can be collaborative, but its main advantage is that it offers writers, alone or in groups, a way to collect and then comment on the information they gather. Other similar online tools include LiveBinders and Zotero.
- Talking. Talking can be an aid to writing if it's encouraged appropriately. One way of talking to develop ideas is to conduct interviews with

knowledgeable people about the topic or question. As the writer listens and poses further questions, she can develop ideas to use in her writing. In a study on the development of persuasive writing skills, researchers found that age doesn't necessarily indicate an ability to develop a good argument for persuasion. Instead, researchers suggest encouraging students to "discuss a topic in detail before [they] actually begin writing" (Nippold, Ward-Lonergan, and Fanning 134). In other words, talking to other people can help students see perspectives that they might have missed without the talk. This ability to consider other viewpoints may then help students develop their ideas for writing.

Prewriting to Shape or Organize Ideas

- Graphic Organizers. Specifics about where to find these are in the applications section of this chapter. The key to effectively using graphic organizers is to help students find one that allows them to plan the shape of their paper, not to impose a shape and ask students to fit their ideas to that shape. Therefore, it's a good idea to investigate several organizers with students ahead of time, and ask them to envision the genre that the organizer would help them write. Help them see the organizers as tools, not as formulas.

- Outlines. Although it often frustrates students, outlining has "improved the quality of the final document, both in terms of its style and content," according to Kellogg's research. His overload hypothesis suggests that creating some sort of macrostructure will prevent writers from having too many concerns when they are ready to begin drafting. With research supporting its use, outlining can be a good strategy to help students prepare to write by giving them a framework to apply. But the research shows that outlining, like all prewriting strategies, is task specific. It has worked best for tasks "that required the writer to both generate and organize ideas" (339). According to Kellogg, outlining may be less helpful for tasks such as fiction writing, and much more effective for factual or informative writing (340). This makes sense. In fiction writing we have a plot line to follow, and even beginning writers have more familiarity with the organization of a story than with almost any other organizational structure. Informative genres, however, include a wide range of organizational options, so an outline may benefit that kind of writing.

Applications

Finding a Good Topic

One of the hardest tasks for novice writers is to figure out what to write about. In a children's book by Roni Schotter, *Nothing Ever Happens on 90th Street*, a girl is told to write about what she knows. She observes her street and sees nothing happening, nothing to write about. To the reader looking at the illustrations, though, there is much going on. The girl just can't see it. Our students are like that. They think they have to find the *perfect* topic. In fact, Ray notes that inexperienced writers "believe the life topic must be extraordinary in some way." She continues, "These young writers do not know yet that it's not what a piece of writing is about, but how it's written that makes good writing *good*" (*Wondrous* 93). And Boiarsky agrees: "The ability to find a unique angle separates good writers from average ones" (46). So one aspect of prewriting can be to help students learn to find ways of considering everyday topics from unusual perspectives.

A website teachers might consider to introduce the concept of differing perspectives is The Rolling Exhibition, which presents the story and photos of a young man without legs. He travels the world on a skateboard and takes pictures from his perspective closer to the ground. His insights could be useful when students begin considering how perspectives matter.

To help my students practice considering new perspectives, I bring in a clay hippo that my children gave me years ago. It's about the size of a baseball. It makes my students smile because it's got wrinkles on its body and a goofy smile on its face. After we enjoy it for a moment, I turn it upside down and ask them to describe it. It's not a hippo now. Now it's four circles, each with an opening about the size of a quarter (not all completely round). To the side of the four circles is a clump with some grooves. Through the holes, we can see that the inside of the object is hollow, with some rough edges. I walk them through this so they understand that everything can be seen from more than one angle—and things often look completely different from a different viewpoint. Teachers can, of course, use any recognizable object for this practice.

After introducing the concept, have students form groups and give them common objects from the room: the tape dispenser, a pencil sharpener, a bookend from the bookshelf. Their job is to look at the object from a new perspective, and to describe it so that other groups can't tell what it is at first, but can eventually. This helps students begin thinking about ideas from more than one direction (much like the listing activity described earlier).

Some questions (heuristics) have been developed by others to support this effort to see topics from new perspectives, and teachers can find them in many places (Lindemann, for example, provides some in her chapter on prewriting). One set of creative questions comes from a textbook for ninth graders. These "what if" questions can help writers identify hidden ideas in a topic:

- What if I combined my topic with something that is normally separate?
- What if I used my topic in a new or unusual way?
- What if I changed one aspect of my topic? What would be the result?
- What if people changed their ideas about my topic?
- What if my topic never existed? How would things (the world?) be different? (McDougal, Littell 34)

I also use a cooperative questioning strategy I modified from an idea I read in Ballenger's *The Curious Researcher*. Have students write their topics at the top of a piece of paper. Then pass the papers around the room, and have each person (one at a time) write a question about the topic on the paper. When the original person gets the paper back, he or she has plenty of questions that provide unique ways to look at the topic. In one section of his book, titled "The Myth of the Boring Topic," Ballenger endorses questioning with students:

> A good question is the tool that makes the world yield to wonder, and knowing this is the key to being a curious researcher. Any research topic—even if it's assigned by the instructor—can glitter for you if you discover the questions that make you wonder. (35)

Ballenger encourages students, after they know enough about their topic to speak for one minute on it, to share their knowledge and then let others in their group generate questions for further investigation. Getting students to generate questions, however we do it, can help them find a good topic—or a good angle on a topic.

Using Poetry as Prewriting

One of the ways I help students generate ideas, or see if they have gaps that suggest a need for additional inquiry, is through the use of poetry. As Holbrook describes in her book about using poetry in a variety of content area classrooms, poetry is like stringing popcorn:

I have to hunt around my memory for the pieces, taking extravagant care to arrange in a certain order, then I remember something else and have to unstring. Working my memory over, I prioritize, make order out of chaos, rediscover details, and put events in sequence. Poetry is a practical route to learning and remembering. (4)

I agree. Poetry encourages just the kinds of thinking we hope for from prewriting. And Buis finds poetry during the writing process a valuable way to encourage reluctant writers, as it provides a measure of success for them while showing that "they already have a good flow of ideas." She acknowledges that using different kinds of poetry can help student writers to prepare for a variety of genres they write: "For example, free-verse poetry fits well with descriptive writing, bio-poems go with biographies, and diamantes fit well with information text" (57). It's important to select a poetic form that matches the genre that students will eventually be writing, but I can see wider uses for some of the forms, and some of them may serve multiple purposes.

For example, I've adapted the bio-poem, usually written about people or characters, to nonfiction topics. By completing the prompts of the poetic form, students have to think deeply about their topics, making connections and inferences. If they can't complete the poem, it's a signal that they need to conduct more inquiry or research. Here is the adapted form I use, with my own poem on the topic of whales following the form:

- Line 1: (Name or Topic)
- Line 2: (Four traits that describe)
- Line 3: *Related to* (…)
- Line 4: *Lover of* (list three things or people)
- Line 5: *Who feels* (three items)
- Line 6: *Who needs* (three items)
- Line 7: *Who fears* (three items)
- Line 8: *Who gives* (three items)
- Line 9: *Who would like to see* (three items)
- Line 10: *Resident of* (…)
- Line 11: (Another name or synonym)

Whales
- Intelligent, Warm-blooded, Social, Air-breathing
- Related to dolphins and porpoises
- Lover of plankton (baleen) and squid and fish (toothed)
- That feels no cold, vibrations, and a need to communicate
- That needs unpolluted seas, companionship, and freedom from hunters

- That fears nothing except man
- That gives oil, food, and baleen
- That would like to see something! And below 4800 feet
- Resident of all the world's oceans
- Cetaceans

From the form and the example, it's evident how the writer would need to know information—or know what information to seek—in order to complete the poem. The poem can function as a sort of outline or record of notes; after completing it, students are then prepared to write their report, editorial, or description on their topic.

Another poetic form that I've used with success is the poem for two voices (Dean, *Strategic* 39–41). Fleischman is the originator of poems for two (or more!) voices, which are structured to allow the two voices (a queen bee and a worker bee, for example) to speak to, with, and against each other. This poetic form works particularly well as a prewrite for persuasive writing when students need to see if they've considered opposing viewpoints, or for reversal papers in which students need to frame one part of their paper against another. It helps them generate or gather ideas for their writing. Here's one I wrote on two perspectives about living in Alaska:

It's big.	It's big.
And cold.	
	But only in some places,
	And at some times of the year.
There are bears	There are bears
That attack you	
And eat people.	
	But only if you go
	Where they are
	Without bells
It's wild and natural	It's wild and natural
	Evergreens
	Mountains
	Rivers
Yes, and tundra,	
And vast, windswept emptiness	
People live in igloos	People live in igloos no more
Use dogsleds for travel	Use dogsleds for recreation
	And sport

Wear fur parkas

       If they're native

Winter has short days
Dark going to school
Dark coming home

       Summer has short nights
       Baseball at midnight—
          Without lights
       Huge turnips and cabbage

SNOW   SNOW
                In winter.
                Swimming in
Cold.   Cool water in summer
It's big   It's big.

Annotated Bibliography

Atwell, Nancie. *Lessons That Change Writers*. Portsmouth: Firsthand / Heinemann, 2002.

> This book has lots of ideas for the entire writing process, but given that Atwell works primarily through a workshop method, I find more ideas for prewriting than for other parts of the process. Although there is a slight emphasis on creative and personal writing, there are some ideas for other genres ("Itches to Scratch in Essays"). Some of the prewriting strategies Atwell uses for personal or creative writing could be adapted appropriately to other kinds of writing. For example, one strategy asks students to record in their notebooks over the weekend "Twenty Actions That Could Be Poems." In doing this, students brainstorm a list of possible topics for poems from their everyday experiences. The same strategy could lead to "Twenty Actions That Could Be Letters to the Editor" if students were coached to consider it that way.

Burke, Jim. *Tools for Thought: Graphic Organizers for Your Classroom*. Portsmouth: Heinemann, 2002.

> If you're at a loss for an appropriate note-taking or organizational pattern, this book will help. It's full of patterns that meet a variety of needs and that set up a variety of structures. Students can keep notes with these patterns, or use them to determine what information goes where in a piece of writing. Although teachers should be careful not to put too tight a structure on students' writing, this book is useful not as a book of forms, but as a book of potential solutions to students' writing challenges.

8

Inquiry Activities

Inquiry [...] lies at the heart of writing of any kind.

—*George Hillocks Jr.*

Overview

In *A Short History of Nearly Everything*, Bryson explains how he came to write the book. The story begins when he was in fourth grade, and he saw a diagram common to science books: a picture of the earth with a wedge cut out to expose the layers beneath the surface that led to the core. Bryson wondered, first, how anyone knew what was down there. Then he wondered about cars that might drive across the central plains of the United States and suddenly fall into the chasm made by the cut-out wedge. But his wondering stayed with him, until, as an adult, he finally did something about his questions—he wrote a book. In the back of *The Dinosaurs of Waterhouse Hawkins*, Kerley explains how she came across a picture of Hawkins holding a formal dinner party inside a mock-up of how he thought dinosaurs might have looked. She wanted to know what was behind the picture—and her wondering led to her inquiry and, eventually, to her book.

Inquiry is wondering and questioning. It's looking for answers and finding more questions. It is a process that helps writers find and develop ideas for writing. It's about writers learning what they have to say—and how they might be able to say it—by actively engaging in thought-provoking experiences. For Hillocks, inquiry is a process "that originates in doubt and moves in a rational way to resolution" (*Teaching* 30). And, as Whitin and Whitin emphasize, it's not just "a question or activity but [. . .] a perspective on learning that celebrates surprise, thrives on doubt, and flourishes in tension" (143–46). For them, "a sense of wonder" (x) is at the center of inquiry. In some ways, then, inquiry is the essence of teaching and learning *and* writing.

Traditionally, inquiry is called research—and it's most likely to be associated with one kind of writing: the research paper. But Hillocks, the researcher most associated with the concept, contends that inquiry involves more than looking in books or on the Internet. Instead, inquiry involves a series of activities that might not normally be considered part of traditional research. According to Smith and Hillocks, inquiry involves "observation, description, comparison and contrast, definition, generalization, and the testing of generalizations against further data" (58). Adding to that list, Whitin and Whitin contribute these additional aspects of inquiry: "critical uses of resources, collaborative communities, focused and refocused investigations, exploratory conversations, and changed visions" (xi). Inquiry, then, involves more engagement with information, more "messing around" with ideas—by ourselves and with others—and more exploring. In a word, inquiry is experiential.

Graham and Perin's report *Writing Next* makes a distinction between prewriting and inquiry. Prewriting is more likely to be used to generate possible topics (as in brainstorming), to probe what is already known about a topic (as in freewriting), or to look at the ideas subsumed by a general idea (as in webbing). Prewriting might also include gathering information (reading books and taking notes) and planning for writing (as in making an outline). All of these activities are important to writing and to writers, but they are often less helpful in generating the kind of content that Hillocks and others believe results from true inquiry. Reither notes this gap in the applications that moved from research into the writing process: "Process research—precisely because it has taught us so much—has bewitched and beguiled us into thinking of writing as a self-contained process that evolves essentially out of a relationship between writers and their emerging texts." He asserts that "this model of what happens when people write does not include, at least not centrally, any substantive coming to know beyond that which occurs as writers probe their own present experience and knowledge" (622). And he argues that the model we've been using needs to change to include "strategies and techniques that will enable students to search beyond their own limited present experience and knowledge" (624). In keeping with Reither's call to action, inquiry moves beyond simply "looking up sources" or googling to get information, information that is often cobbled together to create the "paper" that teachers have assigned. Inquiry moves beyond more superficial knowledge gathering, to include thoughtful interaction with ideas and data.

Inquiry also differs somewhat from invention in traditional rhetoric. As described in Chapter 7, invention is often linked to prewriting because both are meant to help the writer select and develop ideas. But traditionally, invention was also more encompassing than prewriting as it is generally conceived. Plato's version of invention seems more closely related to prewriting because he believed that by searching inside themselves, people could discover truth. The memory-probing activities that constitute much of prewriting as it is commonly practiced reflect this aspect of invention. Aristotle's idea of invention, though, positioned individuals to seek outside themselves for truth; and this seeking, although it might take the form of reading sources as described in Chapter 7, might also take the form of experience, which would be more like the concept of inquiry described in the studies referred to by Graham and Perin. In some ways then, inquiry could be seen to encompass both prewriting and invention—and to move beyond them.

Primarily, an interest in students' experience and their active involvement in meaning making are at the heart of inquiry. An elementary school in my town exemplifies Hillocks's interpretation of inquiry: students there wondered which of the local television channels gave the most accurate weather forecasts. They devised an experiment in which they would compare each station's forecast against the actual weather and temperatures for a specified period of time. They calculated the ranges and derived percentages of accuracy in order to find an answer, which they published. This experience is an excellent example of the kind of inquiry that Hillocks envisions as valuable to writers.

With all that it entails, why should teachers incorporate inquiry into their classroom writing process? Hillocks offers a good reason: the skillful use of language and conventions without substantive content, which comes from inquiry, will likely result in writing that is "trivial and inconsequential" ("Inquiry" 659). How many pieces of this kind of writing have we read as teachers? How many research papers that bore us to tears because they are nothing about real learning or real inquiry (our hope for the assignment!), but merely a string of other-people's-ideas masquerading as a student paper? Research reported by Nippold, Ward-Lonergan, and Fanning reveals that "children's knowledge of the topic at hand greatly impacts the quality of their writing" (126). In other words, the more we know about our topic, the better we can write about it. Inquiry is the heart of good writing.

In the world outside of school, writers wouldn't think of writing without inquiry, without experiencing—and thus, knowing—what they are talking about (although some letters to the editor in my local newspaper might seem to provide evidence to the contrary). But in school, students are often prompted to write just from what they know (think of state tests of writing). Hillocks presents the following stinging indictment of the lack of inquiry in school writing:

> The point is that in no place other than school and college writing classes is writ-
> ing treated as something that can be accomplished with little or no inquiry. To
> satisfy this requirement of no inquiry, students are asked to write about topics of
> such a general nature that they can be expected to fulfill the assignment off the
> top of their heads. Such topics hardly ever allow for real meaning making. They
> encourage students to rely on texts that float in the community mind, much as
> waste paper blows about the windy streets of Chicago. (*Teaching* 16)

Reither agrees, observing that "composition studies does not seriously attend to
the ways writers know what other people know or to the ways mutual knowing
motivates writing" (622). Inquiry can contribute that to the writing process and
to student writers' development.

Besides contributing to the content of their writing, the process of inquiry
can help teach students how to think. Gage states, "Robert Frost once remarked
that students cannot be taught to think by rapping them on the knuckles and
shouting 'Think!' They can, however, be put into situations that require thinking
from them" (20). Inquiry activities should provide just such a situation. When
students are confronted with a question or a discrepancy that matters to them,
they will seek an answer. According to Hillocks, the inquiry process that follows
the desire for an answer is like the development of an argument, "an argument
whose claim is continually reshaped by our changing perceptions of the problem, its data, and its context. The more we work with a problem, the more likely
we are to deconstruct and reconstruct our thinking about it" (*Teaching* 129).

Brian Saxton, a teacher I know, offers his classes an example that portrays
just what Hillocks was explaining about how inquiry creates an argument. Brian
describes his inquiry into which World War II fighter, the German Focke-Wulf
FW-190 Würger or the U.S. Navy's Vought F4U Corsair, would win in a fight.
Each was its nation's best plane, but they had never faced each other because the
U.S. plane had served in the Pacific. At first Brian looked at air speed as a determining factor, finding that the German plane had an advantage. He thought
he'd found his answer—until he learned that the top speed advantage applied
only at higher altitudes, and that the German plane couldn't sustain the high
speeds without causing a fire. In a lower altitude fight or with sustained fighting, the American plane had the advantage. But his inquiry wasn't over:

> As I pushed on with my research, it became clear that, though energy is the *most
> important* factor in determining dogfight success, it is certainly not the *only* fac-
> tor. For example, the Würger could out-climb the Corsair at most altitudes and
> at higher speeds. This gave the German plane a distinct advantage in the use
> of "boom and zoom" dogfight tactics (fighting in the vertical) as it could gain

enough altitude over the F4U to control the fight. However, the Corsair could significantly out-turn the FW-190 at any speed or altitude which gave the American aircraft a strong advantage in "turn and burn" (fighting in the horizontal). A Corsair with a 190 on its tail could turn inside the Würger and be behind the German in three turns. The 190 had a higher roll rate, but the F4U pilot had better forward and downward vision despite its long nose. The 190 had more powerful armament, but the Corsair had better armor and durability. The list goes on and on.

Eventually, I realized that every advantage I could find in one aircraft's characteristics could be equaled by an advantage in the other's. Every time I thought I had found my answer and could make a solid argument for or against one of the two aircraft, I found further information that made my argument moot.

As he conducted his inquiry, Brian built, and rebuilt, an argument. His inquiry process is exactly what Whitin and Whitin explain should happen when students practice inquiry: they should learn that "increased knowledge leads to new questions, and that there will always be spaces in their understanding that only their imaginations can fill" (48). That continual movement between questions and the search for answers that leads to more questions is the same kind of thinking that writers need as they move through drafting and revision cycles. Inquiry, therefore, not only informs writing, but it also develops in writers the kind of thinking that will help them write more effectively.

Although there has been an emphasis on inquiry for developing content, Hillocks actually sees inquiry as necessary in two avenues: one is for content, or what Hillocks calls "inquiring into the substance of writing" (what I call *strategies for knowing*); the other is for "strategies for producing various kinds of discourse" (what I call *strategies for genre*) (*Teaching* 99). Both kinds of inquiry are important because writers need to know what to say as well as how to say it. Hillocks's work mainly focuses on the first kind of inquiry, and he worries about teaching practices that reduce the second kind of inquiry to a kind of formulaic instruction (teachers giving students formulas for writing in a variety of genres). Ray, on the other hand, has done extensive work on the second kind of inquiry—inquiry for genre strategies—and she uses the same experiential focus that Hillocks asserts is essential for development as a writer.

Ray's approach coincides with the one that Hillocks proposes because it gives students ideas about writing—more about the shape and context than the content—but it uses an inquiry process all the same, inquiry in the spirit that Hillocks envisioned. Her inquiry follows a series of stages, not in a linear progression, but in what she calls a predictable rhythm for inquiry into texts and how they work. The stages include gathering texts and setting the stage, followed by immersion and close study, before students write "under the influence" (*Study*

112). The recursive part of the stages Ray describes comes in the middle; at the beginning students need to know the kind of texts they'll be investigating, and at the end they need to write that kind of text. But in the middle, they can return again and again to the inquiry that will enable them to write.

Ray's inquiry follows the activities that Hillocks and Whitin and Whitin establish for inquiry. Students investigate texts that fit a specified genre, texts the teacher has identified for them to use, and eventually texts that they find themselves to see if they fit the genre's characteristics. In this investigative period, students describe the characteristics they observe through multiple readings, and then compare or contrast their findings against each other; in this way, they refine a theory of what a genre is, what it does, and how it does it, as they collaborate and immerse themselves in the exploration of texts, testing their tentative conclusions against further examples as they continue to inquire. During this investigation that clearly matches the expectations of inquiry established by Hillocks, students focus on these questions:

- *What kinds of topics do writers address with this genre and what kinds of things do they do with these topics?* This question helps students understand the human intentions this kind of writing serves in the world of writing.

- *What kinds of work (research, gathering, reflecting, observing, etc.) does it seem like writers of this genre must do in order to produce this kind of writing?* This question helps students understand the preparation and process writers use to write in the genre.

- *How do writers craft this genre so that it is compelling for the readers?* This question helps students understand how writers do this kind of writing *well*. (Ray, *Study Driven* 125)

By developing and testing answers to these questions, students are prepared then to conduct inquiry into appropriate topics and develop their writing appropriately for the genre. Inquiry, at two levels, makes this possible.

Some might see this emphasis on inquiry as a stance against the idea that writing leads to discovery. Hillocks notes this, and agrees that "writing is a process of discovery; without question there are, in Donald Murray's words, 'always surprises on the page.'" At the same time, though, Hillocks argues that some of that discovery may include what a writer gains that does not show up on the page: "part of the writer's perspective and, therefore, personality" (*Teaching* 15). I explain to my students, who often think that they should include every piece of information they find during inquiry, that to be a good writer, they need to know much more than what they put on the paper. I hold my arms straight out to my sides. "You need to know this much," I say, and then move my arms so that my hands are now about a foot apart in front of me, "to write effectively about this much of your topic." Sneed Collard says it more poetically: "A draft is never an inflated version of your research; it's a tiny fragment of what's best or most interesting" (qtd. in Spandel 60). Only by discovering more than they need will students understand what's important to say about a topic, what aspects are worth sharing, and what ideas are just good to know so that they can write with some authority.

So what does all of this mean for us as teachers? Of course we should help students see the value of inquiry in their development as writers and learners. Beyond that, though, we should help them become independent users of inquiry in seeking answers to their own questions, not just in our classes and for our projects, but for life.

Principles

Questioning Environment

Curiosity must be an essential part of inquiry; therefore, we need to help students learn to generate effective questions, to return to the curious natures they had as small children, when they asked questions about everything. Questioning requires that the classroom be a safe place to be curious. If students really do have thoughtful questions, we can't, as I've sometimes done, worry more about finishing the planned lesson than about answering their questions. We have to allow the time for questions, and we have to be willing to be asked questions when we don't know the answers. As one of my students said recently, when I asked why students give up asking questions, "Some teachers just pose questions that they know the answer to and know we don't. They just want to show how smart they are." When teachers do that, students quit asking questions—and actually may learn to fear questions when they are used as weapons in the classroom. Another student added, "And some teachers act like we are dumbheads by asking the questions we ask." Obviously, a large part of helping students become inquirers is to help them see questioning as a valued behavior in our classes. That means allowing time for questions, valuing the questions that get asked, and encouraging more questions by our modeling of delving deeper.

We can also help students see how questions inspire writing. In fact, I tell my students that all writing begins with a question. All of mine does, for sure. Fiction often begins with a "what if" question. My poet friends tell me that poetry is written in response to a question; the poem is the answer. Many books even tell us the question that started the inquiry that led to the book. Shields wrote *Mockingbird* because his students asked him (over and over again) why Harper Lee wrote only one book. *Mockingbird* is his answer to that question. Ballenger describes writing a book about lobsters:

> Even though I grew up in landlocked Chicago, I'd always loved eating lobsters af-ter being introduced to them at age eight at my family's annual Christmas party. Many years later, when I read the article in my local newspaper about the van-ishing lobsters, I was alarmed. I wondered, Will lobster go the way of caviar and become too expensive for people like me? (25)

Ballenger's wondering led, eventually, to a 300-page manuscript. As McPhee passed through Rockefeller Center on his daily commute, he watched the orange juice in a fresh-juice stand change colors with the seasons. He later saw an ad that pictured four oranges; they looked the same to him, but they had different names. He wondered. Eventually, his wondering led to travel and answers and a book, *Oranges*.

Helping students see that writing emerges from questions can be a good way to help them see that their questions matter and can lead to writing. It also raises the issue of how many questions we have to ask before we find one that leads to the kind of writing we want to see. This is even more reason for learn-ing to ask lots of questions as the initial stage of inquiry: we don't know which questions will take us in fruitful directions and which lead us to new questions. When my students write I-Search papers (Macrorie), they begin with a question, but they often find that the first question leads to another and then another as they inquire. One student wanted to know how to convince his mom to stop smoking. He started with questions about the health risks, but then he ran into an interesting fact about how smoking shrinks the capillaries that feed the skin. As he asked about the implications of that fact, he found that the decreased blood flow actually promoted aged-looking skin. He decided that his mother would be more likely to find that argument convincing, because she already knew about the health risks considered common knowledge. His first question isn't where he stopped—and that's part of the benefit of teaching students to conduct extended inquiry: they learn to ask questions about the information they get from their initial questions.

Additionally, as part of their questioning, students should inquire into the genre they are writing. How many times in school do we ask students to write in a genre that they have never read? How much better are we at writing in a familiar genre, one we've read many times? The first time I was asked to write an author's blurb for a piece I contributed to a journal, I didn't think: I just wrote. When the journal came out, I was embarrassed. My author's blurb was noticeably different from anyone else's. It showed my outsider status: I didn't understand the expectations of the genre. Now, I'm more careful, because I realize that all writing is a genre of some sort.

When we want students to write memoirs, they should be reading memoirs and asking questions about what the genre does and what it doesn't do; what it talks about and what it doesn't; the writer's stance; and the ways the genre could be shaped. The same holds true if we want students to write a letter to the editor or a literary analysis paper (try finding some of those!) or a journal entry. Even if we've read a genre many times, if we haven't read it from an inquiry stance, we might not know how to write that genre. If we haven't read it and then compared and contrasted it with other genres, questioning and formulating hypotheses about how the genre works and then checking our hypotheses against other examples to refine and clarify our thinking, we might not know how to write that genre. This kind of questioning and inquiry should be a part of all the writing that students do.

Broad Perspectives

It's essential for students to understand that inquiry—even when more traditional and less experiential—should be more than googling a topic on the Internet. Hillocks explains that "not infrequently the serious writer's inquiry takes place over a lifetime" (*Teaching* 13). He then provides examples of the kinds of inquiry that some writers use. Upton Sinclair, for example, lived for seven weeks among the people whose lives he would portray in *The Jungle*; later he developed characters from those he observed in a wedding party he happened to watch. As Hillocks elaborates, "Clearly with Upton Sinclair, as with other writers, the process of inquiry is integral to the writing process. The 'texts' from which he borrowed were the scenes he observed, the lives of the people he met and spoke to" (*Teaching* 15). Students can benefit if they realize that they can be conducting inquiry throughout their lives.

Inquiry of both content and genre should be part of all the writing that students do. Although this doesn't always have to mean the formal type of inquiry often associated with research papers, some type of inquiry is important. Even in writing personal narrative or memoir, students can conduct a variety of kinds of inquiry: they can make lists of sensory impressions as they remember the events they are describing; they can interview people who were present at an event, to compare different versions of the event; and they can reflect carefully on the meaning of events. As Hillocks notes, even in the cases of personal narratives and poetry, "various strategies of inquiry frequently come into play, consciously or not, as the writer pushes, prods, compares, interprets, and reinterprets the stuff of the experience as it exists in memory" (*Teaching* 15). Helping students practice inquiry with all their writing aids in establishing inquiry as a part of the writing process.

To help my students understand this concept, I share with them the inquiry used by published authors, and I encourage them to look for evidences of inquiry in the books and articles they read. We can often find this information for picture books in the author's note (even in the illustrator's note, as illustrators also conduct inquiry) or in the prefaces of other books. For instance, in the preface to *Mockingbird*, Shields recounts the books he read, the libraries he visited to find primary sources, and the variety of people he interviewed. Rubin, the author of *The Yellow House,* explains in the author's note that she visited museums, read books, letters, and journals, and viewed paintings in order to write the book. Crowe told me that when writing *Mississippi Trial, 1955,* in addition to more traditional research, such as reading books and newspapers, part of his inquiry included visiting the setting of the book to smell the smells, taste the local food, and listen to the cadence of the speech. This was all essential knowledge for him to write the story.

I recently read Roach's book *Stiff,* about what happens to (or is done to) our bodies after we die. I was intrigued by the variety of inquiry methods Roach used to answer her question—and to inform her readers. What follows is only a short list meant to show the variety of her inquiry.

A Wide Variety of Reading Materials

- *Diary of a Resurrectionist* (early 1800s)
- *Journal of Food Science*
- Web search: *the father of*
- *The Chemistry of Death*
- *Proceedings of the Ninth Stapp Car Crash Conference*
- *Gunshot Injuries*
- Thomas Edison's diary
- *My Art, My Life* (memoir of painter Diego Rivera)
- *Surgery* (a journal)
- *Chicago Tribune*
- Government reports
- *Handgun Stopping Power*

- *British Medical Journal*
- *Buried Alive*
- Cemetery Scrapbook I

A Wide Variety of Observations

- University of California–San Francisco gross anatomy lab
- Oak Ridge National Laboratory and Shooting Range, University of Tennessee
- San Francisco College of Mortuary Science
- Wayne State University impact lab
- Smithsonian National Museum of Natural History
- A crematorium in Haikou, China (because of an article found online, published by the *London Daily Telegraph*)
- Colorado State University Veterinary Teaching Hospital
- University of Tennessee human decay research facility
- Business meeting on composting in Stockholm, Sweden

A Wide Variety of Conversations and Interviews

- Man in Colombia reported to have escaped from a murder-for-medicine plot
- Representative of the W. W. Chambers chain of funeral homes
- Injury analyst
- Los Angeles Police Department officer
- US Army's Intelligence and Security Command
- Neurosurgeon in Cleveland
- US Conference of Catholic Bishops

What all of these (and other possible) examples should show students—and us!—is that inquiry can take many forms beyond our expectations. When my students research, I encourage all sorts of experiences for their sources. A girl who was inquiring about astral projection interviewed a psychic and a palm reader. A boy who was considering auto body work as a career visited several garages to interview the mechanics and owners. These interviews and observations were in addition to more traditional types of inquiry. Larson argues that students "should be encouraged to view research as broadly and conduct it as imaginatively as they can" (220). I agree. We should help students see that inquiry can be conducted in a wide variety of ways, almost as many as they can imagine—and they *should* include their imagination.

Connection to Task

Hillocks asserts that "the kind of knowledge involved in inquiry is not general, but rather task specific" ("At Last" 243). What this means for our students and inquiry in writing classes is that we need to consider—and have students consider—the kinds of inquiry strategies that would be most helpful for the task at hand. Following Hillocks's explanation of an observation activity, Cucci and Kowalczyk explain a writing task in which students describe a shell so that other students, after reading each description, will be able to pick that particular one out of a collection of shells. Students do the same thing with pictures of people from *Life* magazine. These inquiry activities are excellent for developing observation skills, and will apply specifically to students' writing of descriptions and stories, even poetry.

If students are going to write about a character in a piece of literature, however, the kind of inquiry just described isn't as helpful. Probably, no picture will be available. What is the most appropriate kind of inquiry for this task, then? Certainly it involves observation, but of a different sort. I suggest having students do what I call the Big People activity (*Strategic* 36–37). In this activity, students collaborate on the general traits of a character in a piece of literature, and then search for the evidence—details—that would support the generalization in a piece of writing that students eventually will complete. Thus, the inquiry matches the type of question and task assigned.

As teachers plan inquiry activities that match the tasks and questions assigned, students will learn a variety of inquiry strategies; they should begin to see how to match strategies appropriately to a task. For example, the following inquiry activities might be specific to each corresponding task:

- Posing "what if" questions and imagining the unheard-of: to write a story
- Interviewing a family member: to write a memoir or biography
- Making something (for example, bread or a ceramic bowl): to write a process paper
- Conducting an experiment: to write a lab report
- Watching a play or movie: to write a review

Applications

Writing about a Concept

Teachers often have students write about concepts. I think it's a good way for students to analyze and synthesize—and then articulate their thinking on these concepts. One of the more interesting concepts I have used is the idea of hero, a fairly common topic. This concept also lends itself to the inquiry process. I like to have the inquiry grow out of what we're already doing in class, so I'm going to frame my explanation as part of teaching Lee's *To Kill a Mockingbird*, particularly the point in Chapter 10 when Atticus shoots the mad dog. But we can make the introduction to the inquiry in any way that fits our situation and our students' needs.

As we finish reading the chapter and begin discussing it, I guide our talk to this question: Is Atticus a hero for doing what he did? Students' discussion of this question leads us to the beginning of a definition of *hero*. As students start naming aspects of heroism, we compare these to Atticus's actions, and I list these criteria on the board. Then I have students develop the definition over the course of the next couple of days, as we read a variety of articles and essays, each time addressing these questions:

Do the actions of the person in the article make him or her a hero?

Why or why not?

What does our answer add to our definition of *hero*?

I begin by having students read a favorite essay of mine, Rosenblatt's "The Man in the Water." We work through the questions in response to this essay. The process continues with a series of readings. Teachers can, and should, find pertinent examples in their community or online. If I were doing this now, I would bring in a current newspaper or Internet article, such as the 2009 CNN online account of the US Airways flight that landed in the Hudson River. In this article, we read, "As the situation began to settle Thursday evening, the flight's pilot, Chesley B. 'Sully' Sullenberger, emerged as a hero, with praise being heaped on him by passengers, officials and aviation experts" ("Airplane" par. 11). Articles or essays that describe someone as a hero are perfect for this activity, as they allow students to refine their definition through inquiry. It's also a good idea to ask students to find their own news articles online and bring them to class for use in this inquiry.

I have students write up short scenarios, such as the following, for use in class discussion: A firefighter runs back into a burning building to save a dog. Is that being a hero? That particular scenario is challenging for my students because they have to consider (1) if doing your job can be considered being heroic, and (2) if going back for a baby would make a difference, in their view. If it does, what does this insight add to the definition of *hero*? We review the students' scenarios as further inquiry into what it means to be a hero. We observe (through reading how other students define *hero*); compare and contrast (by comparing the actions of one person to another); generalize (by listing criteria on the board); and test our generalizations (by measuring the criteria against our written scenarios). Then students write an essay explaining their personal definition of *hero*. In my experience, there is still not consensus—but that's okay. I don't expect students to come to agreement; I just expect them to consider all the things we've read and discussed. Usually, at this point, they write articulate and passionate descriptions with concrete evidence because the inquiry process has allowed them to acquire all the information they need to do so.

Even though this application deals with a specific concept, the process can be applied to any number of concepts that teachers might want students to use for inquiry: courage, justice, or equality, for instance. The process begins with a question, then continues with the search for examples to observe and compare until generalizations can be made. Then students need a chance to consider other possibilities as ways to test their generalizations before they write. Hillocks taught observation as an important part of inquiry. It can be valuable, even when the observation is not of concrete objects, but of ideas and actions in human stories.

Writing for Wikipedia

Recently I was trying to find an article I wanted to reference for my class. I couldn't remember the exact title, so I googled *metaphor*. I was surprised (though I don't know why) to see a Wikipedia entry appear for *metaphor*. For fun, I clicked on it and saw a page with this message at the top: "This article may require cleanup to meet Wikipedia's quality standards." I was intrigued. A little further down the page, I found this message: "This section does not cite any references or sources. Please help improve this section by adding citations to reliable sources. Unverifiable material may be challenged and removed." ("Metaphor"). I was even more intrigued. I knew that Wikipedia is written collaboratively, but I had never considered that I might be one of the collaborators. Then I read Crovitz and Smoot's *English Journal* article about having students contribute to a Wikipedia page. It's a perfect way to incorporate inquiry into writing.

First, have students talk about their experiences with Wikipedia and their understanding of how it works. They *should* understand how it works, and know why some teachers might not want them to use it as a source. This can create quite a discussion—and that's okay. Compared to their teachers, today's students are often more accepting of the democracy of online practices and the idea of sources being written by a fifteen-year-old somewhere in the world. Encourage students to find their own pages requiring "cleanup" on subjects that interest them. Students should each find a page with a question or questions that need to be answered, or a page that needs the addition of reliable sources.

Next, have each student conduct the inquiry needed to answer the question or supply the required information. Much of this inquiry may be conducted online, but I also encourage students to email academics who are specialists in the area they are researching, and ask them to recommend sources or to help with answers. Talk with students about appropriate ways to approach these academics, explaining that the kind of emails they send to their friends may not be appropriate for these queries. As they gather information, have students analyze what they find, comparing and contrasting ideas and results among their sources. Particularly for the outcome of this writing, Wikipedia, students will need to be aware of opposing views or contrasting viewpoints.

When students have their information, they should conduct inquiry into the genre of Wikipedia articles. These are written from a neutral stance. They are not meant to have a voice (unless it is an academic one that will blend with others on the entry page). As with any genre exploration, students should explore several examples and note the patterns in content (use of facts with associated citations and links, for example), in structure (paragraphs with topic sentences), and in tone (academic, neutral) to establish product goals. Encourage students to discuss why these characteristics are associated with Wikipedia, how they benefit users, and how they position both contributors and users. For students to incorporate their understanding into future practice, a genre study should look at more than form (Dean, *Genre)*.

Wikipedia has a style manual, but I found the article "Wikipedia: Version 1.0 Editorial Team/Assessment" more instructive in learning about writing for Wikipedia. This article explains the grading scale associated with Wikipedia articles, links articles rated at each level of the scale, and shows what I find particularly interesting: the evolution of one article from what the editors call "stub class" to the highest ranking, "Featured Article." This information can also contribute to students' product goals.

Students should draft their contributions and receive peer and teacher feedback before posting the writing. A follow-up for this inquiry project is to watch what happens to the contribution over time (each page has a history that can be accessed). Inquiry truly never stops.

Annotated Bibliography

Hillocks, George Jr. *Teaching Writing as Reflective Practice*. New York: Teachers College Press, 1995.

> This book is the foundation of the idea of inquiry and its value to the writing process. Although it doesn't offer many specific ideas for teachers, *Teaching Writing as Reflective Practice* can be an important resource for understanding the implementation of an inquiry approach to classroom learning in a way that will benefit students. Hillocks's overall explanation of the kind of classroom community and procedures necessary to make inquiry effective is invaluable.

Ray, Katie Wood. *Study Driven: A Framework for Planning Units of Study in the Writing Workshop*. Portsmouth: Heinemann, 2006.

> This is a great book to help teachers implement inquiry into students' understanding of different kinds of texts. Although Hillocks's explanation of inquiry focuses on the content knowledge for writing, Ray focuses on the kinds of texts that students can write through inquiry. She presents a plan that will develop independence in student writers, as they learn to practice inquiry for whenever they need to write a kind of text they've never written before.

Process Writing Approach

9

The writing process is an untidy business.

—*Donald Graves*

Overview

Collard describes his writing process:

> Contrary to the way many people envision writing process, I do not bulldoze my way through a rough draft and then revise. Personally, I *can't stand* for my sentences and paragraphs not to flow easily from one to another. If I write a sentence and I know it doesn't work, I make myself get at least a palatable version down before I continue. If a paragraph doesn't follow well from the one before it, I'll either cut it and start over, or go back and change the preceding paragraph. That doesn't mean I demand perfection at each step. It just means I don't want to trip and fall on my face, even during the early stages. As a result, what I call my "first draft" is usually, in reality, my eighth or tenth. Once that draft is complete, the real polishing—and fun—begins. (qtd. in Spandel 61)

Other authors have, in other places, described their own writing processes—and they all differ. The one thing these authors have in common is that they all see writing as a process of one kind or another, structured or loose, messy or neat, always the same or always different.

That writing is a process seems so commonplace now as to be trite. Writing has always been a process of sorts. Bizzell explains that writing process was around in classical times: "Greek and Roman teachers of effective writing and speaking elaborated a five-stage composing process: invention [. . .] arrangement [. . .] style [. . .] memory [. . .] and delivery" (49). It's just that by the 1900s and before the 1970s, writing was a truncated process—at least in school, where students wrote without prewriting or inquiry (with the possible exception of creating an outline), and then recopied their papers (not revising), correcting spelling as they went. It was a process, but a cut-down, linear one that students were often expected to figure out and complete on their own. In the 1970s, researchers gave us a richer view of the process that writers follow to produce polished writing. They showed us the many subprocesses that writers use, and they helped us see the recursiveness of those subprocesses. Together, these concepts provided a fuller perspective on what writing as a process means.

What have we gained as a result of that research? At its foundation, the research showed us that the writing process is variable. That is, we learned that it is not linear and not the same for every writer, or even for the same writer in different writing situations. As Bizzell notes, "[C]omposition scholars agree that the composing process exists or, rather, that there is a complex of activities out of which all writing emerges. We cannot specify one composing process as invariably successful" (49). Indeed, as I read about the causes of variability in the writing process, I found the following possible variables mentioned: a writer's personality, maturity, and work habits (Murray, "Teaching" 4); the kind of writing and "the student's 'ego-strength,'" (Nelms 114); the writer's knowledge about the topic, and his or her past writing instruction (Applebee 96); and the writing situation and many other possible variables. As Fulkerson summarizes, "There are many different 'writing processes'; what works for one writer may be disastrous for another, and what works one time for Writer Jones may completely fail for her at a later time" (98). Early research taught us this variable nature of the writing process.

Early research also taught us about the recursive nature of the writing process—that it could not be acted upon in a sequential way. Researchers investigated many possible aspects of what composing might entail and how these aspects might occur in relation to each other. In trying to explain the writing process, early models depicted it in three stages: prewriting, writing, and rewriting (or rehearsing, drafting, and revising, according to later researchers). But even as researchers named these stages, they knew that the names didn't fully represent the processes and subprocesses associated with writing. Perl explained it this way: "[R]ecursiveness in writing implies that there is a forward-moving action that exists by virtue of a backward-moving action" ("Understanding" 100). Current models of the writing process have elaborated on the early three-stage model in trying to identify some of the subroutines that Perl mentioned and, as a result, to encourage a more thoughtful consideration of the recursiveness of process. These newer models may add thinking, talking, planning, collecting ideas, conducting research, and generating notes to the prewriting, or early, stage. They also add revision, editing, sharing, conferencing, reflecting, and publishing to the rewriting, or later, stage.

Another thing we learned about writing from this early research is that some of the process isn't visible—that is, some of it (some say much of it) occurs when it appears that a writer isn't even thinking about writing. Murray notes that students staring out the window may be writing (*Learning* 32). Brodie reports Henry Miller's comment:

> Most writing is done away from the typewriter, away from the desk. I'd say it occurs in the quiet, silent moments, while you're walking or playing a game, or even talking to someone you're not vitally interested in. You're working, your mind is working, on this problem in the back of your head. (qtd. in Spandel 45)

Because writing is variable, recursive, and not always visible, it isn't easy to explain or to teach. "There are problems," as I tell preservice teachers, "when the writing process goes to school." These problems have raised some concerns and misconceptions about what the writing process actually is and how it is represented in school.

One concern with a process approach as represented in schools is its link to expressivism. The link is so close, in fact, that some people don't see the two as separate. Expressivism is a "theoretical perspective on writing that focuses attention on the writer as meaning-maker and on writing as self-expression and self-discovery" (Yagelski 206). Because process also concerns itself with the personal (early on, we learned that personal attributes contribute to the ways writers use the process) and because some early writing process researchers favored the ideas of expressivism, the two became linked. As Pritchard and Honeycutt note, "The theory behind the process model relied on the genre of narratives about personal experiences" ("Process" 278). Because of that connection, it probably isn't surprising that recommendations for writing about personal topics and using writing for self-discovery, both representative of expressivism, became tied to the writing process approach.

Early researchers and promoters of writing as a process also emphasized the use of writing as a mode of discovery. Murray explains that the writer "writes to discover, with surprise, disappointment and pride, what he has written" (*Learning* 6). Sommers describes "writing as discovery—a repeated process of beginning over again, starting out new" (84). The idea of discovery also suggests an expressive perspective, and many teachers have embraced the idea, suggesting to their students that if they just wrote, they would find what they had to say.

This wasn't quite what some of the early researchers meant by the term *discovery*. Perl explains it this way:

> Yet the term "discovery" ought not lead us to think that meaning exists fully formed inside of us and that all we need do is dig deep enough to release it. In writing, meaning cannot be discovered the way we discover an object on an archeological dig. In writing, meaning is crafted and constructed. ("Understanding" 104)

The idea of discovery still finds expression in classrooms I visit, where teachers exhort students, "Write. Don't think! Just write!" Concerns about the meaning of discovery and the link to expressivism have led to some serious criticisms of the way the writing process approach takes shape in some classrooms, as it seems to ignore issues of thoughtful inquiry and substantive knowledge.

One such criticism is the way this approach favors only certain types of processes (messy) and certain types of writing (personal). Harris critiques these aspects specifically: "Why should writing be a messy, recursive, nonlinear, anguished Beethovian kind of activity? Because that is the process which most seems to lead to the sort of self-expressive writing that Emig (and countless other English teachers) value above all others" (63). When Murray observes that "at the end of the composing process there is a piece of writing which has detached itself from the writer and found its own meaning, a meaning the writer probably did not intend" (*Learning* 17), we have to wonder: if we end up where we intended, did we do something wrong? If our process isn't messy, is something wrong? Because Murray spent so much time prewriting (he recommends 85% of the total writing time), if we spend more on revising, are we wrong? Because Elbow holds off revising until drafting is finished (xxiv), is it wrong to revise as we go? Collard's description of his process, reported at the beginning of this chapter, doesn't really fit with the kinds of process described in lots of books about teaching writing as a process. Collard revises as he writes. Is his process *wrong*? These kinds of questions arise when the language of the writing process research gets interpreted in some classroom practices.

Because of a failure to explain or consider the real purposes of the writing process, sometimes students have been led to believe that they should write only in certain ways and about certain things. Some students write their freewrites and brainstorms and webs *after* they've completed their piece of writing, meeting our need for them to *show* their process, but not meeting any of their own needs to write in the first place. Other students make up the personal experiences they think their teachers want—the self-discovery and self-exploration that some teachers who favor a certain approach to the writing process seem to expect from student writing.

An additional concern is that this interpretation of writing and what it was intended to do marginalizes some groups in the classroom. Ironically, an approach that was meant to fit individuals and meet their needs could actually alienate them. As Bizzell notes, "[T]his style [getting personal] comes more easily to white middle- and upper-class students than to others, thus preserving in personal-style pedagogy the very social discrimination it sought to combat" (55). If our experiences don't seem unusual enough, or if our cultural inclinations don't encourage us to share private or personal information, we might be at odds with such an approach to writing.

A final concern with a process approach, especially when linked to expressivism, is its neglect of the social aspect of writing. With its focus on the individual—on what each individual has to say, and on the way she might want to work through the process and express herself—there is little concern for aspects of writing related to communicating with others or considering the situation of a piece of writing. In the work of early researchers, I can see hints of an awareness of the influence of the social situation on writing. But because they didn't elaborate on this, what came to be the writing process in classrooms tended to be writing that neglected aspects of the social: collaboration (because of an emphasis on the individual and growth); audience (because considering audience might inhibit the use of writing for self-discovery); or context (because writing for self and about self doesn't concern itself significantly with situation).

Despite these issues, research on the writing process has made a huge, positive impact on writing instruction. Attention to the writing process

- turns attention to students and what they need, putting their work at the center of instruction;

- encourages inquiry into all facets of writing in an effort to see how better to engage and instruct students in writing;

- involves teachers in writing—with their students—in ways that were not in place before; and

- increases the potential to help students not only produce better writing but develop as writers in ways that weren't possible without applying process thoughtfully.

All of these are important benefits of the research that initiated what is now called the process approach to writing instruction. Like many good ideas, though, this approach changed as teachers, more and more removed from the original research, implemented its ideas in classrooms across the world. And, as Yagelski reminds us, "[T]here is no such thing as '*the* process approach,' a phrase that implies some sort of monolithic pedagogy or theory of teaching writing" (205). Indeed, what happened in schools was a variety of applications, some more loosely connected to the original ideas of writing process research than others.

In its early application in the classroom, the writing process was often seen as a very loose model of student-centered education. As Pritchard and Honeycutt note, "In the formative years, the process approach was linear and prescriptive, merged proofreading and editing as the same thing, and usually did not involve direct instruction—a sort of anything-goes model whereby process was valued over the product. In this early model, a simplistic pedagogy resulted" ("Process" 276). Even in the late 1990s, Baines and his coauthors noted that in the more than 300 classrooms they observed, teachers implemented the writing process in simplistic ways that did not reflect its full potential. Some teachers implemented selected elements of the process research and applied them without a full understanding of what process was meant to do: improve student writing. Pritchard and Honeycutt (citing Cramer) assert that "the writing process has its weaknesses; it is poorly implemented in many instances; it is not a panacea. But it is a better candidate for improving writing performance than the traditional approach" (qtd. in "Process" 282). I agree. And in its newer applications, it has greater potential than ever to do just that: improve writing performance.

How is today's version of the writing process approach modified from its earlier applications? Today's process approach still puts students and their own writing at the center of the model. It still encourages students to choose (among genres or topics), to accomplish their own purposes, to participate in prewriting experiences before writing, and to work with peers and reading. But in moving away from earlier models, today's approach also involves more explicit instruction from us, encourages reflection and strategy use for transfer, and places more emphasis on revision. With these adaptations, the writing process is proving to be even more effective in helping students develop as writers.

Principles

Time

Even in the early 1970s, proponents of teaching a more robust writing process recognized the necessity of time for an effective implementation of the approach (Murray, *Learning*). What often happened, though, was that teachers brought in the process but treated it as an elongated, linear version of what they had been doing before. Now, instead of students getting an assignment on Monday and being expected to have a polished draft by Friday, teachers engaged students in a rote formula: brainstorming on Monday, freewriting on Tuesday, drafting on Wednesday, peer review on Thursday, final draft on Friday. This form of process really didn't provide the time that students need as writers, despite its additional help through the process. As Dyson and Freedman explain, "[W]riters need [. . .] time to allow the subprocesses to cycle back on each other" (975). Certainly, limited time doesn't help students think about their writing. As Atwell points out, "[G]ood writers don't take less time; they take more. [. . .] We need to acknowledge, once and for all, that writers and writing need time" (*In the Middle* 92–93). Beyond acknowledging this need for time, we must provide it.

One outcome of providing adequate regular time in class for students to work through the writing process is that we show students that we value the process. Casey and Hemenway note that "by not giving them that time, in a sense what you're saying is you're not valuing writing as a process" (71). We can show that we value the process by providing time for writing—both in class and out of it. Atwell explains that "with adequate time to detour—to take risks and reflect on the results—writers learn how to consider what's working and what needs more work, to apply my teaching to their writing, and to take control" (*In the Middle* 93). As all writers know, sometimes there is no substitute for time if we want to create effective products. I have found that students need to at least begin writing in class because, no matter how well I think I've prepared them or how ready they think they are to begin, when they're at home in front of their blank screens or empty sheets of paper, they often can't begin. If they have a start in class, they are more likely to be able to continue outside of class.

However, we all know that there's never enough time to do all that we want or are expected to do. Now we have to add *more* time for writing process? What does this "more time" mean for a classroom? It may require a change in our perception of what it means to teach the writing process. For one thing, writing that is used to assess learning is less likely to be conducive to a writing process approach. If assessment of content knowledge (Did they read the novel?) is the primary purpose of a particular writing task, the process may not make much difference. Students could produce that kind of writing without working through the whole process, perhaps using an abbreviated approach—or even a single draft. The value of the product is in what it tells the teacher about learning, not in the quality of its writing. We might want to consider the purposes of the writing we assign students. If the primary purpose is to assess learning (the theme of the novel, or the information they've learned about the Civil War), might there be a better method for assessing? If not, maybe the assignment should be one that doesn't require using the writing process—thus saving time to work through the writing process for other assignments, ones that matter more to students. If we do that, our students are more likely to use the writing process in ways that will help them as writers and will teach them the value of that process.

If we believe that the writing process is not simply a series of steps a writer takes, but is instead a way of solving writing problems; and if we believe that the aspects of process employed are specific responses to differing problems in different writing tasks, then students—and teachers!—might approach the whole process differently. First, explains Applebee, "writing assignments would themselves be broadened to give scope for students' opinions and solutions" (111). That means that we would encourage students to write in a variety of genres and for a variety of audiences, so they would see how the process adapts to the needs of the individual and the writing situation. These kinds of considerations—genre and audience—would present a variety of challenges that students could resolve through their use of the writing process. But this kind of detection and solution takes time. Writing, when it moves beyond knowledge telling, encourages a richer view of writing process in our classrooms. And this requires us as teachers to provide appropriate time for students to resolve problems that occur with different kinds of writing.

Many teachers follow the models exemplified by the work of Atwell, Graves and Kittle, and Calkins when establishing a writing workshop in their classrooms. A writing workshop sets up student work and student choice as the centerpiece of the classroom; as such, it is "a classroom structure that takes a healthy chunk of time" (Lain 20). Workshops require time for students to think and to talk about their writing. That thinking and talking is often facilitated by teachers but directed by students. However, as Lensmire points out, "children's talk and actions can be turned to worthy and less worthy ends, and [. . .] as teachers we have the responsibility to push for worthy ones" (125). Atwell's revised workshop encourages teachers to take a more active role, moving toward what Taylor calls "interventionist pedagogy" (48). As Atwell describes it, "Just as there are times when kids need a mirror, someone to reflect back their writing to them, there are times when they need an adult who will tell them what to do next or how to do it" (*In the Middle* 21). In the more current models, writing workshops seem to be based on a few principles more than on rules of structure: "[K]ids need time to write, they need to own their work, they need to share, and all of this needs to be wrapped up in a safe classroom cocoon that inspires enough trust to get to the heart of writing" (Lain 20). With these principles in place—including time—writing workshops can teach students more about their writing processes than more structured environments might.

Even if we don't have the time or setting for a traditional writing workshop, time is still a key factor in teaching the writing process. Lain considers having "a predictable time" important in helping students "gain control of their own writing process" (21). I know what it's like to try to fit everything in, to make every minute count, especially as more and more time is devoted to classroom interruptions or testing. Still, we all must decide what to teach and what not to teach, what is a priority and what is not. When we make writing a priority, we find time for it. As Atwell asserts, this time is crucial for students: "When [students] can count on time always being there, they learn how to use it—when to confront and when to wait" (*In the Middle* 93). Although they may be staring out the window, what they know about the process should eventually lead them to put words on paper.

Flexibility

Because the writing process is not the same for all writers, nor even for the same writer at different times, flexibility in its practice is important for helping students use the process strategically to meet their varying writing needs. The problem is that schools allow only a certain level of flexibility. We can't let students take six months to write an essay—grades must be turned in at regular intervals, after all—and we are expected to address state standards and cover content. We can't let students play loud music when they write in class—other students might be distracted from their writing. Students can't just go for a walk to think about things—schools require that we monitor them for their own safety. With all of these considerations, only limited flexibility can occur at school. But that shouldn't mean that we take away what little room we have to make the process as flexible as possible. We don't have to force all students to work at exactly the same pace, but we can establish points at which we want most of them to show a specific level of progress. And they all don't have to work in the same way. Some of my students sprawl on the floor to write; others like a desk or computer. I have tried to accommodate productive flexibility when possible.

One way I learned to help my students see the writing process as flexible came as a result of a student's comment that the expectations in English class were unrealistic. He said something like this: "There isn't anyplace else in the world where I have to turn in drafts of my writing." He may be right. But that doesn't mean that writers in all walks of life don't work through at least portions of the writing process. Then I ran across Maxwell and Meiser's description of levels of writing. They use it to explain the intensity of grading that may occur with different kinds of writing, but I adapted it to use with my students to help them understand the writing process as it relates to writing inside and outside of class.

Level one (L1) writing doesn't really use the writing process. It's spontaneous writing. This kind of writing is probably personal and doesn't go far: to a friend or family member, or just for self. It isn't going to be judged or matter in big ways in a person's life. Emails to friends, text messages, grocery lists, and class notes might qualify as L1 writing.

Level two (L2) writing may use portions of the writing process. Writers may make a list and then a quick draft, or they may draft and then reread for a quick revision. When doing L2 writing, we need to think—at least a little bit—about the audience. This writing might not do its job if it isn't at least slightly polished or a little thoughtful. It has some influence, so it needs to have some process. What kinds of writing are L2? Emails to teachers asking for extra time on an assignment, letters to grandparents thanking them for the graduation gift, essay answers on tests, and personal blog posts might all qualify.

Level three (L3) writing uses the entire writing process. It usually involves inquiry of some kind, drafting, consideration of audience, revision, and editing. This writing is published in some sense of the word—either to a teacher or to a broader audience. Its quality will have an impact on how people think of the writer or her ideas. Examples of L3 writing could include college entrance essays, résumés, important papers written in English class, and letters of complaint to get money refunded because of poor products or service.

Helping students consider the writing process from the perspective of levels makes it flexible. This perspective also makes the writing process strategic because it encourages students to see that the process isn't just "something we do in English" but is something that they can use to help them in a variety of writing situations. Considering levels also helps students think of writing as situated: genres vary in their expectation of how much of the writing process needs to be practiced. Audience is also a factor in how much process should be used. By considering levels as a format for understanding when and how to use the writing process, student writers can begin to see the appropriate use of the process as Applebee describes:

> In a given classroom, the kinds and extent of process-oriented activities would vary from task to task in response to the difficulties posed by each task. Some tasks would require extensive prewriting activities; some would involve help with drafting; some would go through a variety of revisions; some would be edited to share with others; some would emphasize competent first-and-final draft performance. Running through all these variations would be an awareness, on the part

of teachers and students alike, that there are many different kinds of writing and many different strategies for approaching each task; and both tasks and strategies would be varied in a principled way. (107)

With a more flexible view of the writing process—not "anything goes," but not everyone doing the same thing or even everything every time—students can begin to see their processes as individual in meaningful ways, in ways that will matter to them outside of the classroom as well as inside it.

Ownership

Spandel makes this interesting assertion about the writing process and writers in today's classrooms:

Twenty-first century writing instruction can and should take student writers toward independence—toward greater control over their writing and the process by which they create it. Such independence can occur only when process is personalized, shaped to fit the writer—because process at its best, at its most functional, is different for every person. (40)

Ownership, the sense of how the writing process fits you and me and each one of our students, is key to developing lifelong writers. Even from the earliest applications of writing process theory, basic principles of student ownership of text, of choice of topics and genre, of voice and language—all aspects of writing—were essential to process approaches. Yet how we help students gain a sense of ownership might require a delicate balance between structure and freedom.

One classroom application of the writing process already mentioned is the writing workshop. Early on, Murray stated, "In teaching the process we have to look, not at what students need to know, but what they need to experience" (*Learning* 25). That experience of writing is essential to applying the writing process in classrooms. Students need to write. They need to write often. And they need to have some sense of ownership about what they write. These ideas are essential to a writing workshop. Atwell notes that in its early implementation, the workshop allowed her to reject certain orthodoxies, but "as part of my transformation I embraced a whole new set of orthodoxies" (*In the Middle* 17). She found that having no teacher in the center—turning all choices over to students—can be as limiting as having the teacher be the sole focus of the classroom. Atwell now has a more instructional role than before, but she still places students' writing and students writing at the center of the workshop, because those two elements contribute to the sense of ownership that is crucial in developing students' sense of themselves as writers, and to their understanding of writing process. If someone is always telling me what and how to write, how will I ever develop my sense of what the writing process can mean to me? That is key to ownership's importance as a principle of process.

Beyond having choice, though, students can also gain a sense of ownership over their writing processes through reflection, the opportunity to think metacognitively about how these processes help them as writers. Mostly, this thinking can help students reflect on how the processes they've used in the past have been beneficial in solving the problems posed by a particular writing task. Reflection should also move students to consider how those same processes might be useful in other writing situations and with other writing tasks. This forward movement of reflection is essential in developing ownership because it helps students see beyond the immediate product to themselves as writers.

Yancey makes these connected observations about the power of reflection in helping students develop as writers: "Through reflection, students invent identities" and "[t]hrough our own reflections, we make knowledge and compose understandings" (202). If we hope to have students see themselves as writers who can adapt the writing process to their own purposes and needs, we must ask them to reflect: to see their writing identity, and to compose their own understanding of what it means to be a writer. To do this, students should look back *and* look forward: "To develop as writers, students also need the opportunity to articulate their own awareness and understanding of their processes in learning to write" (National Writing Project 82). Reflection is essential, then, to ownership of the writing process.

Connection

A final key principle in using the writing process effectively in classrooms involves its connection to product. Many researchers have addressed the varying ways that individual writers use the writing process, but sometimes, in the rush of school days, we may forget that those expressions of difference also apply to varying writing tasks. As Applebee reminds us, "In the original studies [. . .] the choice of appropriate strategies was driven by the task at hand—not by a generalized conception of the 'writing process' that the writers used in all contexts" (102). What this means for teachers is that we must help students see that elements of the writing process, and the ways we use them, are determined largely by the specific tasks we are performing. I've already addressed levels of writing as one way to approach this kind of strategic use of the writing process, but there are more ways we can help students learn about the connection between process and product in our classrooms.

One of those ways is to draw attention to the writing problems posed by different writing tasks. It's easier for me, I know, to consider the problems I think my students might encounter in a writing situation, and then design process strategies that will address them, than it is to let students encounter those problems and then discuss possible solutions—a way of teaching that would be more beneficial to students, despite its difficulty for me. It's also easier for me to keep everyone on the same "schedule," especially when I have thirty-eight to forty students in each class, and I'm trying to help each one work through the writing process toward a specific goal. But that ease doesn't help my students. Instead, they often begin to rely on my direction of their process or on my dates to determine when they'll write. I'm afraid that in trying to accommodate the writing process in large classrooms, I've been guilty of doing what Applebee describes in his research into classroom practice: "In many excellent classrooms the various process activities have been divorced from the purposes they were meant to serve" (102). I appreciate the fact that he still might consider my classroom "excellent," but I know it could be better.

Applebee also offers a solution to help our students become more aware of how the writing process is connected to product. I think his solution is achievable even in large classes: "The novice must come to recognize not only that there is a range of prewriting, revising, and editing strategies available but that a writing task can be seen as posing problems for which those strategies offer particular solutions" (102). I can do that. I can help my students practice a variety of strategies, and I can help students see how the strategies of process address specific problems in writing. Even if I practice a less-than-ideal process in my classroom, reflection can help me move students to a fuller understanding of their own uses of those elements of process, an understanding of how the elements worked for them as individual writers and for the specific problems they faced (because we don't all face the same task in the same way). My talk in the classroom and the implementation of effective reflection can create a richer view of process than I might otherwise provide for my students.

In looking at all the research and application on writing process, I've sometimes found it overwhelming to determine how to make the best of the ideas work in the less-than-ideal context of public school classrooms. I find in this comment by Dyson and Freedman a comforting and thought-provoking way to continue my work on writing process with my students:

> Thus, process research, like all research, does not offer any simple prescriptions
> for practice, but it can offer a vocabulary for talking about the nature of writing

—planning, revisions, editing—and insight into how these processes work for particular writers in particular situations. (974)

I can use what the writing process offers—especially vocabulary and insight—to help my students develop as writers.

Applications

Developing a Sense of Process

One aspect of a process approach involves helping students develop their own sense of process—what it means to work through a writing process and what options are available to them as writers. Because students have only so many process options available to them in school—they can't take a bubble bath or a long walk through the woods during class, for example—I try to help them see wider options beyond the classroom through reviewing the processes of published writers. Murray advocated a similar experience decades ago (*Learning*), and I think it's still viable. And today, finding what writers have to say about their processes is even more possible because so many interviews are available online. If students can't locate published interviews with a favorite writer, they can often find information through the writer's Web page, and can email to ask specific questions about the author's processes.

This is how I did it. Every third Friday (or any other regular time that worked in the schedule), I set aside time for students to read interviews of published writers. I made several copies of chapters from books, including Strickland's *On Being a Writer* and the *New York Times*'s *Writers [on Writing]*. I also found some chapters online and printed them. I kept these resources for students to select from folders. If I had access to computers for all my students, they could find interviews on the following sites:

- The Internet Writing Journal: an online site for author interviews
- Powell's Books: interviews of authors whose books are currently in the public eye
- Bill Thompson's Eye on Books: oral interviews with authors of current books

Now, I also suggest encouraging students to find or interview writers of nonfiction. Because we know that writers use different processes for different kinds of writing, focusing only on writers of novels (or sometimes poetry) lets students see only some of the processes that are open to them. Compared to fiction writers, people who write at work often use very different processes—for one thing, there is usually more collaboration involved. Students should have a chance to consider strategies used by other writers besides the easily accessible literary ones. It would be a nice project for students to interview working people about their writing and writing processes—and then write up the interviews to be used as sources for future students investigating writing process in class.

With whatever sources, online or in print, those of fiction writers or other professionals who write, every few weeks have students read at least one interview of a writer who is unfamiliar to them. Then have each student write a reflection about the author's process as it might connect to his or her own: What did the author do in the writing process that might work for you sometime, and why? What did the author do in the writing process that would never work for you, and why? Because students know these questions ahead of time, they can take notes as they read. Then they can write their responses carefully, revising as they go. These are L2 writes; that is, they are not spontaneous writing, but neither are they writing that follows the whole writing process.

I collect the responses, just to read them over but not to grade, and return them to students to use in reflecting on their own writing processes and their development as writers. I ask students to identify in their ongoing reflections of L3 writing any new strategies they've learned from their reading of others' writing processes. Through this process, students begin to determine their own processes and learn that the options for writers are wide open—almost anything that will help them write more effectively can be a strategy.

Working with an Unfamiliar Genre

I first learned about the Unfamiliar-Genre Research (UFG) Project from the article "Researching Writing: The Unfamiliar-Genre Research Project" (Andrew-Vaughan and Fleischer). The authors have also published a book, *Writing outside Your Comfort Zone* (Fleischer and Andrew-Vaughan) that provides more details on the project. Essentially, the UFG Project encourages students to use the writing workshop model (a supportive environment) to work through the process of learning a genre that is unfamiliar to them. In her introduction to *Writing outside Your Comfort Zone,* Lattimer explains how the UFG Project bridges genre-based instruction with the process approach by incorporating many of the principles found in traditional writing workshops, particularly students' ownership of the writing process and product, and teachers' fostering a sense of community in the classroom.

In doing the project, students select a genre they want to explore, analyze multiple examples, keep a research journal about their explorations, attempt to write in the genre they have explored, and then reflect on the process and learning. In addition to the opportunity to learn a genre, students learn a process that, as the authors state, can help students "learn the strategies they'll need to take on the new genres that will confront them in their future worlds" (Fleischer and Andrew-Vaughan xiv). They also note that "an emphasis on genre studies can help students begin to understand that while the notion of process writing is absolutely central to the world of writers, different genres may elicit different processes" (3). I found this to be true when I asked my students to work through the process of learning and writing an unfamiliar genre: the UFG Project teaches writing process as well as genre.

With my students, I use a process patterned after the one in the original article. After some initial classwork on the concept of genre, I model the beginning inquiry process. I have selected a genre—wedding announcements—and I explain to my students why I am investigating the genre: when my eldest daughter was getting ready to have her wedding announcements printed, we had no idea what to do. We eventually settled on a formula the printer made available and just plopped in our specific information (names and dates). When another daughter was preparing to marry and was printing her own invitations, we needed to know how the genre worked so we could write our own. Because students will eventually select their own unfamiliar genre and provide a rationale for the choice, my experience helps to model this process for them.

To show the inquiry process this project entails, I share several examples of wedding announcements for us to analyze in class. We make a list of characteristics we notice. To this discussion, I add an aspect I learned from my own genre studies. I ask students to categorize the characteristics: which are mandatory, and which might be considered optional? I also ask students to hypothesize about why the characteristics exist in the genre; that is, what purposes do they help the genre accomplish? To which characteristics do audiences respond? What do these characteristics reveal about the situation and context of the genre? In this way, students move beyond looking at genres as a form and instead (I hope) see it as a response to a social situation (Miller).

After modeling this inquiry process so that students have an idea of how to work through it, introduce the assignment. First, ask students to brainstorm possible unfamiliar genres. This isn't easy, so I suggest giving students several days to consider the different genres they encounter during that time. To give students other ideas, teachers can also provide the list of genres that Andrew-Vaughan and Fleischer include in their works. Brainstorm as a class as well, to make sure that most, if not all, students have options and can make a selection.

Next, once they've chosen a genre, ask students to write a proposal: what genre will they investigate, and why? Expect a wide variety of responses; one of my students emailed that she wanted to investigate newspaper restaurant reviews partly because "the topic of food is anything but boring to me."

After introducing the assignment, follow the pattern established in the UFG Project outlined by Fleischer and Andrew-Vaughan. Have students keep a research journal, annotate examples of the genre, attempt to write the genre, reflect on the experience, and turn everything in as a portfolio of their learning. Although students do attempt to write the unfamiliar genre, the focus of this project is on the process of learning about the genre. Andrew-Vaughan and Fleischer explain that it's important to remind students that "this is primarily a research project, and although original writing in their chosen genre will be the centerpiece of the presentation, the writing quality is only worth a fraction of the final grade" (36). To me, this focus on process is essential. The project gives students experience with one genre; but the process prepares them for writing all through their lives. Have students consider how this process (exploring an unfamiliar genre) could become part of their overall writing process, a pattern they could use throughout their writing lives.

In their reflections about this project, several preservice teachers commented on how valuable it was to examine multiple examples of a genre in depth, something these successful students had not done before. One wrote, "In the past I have looked at maybe one or two examples and tried to go from there." Another wrote, "Without having done this I would have simply looked at one example [. . .] and tried to copy its style, form, and tone. Having read several and looked at what the writer did, the conventions became strategies in my head rather than just a style of writing particular to [this genre]." For these preservice teachers, their understanding of genres and how to get at the underlying conventions and principles would extend beyond their learning of a single genre. And now they would be able to help their future students learn the value of this process at a younger age than they did.

Annotated Bibliography

Atwell, Nancie. *In the Middle: New Understandings about Writing, Reading, and Learning.* 2nd ed. Portsmouth: Boynton/Cook, 1998.

A list of resources on the writing process in classrooms can't be complete without Atwell's well-known text. For teachers who have seen only the first edition, I recommend the second. I've found it much more applicable to the needs of large classes of secondary students, where I didn't always have the types of students that Atwell describes. The principles and practices she explains, though, can be adapted (and I think she'd say they *should* be) to fit the needs of a variety of writing classrooms. They help students learn to write by utilizing the findings of the writing process movement for a better learning situation.

Graves, Donald, and Penny Kittle. *Inside Writing: How to Teach the Details of Craft*. Portsmouth: Heinemann, 2005.

Although the DVD accompanying this book examines younger students and their writing, the principles the book addresses about effective writing instruction are not limited to a specific grade level. Beyond the information in the book itself, it's rewarding to be able to see and hear Donald Graves share his perspective on teaching writing from a process approach.

10

Study of Models

Reading is the creative center of a writer's life.

—*Stephen King*

Overview

In Chapter 1, I described my granddaughters writing books. They both knew, at a young age, what books were. They had books in their homes, they were taken on trips to the library to borrow more, and they were read to by parents, grandparents, aunts, and uncles. Unlike the reports my granddaughters would eventually write in elementary school or the papers in secondary, the books were pages stapled together along the left side. Books had pictures on each page helping to tell a story that was usually "pretend." One granddaughter, when she was six, wrote us a letter (see Figure 10.1). The envelope shows a stamp she drew in the top left corner, and both our names and hers in the place for an address.

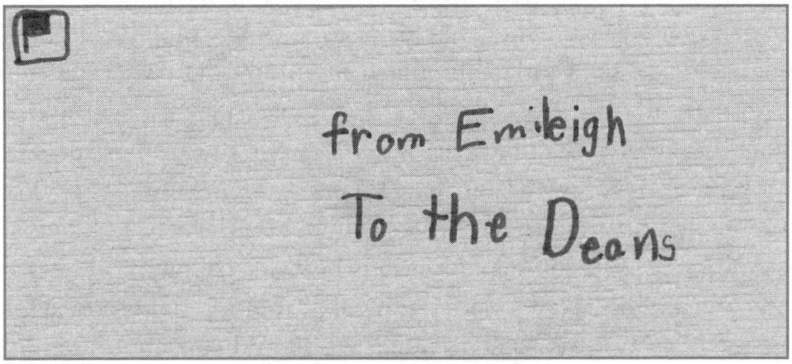

FIGURE 10.1. Envelope for my granddaughter's letter.

She knew, from exposure to letters, something about them and how they work. These examples—like others most of us can recall—remind us how influential models are to writers.

Studying models is an ancient—and persistent—tradition: Plato, Isocrates, Aristotle, and Cicero all comment on imitation as essential to learning. From the classical period to our time, other renowned writers, teachers, and philosophers have spoken of the value of studying models as a way to learn to write. In response to this long tradition, writers as varied as Malcolm X, Benjamin Franklin, and Winston Churchill all offer testimonials to the value of imitation, of studying models, in their development as writers.

Part of the reason for the lingering attachment to studying models is that language is learned by imitation, by studying the spoken models of people around us. The extension of this idea of using models to learn writing, then, seems natural. Chapman, referring to Bahktin's ideas on the interconnectedness of all language, notes that "even when we write to and for ourselves, we use words in ways that we have learned from our communities and cultures" (470). When we are writing for others, knowing how to learn expected conventions from the communities we are writing in is even more vital—and more dependent on an ability to study models for our understanding. Looked at from this perspective, studying models is not about "copying or reproducing the work of another, but transforming it in some important respects" (Butler 3). As the research supports it, studying models is supposed to aid students' writing development by helping them learn about how others use language as a way to build options for their own use, not to have them become slaves to forms or styles that others have created.

Another reason to include the study of models in a writing curriculum is the close connection between reading and writing. Researchers in the 1980s were able to show the influence of reading on writing. Stotsky, in particular, stresses the importance of that influence: "It is possible that reading experience may be as critical a factor in developing writing ability as writing instruction itself." (17). More recent research into the social aspects of composing characterize the relationship as one of intertextuality. Butler notes that "we often gain from interaction with other texts, people, and environments." In fact, he continues, "[W]hether we mean to or not, we are drawing upon those other and prior texts when we produce what we write." (3). Helping students understand how their texts relate to and borrow from other texts in the world around them is crucial for their continuing development as writers beyond school.

Genre theory, with its emphasis on the texts that writers use to act in situations outside of school, also suggests that we should consider the influence of reading on writing. Genre theorists credit a writer's immersion in a situation as key to being able to create the genres of that situation—and reading the texts produced by others in that situation is essential to such immersion. As Chapman points out, "[C]urrent thinking suggests that we learn new genres by forming analogies and making connections with the ones we already know" (472). In order to make those connections, to make comparisons that allow writers to know how to adjust writing to fit different situations, students need exposure to a variety of texts. They need reading. It's central to writing.

Despite its long tradition, though, the effective study of models has disappeared from many modern writing classrooms, to the degree that compelled Ostrom to observe, "One conclusion to draw from the apparent plight of imitation, especially if you're a contrarian, is that a concept so grossly out of fashion must have a lot going for it" (165). What happened? Like most things, no single factor accounts for the decline. With the rise of the process approach, for instance, the use of models was seen as too focused on form to be a valuable aid for teaching writing. Researchers worried that attention to a model might reduce writing to formula—and with the five-paragraph essay as the main model used in many secondary classes, they might have had good reason to think that.

From a related perspective, some teachers believe that studying models means a return to product-oriented instruction over process. Looking at a finished product doesn't make it easy to see what might have gone into the process of writing to arrive at that product: "It is one thing to know what the forms and rhetorical devices are [. . .] and quite another to generate the ideas and operate upon them so that they may be used in a new example of the form" (Hillocks, *Research* 228). And because process advocates envision a messy writing process as the ideal, asking students to study finished products seems even more likely to diminish their understanding and use of the writing process. Students, looking at a model, might imagine that their goal is to produce a similar, finished-looking piece, probably in one sitting, as they imagine that other writers might do. Such feelings could undermine a process approach and students' understanding of the writing process.

Some teachers also worry that students might feel intimidated or have their creativity stifled by studying models. And some students, seeing a polished product, might believe that they, too, are expected to achieve that level of success; that they, too, should have the kinds of insights and use the kind of polished prose they are reading in the models. Such beliefs could either block students' writing (because models inspire feelings of inadequacy) or encourage robotic imitations, void of voice or creativity (because students might not be able to imagine doing anything other than what they see in the models). Either of these responses is undesirable, of course, so some teachers avoid having students study models as part of writing instruction.

On the other hand, Ray predicts a different outcome from the study of models:

> Experienced writers, those with a well-developed sense of craft, of how writing can be fashioned, have the ability to envision more possibilities for their writing than less experienced writers because, to put it simply, experienced writers know more things that they might do with writing. They have read like writers over time, and over time this reading has given them a storehouse of knowledge about how to write. (*Wondrous* 49)

For Ray, and for teachers like her, the study of models, if handled appropriately, instead of stifling students has huge potential for helping writers envision possibilities—for their writing and for themselves as writers.

Less obvious reasons for the declining study of models include the difficulty of using models as an approach in writing instruction. In wondering why the study of models works so well in other areas, Charney and Carlson observe that the challenge has to do with the nature of writing: "Writing tasks are less well-defined. [. . .] The conventions of a genre are not hard-and-fast rules" (90). Indeed, there isn't one correct way to write for every situation. And interpreting what is needed from a model is a challenging task. As Charney and Carlson explain, writers need to determine the salient features of the model text, compare the situation of the model to their own, and then figure out the similarities and differences between the two, so they can work out which elements they should use from the model and which they should drop. Complicated! And teachers need to help students through this complex process.

A final blow to the use of models came in 1986, when Hillocks published his research on different approaches to writing instruction, along with various emphases of that instruction. His findings showed that "emphasis on the presentation of good pieces of writing as models is significantly more useful than the study of grammar [. . . but] less effective than other available techniques" (*Research* 249). Hillocks felt that using models provided sound declarative knowledge, but didn't help with procedural knowledge; that is, students might understand the nature of the finished product but not be able to take the steps to produce it.

What Hillocks supported through his book *Research on Written Composition* was an environmental approach with an inquiry focus. As a result, many teachers interpreted what he wrote to be that the other approaches didn't work. In fact, what Hillocks wrote was this: "It is clear that the study of models has potential for helping writers at a variety of grade levels" (155). There is value in this method—as Graham and Perrin concluded in their later study *Writing*

Next—but the use of models needs to be clarified, and the practice of studying models to teach writing needs to be developed. In research where students were simply given a model and told to replicate it, writing didn't improve (are we surprised?). The study of models also didn't improve student writing when students were given only one model or were allowed to look at the model only prior to writing. Hillocks found—and research since then has supported this finding—that it isn't the study of models alone that is problematic. Instead, it's *how* models are used that determines whether they will be effective instructional tools.

There are plenty of reasons that the study of models *should* work in writing instruction. The first is its logic: many fields use models as a way to help novices gain experience. Despite the complexities of writing just mentioned, imitation is so much the way we learn in other areas that it just makes sense! In fact, Ianacone affirms the necessity of the study of models (at some level) to writing instruction:

> I have never had any reluctance to use models in my teaching; it never occurred to me that there could be any harm. [. . .] It was, after all, my own reading that inspired me to try to write; it is also a truism that you will never be a writer if you are not a reader. You simply cannot do (or, at least, cannot do well) what you've never seen done. Can you imagine a Little Leaguer never watching a baseball game? A painter never looking at paintings? I have absolutely no fear that the insights and examples provided by models will ever stifle the student's own voice; we, each of us, will always do things our own way. (20)

Like Ianacone, my own experience has taught me that if I didn't have my students study models, they used models from their lives instead—so persuasion sounded like television ads: *If you call within the next fifteen minutes . . .* The study of models is just logical.

A second reason for studying models is that it benefits students. Fisher and Frey, in their work with struggling adolescents, find that "using existing writing as a model for new writing is another way to engage young writers." Besides engaging students, these researchers also find that studying models offers them "increased [. . .] control" because of the "framework" provided by the models ("Writing" 400). Creativity theory suggests that studying models isn't necessarily constraining: writers need to know what is possible and what is "usual" in order to make choices about following expectations or doing something different, something creative. Ray's work with elementary students shows the same benefits: students learn their options as writers because of their study of models. The study of models can give students more than just an idea of how to proceed with a particular writing task. It can teach students a *practice* they can use throughout their lives as writers. Knowing and using options is both engaging and enabling.

Of course, one concern—that looking at a product can't tell us about the writer's process—is a valid issue. From the final product, we can't see what gave the writer the idea, or how the writer conducted inquiry or decided on an organizational pattern. It's true that we might not see the writer's entire process, but students can learn part of the process for themselves. They can know that at some point, that writer—like all writers—looked at how other writers did things in order to get ideas for her own writing. Without this study of models, teachers are often left with only simplified visions of writing: formulas. And, as Ray notes, "When teachers give students a simple way to write something, not only are they not true to the product, they aren't true to the process either" ("Exploring" 243). The study of models can enhance our students' understanding of process—their own, if not the original author's.

Teaching students how to study models to get ideas for their own writing is essentially teaching them part of the writing process, the process that writers outside of school follow all the time. In life outside of school ("real life"), we use writing mostly to *do* things, to communicate something, so we usually decide (or have told to us) the product before we begin: "I'm going to write a letter to the company about this product's ineffectiveness." Or "Write a memo to the employees in your section to explain the company's position on this matter." Rarely in real life is the sole purpose of writing self-expression, where the shape of the writing finds itself as we write. When we start to write in real life, we often start with the product in mind—and we are left to determine an effective process for the task, much as we might show students to do through the study of models: How might the writer have conceived the idea for this writing? What inquiry do you think the writer had to conduct? How do you think the writer came up with the organizational choices?

The study of models, rather than undermining the process approach, is probably a more accurate representation of how writers in life situations outside of school actually use process, more accurate than the idealized version often presented in classrooms. Studying models can actually enhance a process approach—if we think of it that way. What research and practice tell us is that we should match the model to the task and to our students' needs, and that we need to do more than simply hand out a model for writing. That's where the principles come in.

Principles

Text Selection

One key principle for the effective use of models involves the selection of those models. First, students need a variety of examples to study. A limited number of models might suggest a single way to approach writing any text and could contribute to a perception of writing as having only "one right way." One problem that sometimes occurs with a study of models is that students interpret their use as encouragement from teachers to "copy" the model. Indeed, if students see only limited numbers of models, or samples that are too alike, they're less likely to see options in and flexibility from the study of models. A limited number of models tends to reinforce the idea that a model is a formula, and that the only way to complete a writing task is to follow the model slavishly.

A second aspect of selection is that the models should not be too long. Hillocks's research showed positive results when teachers used "models [that] were relatively brief [. . .] and [that] were selected to illustrate relatively few but specific points about good writing" (*Research* 155). Smagorinsky later found the same thing: "[M]ore successful models targeted one or two writing features rather than a whole complex of features (referred to in Charney and Carlson 91). From this research, we should conclude that we can't expect a single lengthy model to do too many tasks. Instead, students will benefit if they don't have to attend to so much at one time. In my experience, if I want to use a longer piece, I'm better off taking an excerpt from it for a model study, finding a part of the writing that exemplifies the particular elements I want students to examine. This is more useful than having them look at a long piece and try to find options for themselves as writers. Although research doesn't say this explicitly, my feeling is that cognitive overload occurs when students have too much text as a model; they simply have to hold too much information about content, structure, and style to be able to focus on the options possible for them as writers.

That said, once students have the idea that texts can serve as models, they sometimes effectively use a single model to give them ideas for their writing. One of my daughters did this with a book that my grandchildren loved to have me read to them, Mayo's *Dig Dig Digging*. It's about heavy equipment: bulldozers, tractors, cranes, and so on. Each page has a simple text describing a single piece of heavy equipment. The structure and rhythm of the text throughout is similar to this sentence from the page about bulldozers: "Bulldozers are good at push, push, pushing, over rough bumpy ground, scraping and shoving" (n.p.). My daughter made a book about grandparents, filled it with pictures of us with our grandchildren, and printed it using tools provided on the Heritage Makers website. She used the model of *Dig Dig Digging* for her own text, and it's evident how the model inspired her but did not constrain her to a rigid formula: "Grandmas are good at bake, bake, baking, With wooden spoons stirring, beaters mixing. Take a lick, yummy tasting. Mmmm. Yea. Grandma." From this example I hope it's clear that, although for exploration of options for a genre, choosing a wide variety of texts helps students see a range of possibilities, once they understand how models work, they might sometimes choose one—or teachers might—that offers possibilities students can take advantage of.

Talk

One classroom procedure that's essential for the beneficial study of models is talk. Students need to be able to articulate what they notice about sample texts, and they need to talk about their noticings with other students to help them clarify their findings. Ray recommends five steps in helping students use models as ways to find options for their own writing:

1. *Notice* something about the craft of the text.
2. *Talk* about it and make a theory about why a writer might use this craft.
3. Give the craft a *name*.
4. Think of *other texts* you know. Have you seen this craft before?
5. Try and *envision* using this crafting in your own writing. (*Wondrous* 120)

Notice how important talking—discussion—is to this process? Whether I have students work through this exact process or a similar one, discussion is essential. By responding to what others see and how others interpret what they see, students build their understanding of how texts work. This isn't a process that students can do by themselves, at least at first; when they progress, we hope they can. Even then, they will probably use internal talk to explore this process. To start off, though, and often throughout our explorations of models, there is a need for discussion.

An important part of classroom talk relates to theorizing. What students notice and what they discuss must include analysis and theorizing. While students are examining multiple examples, they need to be able to make guesses, articulate assumptions, and draw some conclusions about what writers do and why they do it. Students accomplish this through theorizing. Hillocks's research showed that a contributing factor in the beneficial study of models is "the types of student tasks accompanying the use of models" (*Research* 156). Analysis and theorizing are two such tasks. Hillocks found this approach to instruction contributed most to student learning and involved the following activities: "careful observation and representation in language of phenomena observed, questioning at every stage, comparison and contrast of the phenomena with what is already known (prior knowledge), interpretation leading to tentative hypotheses, testing of tentative hypotheses" (*Teaching* 105). This sequence of activities, what Hillocks calls the inquiry approach, is exactly what should happen with the study of models: analysis and theorizing, moving into application in writing. Chapman agrees, recognizing the limited value of having students copy teacher-selected models, but reminding us that models "have been shown to be beneficial when students generate criteria and apply them to their own work" (488). Analysis and theorizing: these are key principles.

Theorizing, though, requires a classroom that allows—even encourages—taking risks. When we make guesses about something, especially when we're guessing during exploration, we often follow false paths or make incorrect assumptions. When students theorize about what they notice in writing, they make themselves vulnerable. Our classrooms must be places where this is okay. For me, part of establishing a safe classroom is the way I set up the questioning. I notice that, initially, students might be reluctant to risk guesses, anticipating that I have a specific answer in mind. I may let them work with partners first, which sometimes eases them into the theorizing part of analysis. Even then, though, my prompting can't look like I'm trying to get students to guess the answer that's in my head. I encourage them to look for multiple "right answers" or for another theory in addition to the first one that comes to mind. In so doing, I establish our classroom as a place to explore—and explorers don't know where they are going until they get there.

Another way we create this environment is through our responses to students' ideas. My response to students' comments is, in large measure, a gauge of how the class will feel about taking risks with theorizing. For example, the more I work with models, the more I'm able to anticipate what students will probably notice, and predict the ways they will theorize about them. That said, I am always surprised. Someone always comes up with something I hadn't noticed myself, or something no one before has noticed—and someone always theorizes something so far out that it's hard to rein in the idea to something reasonable. How I respond in these situations goes a long way toward creating the kind of environment necessary for effective exploration of models. I must respect all theories students offer, even ones we eventually reject.

Integration

Timing is a significant part of integrating models effectively: where in the writing process are models most useful? They can be useful all the way through, of course, but the writing task largely determines when models would be most beneficial. As a rule of thumb, I time the introduction of models by how well my students know a genre. The more familiar the genre, the later in the process I introduce its models. Narratives, for example, are a genre students in secondary schools know something about, so I introduce the models just prior to drafting, after students have a solid start with inquiry but in time to help them refine their understanding for drafting. If a genre is less familiar, for example a résumé or précis, I introduce models earlier so that students can develop a general sense of the writing: What kinds of ideas does this genre take up? What is the role of the writer? Who uses the genre and for what purpose? These questions are important in early stages of the writing process so that students know how to begin thinking about their inquiry and writing.

Beyond introducing a genre, though, models should be used at other times during the writing process. Charney and Carlson note Smagorinsky's research on this point: "In several studies in which models failed to improve performance, the models were available to participants only before, and not while, they wrote" (91). It seems only logical that students should have access to the texts that they want to imitate while they write. Otherwise, how hard would it be to use what models have to offer? Charney and Carlson conclude that "consulting models actively during the writing process may provide the writer with a database for testing whether a candidate idea should be included" (114). What this means is that we need to consider when it would be best to introduce and study the models, but also how to keep them ready as references during students' writing processes.

The use of models also should be integrated into effective writing instruction because the use of models alone may not be sufficient for many student writers. Certainly some writers can use models alone. Quindlen describes how her own skills as a writer developed from her reading: "I wrote fiction in college, and then for many years I wrote fact, as best I could gather, discern, and describe it, as a newspaper reporter. Then I wrote fiction again. Reading taught me how to do it all" (*How* 58). She argues that all writers use reading as a way to learn to write—and to a certain extent, she is correct. But many of our students need to be taught, first, how to study their reading material as writers do, and next, how to apply the skills they garner from that study. That's where additional instruction comes in.

From their research, Charney and Carlson report that "students wrote more successful products and reported using more active and evaluative writing strategies *when given models in conjunction with some other instruction* than when given models alone or guidelines alone" (115; emphasis added). Many teachers use mini-lessons as part of writing workshops. McElveen and Dierking recommend using demonstrations in mini-lessons as a "bridge" between the model and the student writing (362). In other words, the model can show what options students have, but unless students have some time to practice the skills exemplified and discovered in the models, they might not be able to use those skills in their own writing and for their own purposes. Without some additional instruction and practice, students might not gain the procedural knowledge they need as writers.

Applications

Using Models to Teach Persuasive Writing

This application uses models to prepare students to write persuasive essays for a general audience on a topic of interest, much like the persuasive essays published in popular journals, a genre we could call persuasive commentaries. This study begins by having students discuss what they know about persuasion as a purpose in communication. They should consider advertisements and other pervasive forms of persuasion, but also address what they know personally about persuasion: when they use it, how they try to persuade others, and what makes it more or less successful. This preparatory work helps students begin to see basic issues related to persuasion: audience concerns, tactics, use of evidence, appropriateness of tone, and so on. With these ideas already in their minds and connected to their experience, students are ready to look at models of written persuasion.

I recommend using of a variety of models, available from many sources: *Newsweek*'s "My Turn" column is often persuasive, although sometimes, like other columns, it's merely commentary; Rick Reilly's past columns in *Sports Illustrated* (available online) are sometimes persuasive, sometimes commentary, and almost always humorous; Quindlen, George Will, and others who write for *Newsweek*'s "The Last Word" vary between commentary and persuasion. Teachers might find editorials in local newspapers that work as well. Mostly, I try to find interesting models that are relatively short.

Over several days, acquaint students with the models, either as a whole class or in small groups, depending on how familiar they already are with the genre.

Sometimes it's a good idea to examine one model together as a class, followed by student examination of additional models in small groups; or work through several models together, to help students begin to see what's in a model that they can eventually use in their own writing. Although teachers will want to have more models than these, for this explanation I will refer to three I have used with my classes: Fleming's "Wrestling's Dirty Secret," Reilly's "Give Casey Martin a Lift," and Quindlen's "Look at What They've Done."

While they listen to a reading of a model, ask students to follow along. After reading an essay (in this case, I'll refer to Fleming's), take some time to discuss students' responses to the ideas and thesis: What did they think about as they listened and followed along? What does the essay make them feel? Then ask what the author is trying to persuade the audience to do or think. Students usually answer that Fleming wants the audience to encourage the National Collegiate Athletic Association (NCAA) to institute, and adhere to, safer practices in college wrestling. When students have identified the main assertion, ask them where it's stated (in this case, about three-quarters of the way through the essay). Discuss this placement in comparison to what students are familiar with, because most of their experience with thesis statements is in school writing, where they find the thesis at the end of the first paragraph. Ask students how this essay would be different if Fleming had placed his thesis in the expected location for school writing. The discussion that follows is valuable in helping students learn about persuasion and audience by drawing comparisons to the models of a genre that they already know. This kind of talk represents some of the theorizing that students should undertake with all of their models for study.

Next, ask students if they are convinced by Fleming's argument. If so, why is the piece convincing (or not)? They should refer to the evidence and the details, particularly the evidence of people dying so horribly. This consideration of evidence is key because it develops students' understanding of how evidence is handled in persuasion: it's not just tossed in without thinking about *how* to make it persuasive. Personal experience, facts and statistics, stories of other people connected to the sport: these are all solid kinds of evidence. And the details? Adjectives like "glassy-eyed and pale" and "self-inflicted," and verbs like "slumped," "collapsed," and "expired" all add weight to the details (134). If students don't notice those aspects of the writing, try to guide them.

When studying Fleming's essay, students usually comment on the introduction. The essay begins, "He died crawling to the scale" (134). Ask students to discuss the effectiveness of this introduction: Does it work? Why—or why not? This gets them theorizing. Prompt them to consider the conclusion. In it, Fleming makes recommendations and then comments on the possibility of ending collegiate wrestling if the recommendations are not enacted: "Better an entire level of competition than one more college athlete" (Fleming 134). This strategy of returning to the idea presented in the introduction (referring to the death of the wrestler) is sometimes called *bookending*. Ask students about the strategies used in the introduction and conclusion, and the effectiveness of those strategies. This discussion engages them in noticing and theorizing—as such discussions should.

Then, when students read the other models, they should compare the aspects they've noticed in this model with what they notice in the other models. They might notice, for instance, that all three essays begin with intriguing (if not as shocking) sentences:

- Casey Martin has a right leg two sizes too small and a heart three sizes too big. (Reilly 140)
- The site is as tidy and anonymous now as a hospital room after the patient has left, or died. (Quindlen, "Look" 68)

Students might notice that the thesis statement in the other essays isn't as close to the end as it is in the Fleming essay, but it's still not in the introductory paragraph. They might notice the choice of details, verbs, and adjectives that help to persuade. They might notice the "punch" endings that serve to reinforce the author's stance. How do these compare? How do they contribute to the writing? Finally, what should students conclude from this noticing, analysis, comparison, and theorizing? That's up to each class, but the process is important in preparing them to write their own persuasive essays: they now have options.

As small groups—and then later, as a whole class—students should use their discussion to develop a list of the options and expectations they see in this kind of writing: the product goals. During this process, also try to make sure that students see how some elements on this list differ from those that apply to persuasive essays they might write for a standardized test, a letter to the editor, or an advertisement. For instance, provide samples of those kinds of writing (a sample test from the state exam, or a letter to the editor) to help them make this comparison. By contrasting the kind of persuasive writing they are writing with other types of persuasive writing, students reinforce their understanding of this specific genre. I recently discovered a book that I plan to use in future, to make this point when I teach persuasive writing. Watt's *Have I Got A Book for You!* parodies many obvious persuasive techniques that are *not* found in the models we study for this assignment but that *are* found in students' lives outside of school. I want students to notice these persuasive elements and consider which genres they would fit, in contrast to the persuasive elements they should use in writing persuasive commentaries.

Once students have a good foundation for understanding the workings of this kind of writing, give the assignment: write a persuasive commentary essay on a topic of interest that might be found in *Newsweek* or *Sports Illustrated*. Work through the writing process with students, helping them select suitable topics, conduct inquiry, draft, and revise. At appropriate times during the process, refer students to the models, encouraging them to see that the models offer options that could address writing concerns that arise. For instance, as students get ready to draft, they sometimes need to revisit the models to determine a way to start, to organize, or to conclude their essay. During revision or peer evaluation, students should also refer to the models to consider the effectiveness of options they've chosen. Thus, the models help students all through the process, not just at the beginning. If students know that models can help them throughout their writing, they are more likely to use them in effective ways—and to produce more effective writing. Regarding persuasive writing, they are more likely to see persuasion as nuanced, instead of seeing all persuasion as an attempt to advertise or strong-arm.

Using Models to Teach Sentences

A variety of books lend themselves to teaching different aspects of sentence structure and how they help to create tone. In the following application, I use Burleigh's *Seurat and La Grande Jatte*, Kerley's *Walt Whitman*, and Aston's *An Egg Is Quiet*.

To begin, make sure that students have a chance to read the books. Prior reading prepares them to discuss the different tones they find in the books, and how these compare to other readings on similar topics (for example, an encyclopedia has a very specific tone). Ask students why these authors might try to achieve certain tones: entertaining, quiet, energetic, or passionate. After students identify the additional purpose of these texts—to entertain as well as to inform—ask them to look again at the Burleigh and Kerley texts to try to identify some of the elements of the writing that contribute to the tones. Most students notice, especially in the Burleigh book, the use of dashes. Because this lesson isn't specifically about punctuation, but is about the structures created by different punctuation, it's important to have students compare the sentences that use that punctuation with similar constructions that use other forms of punctuation (commas, colons, or parentheses).

Make a handout with sample sentences from the texts arranged in patterns, similar to the example that follows. Try to give examples and non-examples in groups—or examples of one structure and then examples of a contrasting structure in groups (as shown in Group One and Group Two). Italicize the parts of sentences that students should notice particularly; the italics help students see what to compare. As students work in small groups to identify the similarities and differences in the structures and in how they work, ask them to give names to the structures. The names they choose allow students to recall and comment on what they see—not match up to a rhetorician's name for a particular structure, even though those in Group One are appositives and those in Group Two are parentheses (a group of words that interrupt the normal flow of a sentence).

Group One

From Burleigh:

- It's fun to imagine that among the many people in the park—*the musician, the soldiers, the pipe-smoker, the man sitting under a distant tree*—the painter might be lurking there, too. (27)

From Kerley:

- He made tiny notebooks—*a few sheets of paper secured with a ribbon or pin*—and carried one in his pocket at all times, so that at a moment's notice he could record what he saw and felt. (n. pag.)
- Walt yearned for a new kind of leader: *an honest, homespun president who could keep America strong.* (n. pag.)
- Barely a month into Lincoln's presidency, Southern forces fired upon Fort Sumter, *a Union garrison in Charleston harbor, South Carolina.* (n. pag.)

Group Two

From Kerley:

- Awkwardly, he held the compositor's stick, eager to see the words form—*letter by letter*—beneath his inky fingers. (n. pag.)
- And as they read, they heard—*in every line*—the voice of the nation. (n. pag.)

From Burleigh:

- So—*for some Parisians at least*—Sunday was a day to escape from the heat of the city. (4)
- On the right, a fashionable couple (*that's the woman with her sunshade and the man in his top hat*) is on a promenade, or stroll. Across the way, another woman—*also well dressed*—extends her fishing pole over the water. (5)

Once students have theorized about the sentences in the groups, have them share their ideas with the class. Interestingly, although the two types of sentences are similar in structure—that is, there's something added using commas, dashes, or parentheses—the kinds of additions strongly differ. One addition adds information, details that focus in on an earlier noun; the other could be seen as a detractor, taking readers away from the idea of the sentence for a moment. Both, though, seem to create a rhythm more like speech than academic writing. Although students may not know it, appositives are not common in speech, but parentheses are. Ironically, in creating speech-like patterns, both authors have used parentheses, but they also have used a more writerly style when they employed appositives. Helping students see how writing can combine these two sentence types is an important part of what they can learn from these models.

Students need to practice what they've learned, so they should write. They could—and eventually should!—write their own sentences using both appositives and parentheses (or whatever the class calls these constructions), but another way to bridge to that independence is to examine a text that could be rewritten with these structures. Many picture books would work for this scaffolded practice. I suggest Aston's book *An Egg Is Quiet*. The pages lend themselves to working with paragraphs because each page begins with a generalization, with examples, often followed by specific details. The picture-book format allows the page design to group similar ideas, but students could take the sentences from one two-page spread and practice using either appositives or parentheses in their rewriting of the information (see examples shown in the boxes).

> An egg is textured.
> There are hard eggs and soft eggs and gooey eggs. Bird eggs are hard. Reptile eggs are often soft and rubbery. Amphibian eggs are gooey. There are smooth eggs and rough eggs. Most bird eggs are smooth.

Here's a possible rewriting, imitating the sentence structures from the models:

> An egg is textured. There are hard eggs (bird eggs) and soft eggs (reptile eggs) and gooey eggs (amphibian eggs). Most bird eggs are smooth, but some eggs—those of the emus and cormorants—are rough.

After this practice, it's valuable for students to reflect on the differences made when they used these structures: How do these new structures change the tone of the writing? When would the new tone be appropriate? When would it not? How does the genre influence the tone—and therefore the options for sentence structures available to writers?

Eventually students should generate their own texts, keeping in mind possibilities for using the structures they have studied. Remind them that they should consider how the structures affect tone, and also consider whether the tone they are creating is appropriate for the genre they are writing and for the situation in which that genre functions.

Annotated Bibliography

Campbell, Kimberly Hill. *Less Is More: Teaching Literature with Short Texts Grades 6–12.* Portland: Stenhouse, 2007.

> This book offers some strategies for using models in the classroom, but I have found its value to be more in the lists of sources for models. There are sources for essays on sports, writing, and reading; short stories; poetry; and graphic novels. I find Campbell's recommendations helpful in locating more models that I can use, even if I use them for purposes other than the ones she suggests.

Ehrenworth, Mary, and Vicki Vinton. *The Power of Grammar: Unconventional Approaches to the Conventions of Language.* Portsmouth: Heinemann, 2005.

> These authors do a wonderful job of using models to teach sentences and punctuation—grammar! They make a case for using what they call *mentor texts* that is similar to Ray's. The authors also explain how to use models as a way to learn about how writers use more local aspects of writing.

Kittle, Penny. *Write Beside Them: Risk, Voice, and Clarity in High School Writing.* Portsmouth: Heinemann, 2008.

> Kittle not only explains how to use models in the classroom, but also *shows* how—through her words and the accompanying DVD. She makes a clear case for the way that reading model texts should be practiced in classrooms, so that students can learn a strategy that moves beyond the writing of any single text to their work as writers in all writing situations. Going even further, Kittle makes a good case for reading in general as a vital component of any writing classroom. Her students' voices show up in the book, endorsing personal reading's importance to them as writers. This book is about models of language, not just models of genre.

11

Writing for Content Learning

Writing is not writing is not writing.

—*Langer and Applebee*

Overview

In a *Peanuts* comic strip, Sally asks Charlie Brown to write her school essay for her. In reply, he asks how she will learn if she doesn't write the essay. In the final frame, Sally's hand holding the paper has dropped to her side in a pose that shouts bewilderment. The word *LEARN* written in caps and followed by a question mark is in a word bubble over her head. It's obvious that Sally has never considered the idea of writing as a way of learning. Writing to learn is another facet of writing, one that applies to all content areas. Referring to an important research study by Boscolo and Mason, Graham and Perin clarify what they mean by writing to learn: "In the writing-to-learn approach, the teacher assigns writing tasks but does not provide explicit instruction in writing skills. Thus, writing is a tool of learning content material rather an end in itself" (*Writing* 21). The importance of writing in the content areas—writing to learn—is that not only can it help students learn, but it also can help them as writers, not through instruction but through practice using written language meaningfully for their own learning.

Using writing to learn is sometimes difficult for students to understand, but that misunderstanding is partly a fault of their experience: most of the writing students do in school is used as a way for teachers to measure comprehension. Teachers also confuse writing to learn with writing to *show* learning when they grade informal freewriting or note-taking. I once observed a teacher have students use the unsent letter strategy as a way to determine what they knew about the characters in the novel they were reading. And then she graded the letters for business letter format! So it's no wonder that students often resist using writing to learn when they fear the evaluation before they know the material—or they fear being judged on their informal writing.

In its most effective uses, writing to learn is short, spontaneous, exploratory, informal, personal, and often unedited and ungraded (Daniels, Zemelman, and Steineke 22–23). It reflects what we know of learning, that "learning is not linear and sequential but instead involves false starts and tentative explorations" (Newell, Koukis, and Boster 77). As Mitchell notes, "Writing to learn involves getting students to think about and to find the words to explain what they are learning, how they understand that learning, and what their own processes of learning involve" (93). Helping students learn the value of writing to learn is an important part of their development as writers. Louis Bloomfield, professor of physics at the University of Virginia, explains his feelings about students using writing to learn:

> Students need to be taught that the act of writing is intrinsically valuable to them. It crystallizes one's thoughts in a way that nothing else can. As a physicist, I find that I often learn more from writing papers and proposals than I do from working in the laboratory. I rarely find writing easy, but I always find it rewarding. (n.p.)

If students can have positive experiences with writing as a tool for learning, they will be more likely to write, even if it is sometimes challenging.

Although some identify disciplinary writing courses in American universities in the 1800s as the origin of the concept of writing to learn (Tynjälä, Mason, and Lonka), most people agree that Emig's "Writing as a Mode of Learning" is the foundational document for the concept and practice of writing to learn. In that article, Emig asserts that writing can enable learning because "writing involves the fullest possible functioning of the brain." After making the case that language is essential to learning, she notes how writing creates an object with language that can provide "a unique form of feedback, as well as reinforcement" (11), something that learners don't have with speech. Finally, Emig notes the slower pace of writing that "allows for—indeed, encourages—the shuttling among past, present, and future" (13). These three points—the way writing encourages thinking, the way it provides a record for further examination, and the way it enables connections—supply some of the foundational principles for the concept of writing to learn.

Although writing can aid learning, Boscolo and Mason remind us that "writing does not automatically mean improvement in learning." Instead, it "activates and fosters higher order thinking skills for learning." (84). Weinstein and Mayer found that four different kinds of strategies lead to learning: rehearsal, organi-zation, elaboration, and comprehension monitoring (see discussion in Bangert-Drowns, Hurley, and Wilkinson). Writing can contribute to all four. Once we've written something, as Emig has noted, it becomes an artifact that we can revisit, thus allowing for rehearsal. When we write, we spend time thinking about a topic; even the time it takes to write something slows our thinking and thus con-tributes to rehearsal. Writing tasks usually require writers to organize material in some manner, either in a way similar to the original presentation of ideas (as in a summary) or in a new way (as when a student writes a poem or a readers theater piece about a topic under study). Either way, writers must make connec-tions that require establishing relationships—so they learn more than they knew before the writing. When a writing task necessitates elaboration, such as writing an analysis of a process or a piece of literature, the task's requirements encour-age writers to extend and connect the new information, which leads to learning. Finally, writing about *how* we are learning, about what activities and processes are most effective for us as learners, is perhaps the most effective way to use writing to learn. Bangert-Drowns, Hurley, and Wilkinson assert that "there is evidence to suggest that self-reflective metacognition is more important than content-focused reflection and elaboration" in helping students learn (32). In all these ways, the thinking involved in writing contributes to learning.

Challenges to the value of writing to learn have been raised, partly because research in this area has been seen as "soft" (Bangert-Drowns, Hurley, and Wilkinson 31) or inconsistent. As Graham and Perin report, only about 75 per-cent of studies show a positive result, and the average of those results is "small, but significant" (*Writing* 20). Several variables have been proposed to account for the research findings; what follows are some of these that may affect the ben-efit of writing to learn. They are valuable not just because they help us under-stand the research, but because they help us see how we can use writing to learn more effectively in our classrooms.

- What students think of writing: Tynjälä, Mason, and Lonka note that "students' conceptions of learning are related to the way in which they see the aim of writing" (13). For example, if students see writing as knowledge telling only, they are more likely to use opportunities for writing to learn superficially, which does not contribute to their learning. On the other hand, if students see writing as knowledge transforming, they will be more likely to use the opportunity to write as a way to learn.
- What we mean by *learning*: Because "the relationship between writing and learning is not simple" (Tynjälä, Mason, and Lonka 15), and be-cause "learning is not synonymous with writing but a possible effect of

writing under certain contextual conditions" (Bangert-Drowns, Hurley, and Wilkinson 31), what one researcher or teacher believes qualifies as learning may not be what another believes. Teachers' hopes for the outcomes of writing to learn may not be what actually develop. And sometimes the learning that occurs is not of a measurable type, because it is related to attitudes, dispositions, or processes—all significant to learning, but not easily measured by tests or immediate performance.

- What students already know: Some research indicates that students' familiarity with the content or the writing task may influence the ability of writing to enhance learning. Bangert-Drowns, Hurley, and Wilkinson report that "the content learning of poor writers may not benefit from writing to learn" (52), possibly because the skills required for effective writing—difficult for these students—reduces their ability to learn while writing. The authors also suggest that the less familiar a student is with content, the more likely that student is to benefit from writing to learn. In summary, they suggest that "combinations of writing ability and subject area competence could produce complex interactions" (53).

Other aspects of writing can affect the potential for learning to occur as a result of writing and can therefore impact the learning that results from writing. One such aspect is time or frequency. Writing tasks that take more time tend to produce smaller benefits to learning, probably because the writing itself, not the learning, is the focus. The frequency of writing tasks that promote learning also influences the effectiveness of the task for learning. Shorter, more frequent writing proves most valuable. And the tasks themselves—as I have mentioned—influence learning. Taking notes by simply writing down the teacher's words or freewriting on what we already know is unlikely to produce significant or effective learning. Instead, prompts that ask students to do something more with their new knowledge—to make something of it, to connect it to other things they know, or to reflect on its value in their lives—are more likely to build new knowledge.

Principles

Context

One important consideration for using writing to learn effectively in the classroom is to make sure that it isn't just an "add-on," something else we are going to try to see if it works. Instead, writing to learn must be part of an entire curriculum that works holistically in seeking learning. To that end, then, teachers should ensure that writing is an integral part of the classroom, a continuation of the classroom talk or course reading, and a way into further reading or discussion. Cruz states it this way: "Any activity in isolation loses its point. Writing-to-learn activities must be part of a whole way of teaching and learning" (74). Nystrand, Gamoran, and Carbonaro refer to the "ecology" of the classroom (81): similar to the interrelatedness of ecology in the natural world, writing to learn must be connected to all the other substantive activities of the classroom to achieve the best results. It must be part of reading, whole-class discussion, and small-group tasks. Writing to learn should be as essential to those tasks as they are to students' overall learning. As Haneda and Wells assert, "To attempt to implement a new form of writing pedagogy, however sound it is in itself, is unlikely to achieve the desired results if all other aspects of curricular activity remain unchanged" (436).

Part of what creates this interrelated environment is the teacher's attitude toward learning and students. In explaining the use of daybooks in classrooms, or writing that documents students' learning, Brannon and her coauthors explain that "a daybook won't work well in a traditional classroom because there is no purpose for it. A daybook works in classrooms that are concerned with what and how children learn and where teachers are curious about what and how children think" (13). Classrooms where the right answer is the bottom line are not likely to promote value in writing to learn.

Haneda and Wells offer another way to consider how the classroom enables writing to learn. They note that a teacher's "commitment to a vision of a community of inquiry in which writing functions, not as an end in itself, but as a tool for knowledge building" (449) will make the difference in students' use of writing to learn and, eventually, in their development as writers. This kind of community, then, must be set up by a teacher who understands the appropriate context for using writing as a way to learn. We must create an atmosphere of trust, where students are willing to take risks in their writing as they use it to learn. This means that, although we do not neglect conventions such as spelling and grammar in polished writing, those are not our primary concerns in writing to learn. Instead, finding and elaborating meaning are what matters most. And finally, we should be aware of the ways that writing can be woven effectively into the fabric of our classes so that it is used appropriately and purposefully to achieve our desired learning goals.

A second aspect of classroom context required for writing to learn to be effective relates more specifically to the teacher's understanding of how children learn and how best to help them learn. Writing to learn is best supported by a constructivist teaching philosophy. Constructivism builds on what students already know and sees students as active participants in their learning instead of passive recipients of others' knowledge. "Rather than considering the content of the academic disciplines and students' experiences and knowledge as mutually exclusive concerns, constructivist views focus on learning in context—how knowledge develops within particular instructional contexts" (Newell, Koukis, and Boster 77). It pays attention to both students and subject matter. Such a conception of learning requires us to set the stage for effective learning and then allow students to work with ideas, take more control of what they are learning, come to their own conclusions, and then test them to discover if their thinking is accurate.

Writing to learn fits well within the constructivist philosophy because it's a way for individual learners to make sense of what they are experiencing through other classroom activities. It's particularly adapted to constructivism because it is individual and encourages connections between what the learner brings to, and takes away from, the situation. As Nelson makes clear, students "must determine what is relevant and what is irrelevant; they must supply organization; and they must generate links between the new and the unknown" (25). In this way, constructivism is the ideal classroom philosophy for writing to learn: students do the real work of learning, and they use writing to do it.

Appropriateness

The appropriateness of the writing task for the desired learning has been a point of interest in all conversations about writing to learn, but this is especially true since 1987, when Langer and Applebee published *How Writing Shapes Thinking*. The authors concluded, essentially, that writing can contribute to learning, but that the kind of writing students do has an enormous impact on the kind of learning they gain: "Different types of written tasks promote different kinds of learning, and choosing among them will depend upon the teacher's goals for a particular lesson" (131–32). Their conclusions provide generalities in example: summaries, note-taking, and answering questions at the ends of chapters all lead to generalized learning, whereas analytical writing helps writers focus on relationships, leading to better learning but of a smaller portion of the material studied. Beyond these, researchers haven't connected many specific writing-to-learn activities to the particular benefits that can be gained from them. From my own research and experience, though, I have drawn some conclusions that I hope will help other teachers begin to see how the choice of writing can create specific types of learning outcomes (see Table 11.1).

TABLE 11.1. Relationship of Writing Choice to Learning Outcomes

Writing Choice	Learning Outcomes
• Write a paraphrase or summary. • Write a letter explaining the concept to _____ (a fictional or cartoon character). • Write an exit slip (a notecard) that explains what you learned.	To clarify understanding
• Write a dialogue between two or more elements from the learning (such as between an electron and a neuron). • Write about your learning from a different role: a reporter, an animal, an astronaut, or an object (a pencil, for example). • Write a nutshelling-questioning sequence: one sentence explaining the importance of the reading (or lesson or lecture). Then ask, "Why ...?" Answer your question, and ask it again, based on the most recent writing. Keep going until you run out of answers.	To extend learning

Other research has suggested that we should consider additional factors when making appropriate choices of writing-to-learn activities in our classrooms. This research shows that teachers should have students write about their thinking, and then go back and review it to see if they can organize, evaluate, or elaborate on the ideas they have generated. Beyond that, teachers can assign genres for students to write, using their new and emerging knowledge about a topic. Genres encourage learning because they require students to manipulate their content knowledge, a critical component in learning (Langer and Applebee 130). Further, genres' varying structures require students to shape information in different ways, thereby creating new relationships and connections that contribute to learning.

So, which genres are better at fostering the kind of learning that teachers might have as goals? Research hasn't determined that yet. I have had my students use a variety of genres to respond to their reading, letting them select from a list of genre options. Then I ask them to tell me what responding in the various genres does for them as learners. In this way, I've used genre as a writing-to-learn strategy (as suggested by research), but I've also moved students' thinking into metacognitive areas, a crucial aspect of writing to learn. In response to this multigenre log reflection, one of my students, Jonathan, noted some ways that the genre responses encouraged his learning: "I had to read and reread. [. . .] I had to use higher levels of thinking. Not just information regurgitation." Other students also commented on the need to reread in order to write in a variety of genres about the texts they were reading. Heather's response is almost word for word the conclusion noted by Langer and Applebee, who stated that "the more that content is manipulated, the more likely it is to be remembered and understood" (130). Heather wrote, "The parts [of the essay] that I read and then interacted with, I remember better than any other part in the essay." What great evidence of the way writing can promote learning.

Finally, we must consider another aspect of appropriateness, one that relates to the students. Kieft, Rijlaarsdam, and van den Bergh's research begins with the contention that "writing-to-learn research has disregarded the different writing strategies used by students" (18). Referring to other researchers who have found that different planning strategies work for different writers (some choose to write their way into what they are saying, while others prefer to make a plan prior to writing), they argue that writing-to-learn strategies may have a similar effect on students. In other words, some writing-to-learn strategies may benefit some kinds of student learners more than others. If this is true, what's a teacher with 150 (or more) students a day to do? How can we design every writing task or writing-to-learn task to adapt to all the learning styles in our classrooms? For that matter, how can we even discover what all the learning styles are? I don't think we can. But we can take care in our choices to see that the kinds of learning most likely to result from a particular writing task are the ones we hope will most benefit the most students. And we can change our prompts—or offer students choices—so that the same kinds of learners aren't always the ones benefitting (or losing out). Simply an awareness that the task should match the desired outcome is an important place to begin.

Some teachers associate only a few applications—journals, note-taking, free-writing—with writing to learn, but the ways in which teachers can use writing to learn in the classroom are far more numerous and wide-ranging than that short list suggests. It's important to distinguish these effective practices from what might be considered mechanical writing: fill-in-the-blank worksheets or notes copied from the teacher's writing on the board. When we begin to think of the possibilities—and consider concerns for appropriateness to the desired learning—deciding what to use can sometimes feel overwhelming. We should remember that "[a]lthough certain techniques are associated with the process of writing to learn, the techniques do not define the process. Writing to learn is defined by its intent" (Galbadon 63). So perhaps more important than the method we select is the need to be clear in our intent: to enhance student learning. Langer and Applebee add two more points to ensure effectiveness of writing-to-learn activities: "Allow room for students to have something of their own to say in their writing" and help students "see the point of the task, beyond simple obedience to the teacher's demands" (141). With these guidelines, teachers can feel some assurance that they are on the right track.

Reflection

In their review of studies on writing to learn, Bangert-Drowns, Hurley, and Wilkinson found that "writing-to-learn interventions that included prompts for students to reflect on their current knowledge, confusions, and learning processes proved particularly effective" (50). Andrews found a similar result in her study of learning logs (141). And McCrindle and Christensen report a comparable finding: "The learning journal group showed more sophisticated understanding of the concept of learning, had greater metacognitive awareness and control of their learning process and used more sophisticated cognitive strategies while engaged in a learning task" (181). Whatever we call the method—journals, learning logs, learning journals, or something else—using writing to reflect on learning and the processes that contributed to that learning is an essential element of effective writing-to-learn practice.

Reflection itself has strong support in professional publications. *Because Writing Matters* identifies reflection as an essential element in learning to write: "To develop as writers, students also need the opportunity to articulate their own awareness and understanding of their processes in learning to write. Research has shown the importance of such metacognitive thinking in becoming a better writer" (National Writing Project 82). Reflection helps learners know what they've learned and how they've learned it. It requires them to consider themselves *as* learners, which means that they're more likely to transfer practices helpful to their learning in one setting to another setting. With its double emphasis, affecting both their development as writers and their development as learners, using writing to reflect is an essential principle to include when incorporating writing to learn into any classroom.

Applications

Journals

Many teachers use journals (also known as daybooks, learning logs, or other names) as spaces for students to write informally and frequently. Journals are often considered the primary way to use writing to learn, and they're probably the most common form such writing takes. But journals encourage learning even more effectively when we give prompts that move students to do something, either with their new knowledge (make connections, for example) or with their process of acquiring that new knowledge. When students write what they already know about a subject, some learning may occur as they make connections or articulate what had previously been a vague notion in their minds. However, research suggests that specific prompts can be more beneficial to students when they write in journals or daybooks.

Guidance for these prompts comes from Bangert-Drowns, Hurley, and Wilkinson, who suggest types of tasks that are shown to be most valuable in writing-to-learn studies:

1. Informational tasks that ask students to "describe processes, construct reports and summaries of other texts, or apply new knowledge to the creation of examples" (37). Prompts that fit this category could ask students to consider what one character—Atticus in *To Kill a Mockingbird*, for instance—might have to say to Romeo about his rash behavior, or ask students to consider a concept they are studying—prejudice or maturity, for instance—and give examples that would help establish a definition of the concept for others.

2. Personal writing that asks students to "link personal experiences outside of class with academic content, or to express what they liked or disliked about particular course content" (37). In this category, prompts might include students writing about a time they experienced something similar to what the characters they are reading about experienced, or evaluative prompts that ask students to rank a short story against other short stories they've read, and then to explain the ranking.

3. Metacognitive reflection where "students [are] asked to reflect on their ongoing learning processes, their current level of comprehension in a content area, comprehension failures and successes" (38). Prompts in this category might ask students to consider their progress as writers and how a particular writing assignment helped them develop their writing skills (or not). Another prompt might be to have students, after a lesson on revision, for example, reflect on what they will take away from the lesson and use in their own writing process.

Although there is certainly a time and place for students to review what they know about a topic, or to consider their feelings about a topic, the purposes of those kinds of prompts differ from the purposes of prompts that can promote learning, such as the ones just explained. If we design prompts along the guidelines I have just noted, students will be more likely to learn than if they simply write freely about whatever they want or what they already know.

Brannon and coauthors promote the use of daybooks, a term they borrow from Murray ("One" 148). Daybooks are like journals, except that they aren't only places for students to write their feelings and private thoughts. They are usually filled with the work of learning: maps of an essay, responses to literature, reflections on students' writing. Teachers do not grade or even write in the daybooks, viewing them as students' records of their learning. Instead, to keep students accountable, teachers have students create a Daybook Defense, like a portfolio, where they photocopy evidence from the daybook to show that they are "truly using their daybooks as thinking tools" (Brannon, Griffin, Haag, Iannone, Urbanski, and Woodward 90). Along with the artifacts students copy as evidence from the daybook, they write a letter to the teacher explaining the artifacts and arguing for their value as evidence of learning.

Although I didn't call mine a daybook, I have used a similar process with junior high students. Students kept track of all their coursework—formal and informal—in a notebook, and then created a portfolio to show evidence of their learning. They wrote me a cover letter, explaining specifically what they had learned during the quarter, and then they choose items from their notebooks to provide evidence of their learning (for instance, an early draft and a later draft to show the development of skill with effective paragraphing). I found many benefits to this process, the primary being that students took responsibility for their learning—and they could articulate it and provide evidence instead of my designing some instrument to measure what I hoped they would learn. This is truly what is meant by writing to learn.

Readers Theater

This is a specific genre that can help students learn while they write. Readers theater is a performance genre, as *theater* suggests, but the performers hold their scripts and read from them instead of memorizing parts. Additionally, it often involves gestures and sound effects, and can include audience participation. According to Flynn, whose book on the topic is invaluable to teachers using the idea, the purposes of readers theater are "to inform and to entertain" (*Dramatizing* 25). Readers theater benefits students in a variety of ways as both writers and learners. First, writing the scripts is motivating for students, partly because of the collaborative nature of the writing, and partly because the writing will be performed—and partly just because it's fun. Because the scripts are based on content that students must manipulate, they also increase student learning of that content. And the writing, although of a specific type, can help students develop writing skills, especially related to audience awareness.

To begin working on this genre, have students read through some sample scripts as a class. As with any genre study, students should analyze the scripts to determine their characteristics and then establish product goals. Sample scripts for this class reading can be found online at "Curriculum Based Readers Theatre Scripts" (Flynn). Many of the scripts on this website are designed for elementary school, but older students can still generate the criteria for a script by performing one or two of these simpler ones as a class. After students have a sense of the genre and have generated a list of product goals for readers theater, work with them to write a script as a class, using these basic steps:

1. Choose a topic.

2. List the information about that topic to be included in the script.

3. Decide on a context and on characters.

Flynn explains that "all speakers function essentially as narrators" in readers theater, "but individual speakers can also play characters or historical figures" (*Dramatizing* 31). In addition, speakers can also play one or more of the following roles that make presenting information a little more practical:

- someone in need of information
- someone who knows the information
- the doubter
- the joker or punster
- the enthusiast
- the clueless one
- an announcer or emcee (*Dramatizing* 31)

Flynn also recommends several other character possibilities (superheroes, reporters, spies, or literary characters) as well as a variety of possible contexts, including an awards ceremony, a classroom, a commercial, a game show, a tribute, a talk show, and a rally (*Dramatizing* 31).

When the class begins writing the script—and I recommend that the class script be relatively short and simple—it's a good idea to establish the context right away. Flynn suggests creating several lines before worrying about assigning them to speakers, and I think that's good advice. If I try to worry about characters too early, I get bogged down. Flynn also proposes helpful strategies, such as making sure that incorrect responses are corrected by another speaker, or repeating some key ideas, phrases, or gestures. Once lines are written, have students add gestures and sound effects. Ask students to generate suggestions for sound effects or gestures that should accompany key ideas. Because part of the point of readers theater is to convey information, such connections between ideas and gestures or sounds reinforce those key concepts. As a class, revise the script by making sure that the information established before writing is included, that the script is interesting to hear, and that all the voices get a chance to speak. As students can tell from sample scripts, when a script is meant for the whole class, some lines may be said in unison, or some may be broken up to make sure that every participant gets a chance. Finally, perform the script. Here's a portion of one I have written to give students an example:

REPORTER: Hello, I'm your at-the-scene reporter, today at the scene of a football game between the top school rivals in the state. It's a toss-up as to who will win, but spirits are high and the crowds are anxious. The game is about to begin . . . but, wait, [ZOOMING sound] something—or someone—has just zoomed into the stadium. Who can it be?

SPECTATOR 1: It's a bird!

SPECTATOR 2: It's a plane!

SPECTATOR 3: No, it's Adverb Man!

REPORTER: Adverb Man! What's he doing here?

SPECTATOR 3: He's here to help the players run **faster**, throw **harder**, and kick **straighter**.

REPORTER: How does he do that?

SPECTATOR 4: (**Sadly**) Haven't you ever seen what adverbs can do to an athlete?

REPORTER: (Thinking **quickly**) Does he tell them how, when, where, how often, and how much they should run, kick, jump, and throw?

ALL SPECTATORS: YES!

SPECTATOR 1: Now sit down and watch the game! You'll see how Adverb Man can make a difference.

REPORTER: But which team will he help?

ALL SPECTATORS: WATCH AND SEE!

Once students have had a chance to read several scripts, and to work through the process at least once with the whole class, they may be ready to write their own scripts in small groups on topics that you or they select, reflecting the content of the course. If some classes don't seem ready after one class-written script, they may need to do one or two more together before the small-group work, to be sure that the scaffolding they need has been provided.

Annotated Bibliography

Anson, Chris M., and Richard Beach. *Journals in the Classroom: Writing to Learn*. Norwood: Christopher-Gordon, 1995.

> Although this book is not recent, it is theoretically solid: it places journals as a central tool for student learning, not just a repository for writing. *Journals in the Classroom* provides a foundation for the purposeful use of journals in this effective way, along with specific ideas for making them work in the classroom, and ideas for prompts, for studying published journals, and for responding to student journals. In one place, teachers have some of the best advice for making journals work in the classroom.

Brannon, Lil, Sally Griffin, Karen Haag, Tony Iannone, Cynthia Urbanski, and Shana Woodward. *Thinking Out Loud on Paper: The Student Daybook as a Tool to Foster Learning*. Portsmouth: Heinemann, 2008.

> This book gives many specific ideas for helping students see daybooks (possibly considered journals in other classes) as places to use writing to learn. The authors also transfer the concept to computer applications, which may be more interesting and appealing to students.

Daniels, Harvey, Steven Zemelman, and Nancy Steineke. *Content-Area Writing: Every Teacher's Guide*. Portsmouth: Heinemann, 2007.

> *Content-Area Writing* suggests ways to use writing in many content areas. But even if an idea is explained for one content area, it could be adapted for another. One nice feature of this book is that for each application, the authors include a section titled "What Could Go Wrong." I love this—acknowledging how the activities might go astray, as good ideas can.

12

Putting Everything Together

Revision is about change, not mutilation. When your hair gets mussed, you don't shave your head.

—*Vicki Spandel*

Readers might wonder about my choice of the quote to begin this chapter; after all, the chapter is not about revision, but about teaching writing. So why select this quote? Besides the fact that it makes me laugh and it's a great quote for writers to remember, I also think it applies to teaching and to what teachers do at times: they think they have to toss out everything and start from scratch in order to revise their teaching. I don't think that's what Graham and Perin's report *Writing Next*—or this book about it—means to suggest. I suspect that the people reading this book right now are already pretty good teachers and are looking for ways to teach writing more effectively in their classrooms. In this chapter I'd like to offer ways to improve our teaching by adding good practices, not by suggesting that we toss out the good things we already do.

The previous chapters have shown each of the eleven elements of effective instruction in isolation, and certainly each of these can be used individually to benefit student writers. But, as Graham and Perin point out in *Writing Next*, even together these elements don't make a complete curriculum. However, these elements should be *part* of an effective writing curriculum, and that's what this chapter is all about. To begin, I want to address two aspects of these elements that should be considered before we can implement them effectively in their totality. One involves the scope of the practices, and the other involves overlapping principles that we need to bear in mind.

With regard to scope, the eleven elements have a wide range of levels of specificity and application. Word processing is a method of producing writing (like writing by hand or with a typewriter), a tool for writing that affects its production. Word processing is less about instruction (although it influences our teaching) and more about the effects of tools and technology on writing. In a similar way, collaborative writing is a way to structure writing that also impacts writers and their development. Writing for content learning is a specific use of writing, as is summarization: both are ways of using writing that also influence the development of writing and of the writer. The writing process and a strategic approach are broad ranging, applying to curricular levels of writing instruction, even to the way in which writing philosophy is represented in course design and practice.

Others of the eleven elements seem to fall within those broader ones: inquiry and prewriting could be considered aspects of the writing process (and often are), while product goals could be seen as part of a strategic approach. The use of models could be a part of both the writing process and a strategic approach, linked as it could be to drafting, revision, and understanding of genre (product goals). Sentence combining is a practice that could be used throughout a course to develop students' facility with sentences, or applied specifically during revision of a text, thus becoming a subset of one element of the writing process. What I hope is clear is that these eleven elements are not equal in terms of how they impact a classroom or a teacher's practices. They require different levels of commitment because they create different kinds of demands on class time and on classroom practices.

At the same time, each element is built on principles that must be considered to make it effective. Without considering these principles, we might *seem* to implement an element but students might not receive the anticipated benefits. The principles section in each chapter is intended to help us avoid those problems by identifying some key aspects that should be in place for effective application in a writing class. As I review those principles, though, I see some overlapping among them (as I suspect readers have) that suggest overall considerations for a writing class to enable the most benefits from these research-proven practices.

Classroom Philosophy

First, and probably most important, is that classes should be based on constructivist principles. That is, teachers and students should be working together to create understanding, rather than teachers seeing themselves as transmitters of knowledge and students as waiting vessels. Constructivism does not, as some teachers might view it, leave everything up to the learner. Instead, it means that we value what students bring to our classroom, and we design activities that will help students make sense of what is still unknown. Constructivism means that we know our students, select the most appropriate texts (books, essays, websites) for them to study, and then arrange activities that will best encourage learning with and from those texts. This means some prep work—but it offers big results.

Although it might seem that only a few of the eleven elements specifically mention the classroom structure, at least some researchers in each element note that the practices explained in their study are enhanced when students have teachers who value the knowledge they bring to the classroom; who allow students to engage with each other and with the teacher in collaborative ways; and who encourage exploration of ideas and risk-taking as part of learning to write. Indeed, writing itself is a risky adventure, so classrooms built on a philosophy that students should be guided to their own understandings tend to be the most effective for teaching writing. This is why so many teachers report success with writing workshop (despite a lack of the kind of research studies on the practice that excluded it from *Writing Next*). Constructivism allows students choice and room to risk, with a teacher facilitating instruction in mini-lessons and conferences rather than just telling students directions or "rules."

Constructivism also encourages a scaffolded approach to instruction, that is, a supported progress toward independence. Such an approach is key in writing instruction, particularly, because writing is a challenging skill to learn—and it isn't learned once and then always practiced in the same way forever. As students progress, so do their needs as writers, and so do the kinds of skills they may need help with during writing instruction. In scaffolding writing, we model for students, work with them as a whole class and in small groups, and ultimately, work with them as individuals until students are able to perform independently. This gradual release of support is consistent with a constructivist philosophy and crucial to students' development as writers.

A constructivist approach does not, however, mean that we don't sometimes take opportunities to teach explicitly. In fact, Graham and Perin conducted two additional reviews of different types of studies, and found that two practices—scaffolding and explicit instruction—were consistently part of effective writing instruction ("What" 323). Despite some concerns about explicit instruction leading to traditional (nonconstructivist) practices, teachers who consider the different kinds of knowledge that Hillocks identified in his studies will remember that some declarative knowledge is necessary for learners. What good teachers remember is that, in addition to the declarative knowledge that can come from explicit instruction, writers also need procedural knowledge that offers them opportunities to practice and learn through experience, as well as conditional knowledge that allows them to reflect on their learning. This is all consistent with a constructivist philosophy.

A problem with constructivism in practice is that some teachers give up: the time and preparation needed for such learning is much greater than might be anticipated. Especially at a time when testing is emphasized, and when the consequences of such testing are significant to administrators, the time that effective writing instruction needs—time for exploring and developing individual understanding—is usually in short supply. Additionally, although a constructivist approach seems easier (the students should be doing the work, after all), it's actually challenging to apply this approach effectively, because we must create a classroom climate (not an easy task) that may differ from students' prior experiences. We need to create structures and practices in the classroom that sometimes rely on students' independence and motivation, even as students are developing these characteristics. A constructivist approach isn't easy, but it isn't impossible, either. It's a way of thinking about teaching that is particularly important in making many of the eleven elements generate the biggest difference for student writers.

Teacher Knowledge and Beliefs

Another thread that runs through many, if not all, of these practices is the value of teacher beliefs and knowledge, particularly as that knowledge relates to students, writing processes, and the genres that students are asked to write. In their studies, Graham and Perin found that, after accounting for other variables (such as teacher experience, number of students in the classes, and teacher efficacy), five variables account for "30% of the variance in teachers' use of specific adaptations":

> Teachers' willingness to implement particular treatments is influenced by beliefs about (a) how suitable it is for their students, (b) whether it is effective, (c) how hard it is to implement, (d) possible negative impacts of implementing it, and (e) their knowledge about how to implement it. ("What" 329)

If teachers hold positive beliefs on these items, it's more likely that the eleven elements will benefit their students.

Beyond believing that students can benefit from implementing these elements, knowledge of students is crucial to apply many of them effectively, especially writing strategies, specific product goals, and process writing. In these practices, our knowledge of students and their needs as writers is key. Penny Kittle makes the point that "the single most efficient path toward success as a teacher lies in knowing your students in *important* ways" (102). We need to help students find strategies that address their specific writing needs, both in process and in product. When we know our students in the way Kittle explains, we are better able to pace the class time for the writing process. We also understand how to use elements of models, and when to bring them in for the best effect for our students. Collaborative writing is especially dependent on our knowledge of students—we need to know how students work and how they work together.

Knowledge of writing processes is important as we consider inquiry, prewriting, collaborative writing, and writing for content learning. Writing takes time, and teachers who don't understand the writing process might be frustrated by the time involved in students' working through it. Both prewriting and inquiry, in their best uses, require teacher knowledge of how those practices influence other aspects of the writing process and product. Teachers who understand that writing needs time and a certain kind of environment to flourish are more likely to use these approaches—and to use approaches that also encourage writing development but are not included in the *Writing Next* report—in ways that will allow them to achieve the results that research shows are possible.

Knowledge of genres is essential for teachers to help students develop product goals, to help them know the appropriate prewriting and inquiry strategies to use for the specific tasks they are writing. Our knowledge of genres is also important in understanding the ways to use sentence combining to good effect (because different genres use different kinds of sentence structures). Additionally, knowledge of genres is essential for us to know the best ways to use models to enhance writing instead of reducing it to a formula. Writing in the content areas hinges on teacher knowledge of genres and how those genres develop different kinds of learning, as well as how they represent disciplinary knowledge.

None of these expectations for teacher knowledge should mean that a teacher stops teaching writing if she lacks some knowledge; instead, what this thread suggests is that we continue to improve our understanding of writing and genres, and to pay attention to students and their needs—as good teachers are already doing. Additionally, Graham and Perin report that teachers' enthusiasm for writing and high expectations for students also influence the effective instruction of writing ("What" 325). When we exhibit these characteristics, instruction with these eleven elements can be even more influential in students' writing development.

Purposeful Writing

We often hear about the motivational influence of "authentic" writing—writing that serves real purposes for students by moving beyond the classroom, or by doing real work within the classroom (writing a memo to persuade the teacher to change a due date, for example). Related to that concept of authentic writing is making sure that the elements described in *Writing Next* are experienced in contextualized, meaningful ways. In other words, inquiry for inquiry's sake doesn't really help students see the value of the practice; similarly, collaborative writing and studying models also need to occur as students are writing products that matter to them. Another thread that runs through these eleven elements is the idea that they should not stand alone, that they need to connect to regular classroom practices and tasks.

Part of making writing tasks purposeful is creating assignments that are meaningful. Most teachers know that students are less likely to write in ways that encourage learning if they can't engage with the writing task. They might write (because they want the grades or want to make the teacher happy), but they generally don't learn what they need to learn about writing if they don't see value in a task, or if they don't see it as interesting. Today's students write a lot—online opportunities abound for their writing. We need to make sure that the writing they do for class is as engaging as the writing they do in their lives outside of class. When it is, then we can incorporate these elements in ways that allow students to get the most from them.

Time

Over and over again, as I studied each of the eleven elements, I found that time was an essential principle in many. What this suggests to me is that writing and writing development can't be rushed. We have to plan for that slower pace. We can't give up when we don't see results right away. We have to allow time—and more time—for students to practice and practice, until they can not only undertake the eleven elements we are giving them to experience, but also have time for reflection: for seeing how the elements benefit them, and for making the elements their own. And that just takes time.

One of the best experiences of my teaching was having the opportunity to teach a student over multiple years (ninth and eleventh grades). A few students I even taught for three years, through seventh, eighth, and ninth grades. I tried to get their schedules changed because I think that students benefit from different teachers' strengths, but being able to teach them for a longer period of time allowed me to see their real development as writers. What I learned from these rare experiences was that improvement as a writer is almost glacial in its movement—and we can only see glimpses of that kind of movement if we allow time for students to progress through the writing process, through writing and thinking and inquiring and collaborating and reading models and setting goals and using strategies—and then consider how each and all of those help writers. And that takes time.

Most teachers don't get this opportunity to work with students across multiple years, so they often don't get to see what grows out of the seeds they plant about writing. But we can't give up just because it's hard to see improvement, just because we might not be around to see what comes from our efforts with students. We must still give students the time that their writing development needs. I know that's hard; I know there isn't enough time for everything. I've said that to myself so many times that I've lost count. No matter how much I complain, I don't get any more time in my day or in my classes. So what can we do?

First, I think we can evaluate how we use writing now in our classes, and then decide if there might be better, more efficient ways to use it. What writing do we cause—and what do we teach? Are there times when the writing tasks can involve a different level of writing (see Chapter 9)? Can an assessment essay be an L2, for example, so that students can write what they know without working through the entire process (which is time intensive), and then spend time on the writing process with more meaningful writing? Would students benefit from fewer "big" writing assignments and more "short" or less intensive ones? I don't know. It depends on what each set of students needs. But recognizing that students need to write, and write often, is a start. Then, evaluating how I am meeting that need and considering how I can do it better will help me improve my teaching, even if I can't reach my ideals with regard to more time.

With our concern about limited time, we should try to think of how we can use writing in a variety of ways so that it (and we!) can do multiple jobs at once. If we don't have time for all the writing we would like, we should make writing do more. When teachers worry about test preparation, for example, writing doesn't have to get shoved out. Instead, teachers can have students write summaries, practice sentence combining, inquire, and collaborate as part of the test prep. Students can use writing to learn (in English and in other classes), and they can word process their writing for multiple purposes. They can practice the writing process and strategies with shorter pieces of writing, to learn about the value of the process even when there isn't as much time as teachers would like.

There are ways to make time for writing, even in a test-pressed curriculum. We just have to be creative.

Combining Everything

Overall, these eleven elements can be applied to many writing assignments that teachers already ask students to complete in class. What follows are two examples—one traditional, and one current—that show how the eleven elements, along with the principles and concepts explained earlier—could be implemented in the classroom. I don't mean for these examples to be seen as the *one* way to teach writing. And I don't intend to suggest that there are not other aspects of writing instruction that could be used effectively in classes; we know that just because a practice didn't make it into the *Writing Next* report, we should not automatically reject it. And I want to emphasize that what follows is not a curriculum. As I hope I've made clear, sticking one of the following units into a class that isn't set up to sustain the principles of the eleven elements won't make a big difference in how students develop as writers. These are only examples of what could happen within a broader classroom context designed to use the principles throughout all the writing that occurs, not just in an assignment or two. What I am trying to do with these examples is suggest how these eleven elements *might* be implemented in the classroom in meaningful ways—in an already effective classroom—and I've marked in bold the elements from *Writing Next*.

Letter to the Editor or Blog Post

1. First, students should be led to find a topic or issue on which they want to write. Letters to the editor and postings on news blogs are usually based on current events or topics found in social conversation, so these issues are usually related to content in the world beyond the classroom: for example, environmental concerns, social questions, or politics. Often, these topics can develop out of the various courses that students take. Here I've listed the course, some content possible in that course, and a topic that could derive from that point, as an example of how teachers could engage students in selecting topics that derive from course content.
   - Physical Education: exercise . . . bike trails in the community
   - Earth Science: water cycle . . . the move to zero-scape yards
   - History: World War II . . . the use of force to solve political differences
   - English: *To Kill a Mockingbird* . . . the effectiveness of the judicial system

When their topics of interest grow out of content area classrooms, students are more likely to see connections between school and their writing, and to see how writing can help them learn in all their classes (**writing for content learning**).

2. Once a topic is selected, students should conduct **inquiry** into it. They should conduct research, ask questions, interview, engage in debates, or do anything else that will help them understand the topic. They should also investigate the newspapers or news blogs that are potential situations for their writing, so they can begin to see how those various venues might represent different perspectives. As students conduct inquiry, they should **summarize** what they find and share it with others (**collaborate**) in the class, building a library of information that all can draw from as they move forward in their writing.

3. To write a letter to the editor or news blog post, students benefit from studying examples of such writing. I've found that offering examples of good and not-so-good letters and posts can be helpful; students can rank them to discover the qualities that contribute to effective writing in each genre. With the blog posts, students might also need to consider how news blogs differ from personal blogs—and therefore, how the postings on those sites also differ. Students study the **models** and build a list of criteria (**product goals**) for effective letters to the editor or news blog posts.

4. With some understanding of the topic and genre, students are ready to start thinking more explicitly about the **writing process**, and to set goals for that process (**writing strategies**). Some goals and process information might come from the teacher, who may set due dates or interim due dates, but students can still set some process goals themselves. They can determine how much time they will spend each night for the duration of the project, or how much they will write each day or in total. They can decide how to monitor themselves, and they can determine how they will reward themselves as they achieve their goals. Once their goals are set, students can begin their **prewriting**, while working with others (**collaborating**) in small groups to see if initial plans are likely to lead toward success.

5. While students are drafting, teachers can guide them in practice with **sentence combining** so that the sentences they use in their drafts or write during revision are effective. Also, while they are drafting and revising, students

should have access to **word processing** so they can see the recursive nature of writing and get feedback from others that is easy to incorporate.

6. During revision, students should revisit the **product goals** established earlier in the process, and work with each other (**collaborate**) to generate feedback on the effectiveness of the writing and the revising choices that students are or should be making. They should practice **writing strategies** such as Compare-Diagnose-Operate (CDC) (Graham and Harris, *Making* 114) for revision. When the letters are revised, students should send them to the appropriate newspapers or post them to the selected blog site.

7. Finally, students should reflect on the **writing process**: on how well they used the goals for process and product they had set; and on how the work with others, the inquiry and prewriting, the model analysis, the sentence combining, and the word processing all helped them write the letter or post. They should also consider how they could use such strategies to help them write other genres in other situations in the future. In this way, students begin to transfer the **writing strategies** they use in the process for one product to other writing tasks in other situations.

Podcasts

A podcast is a combination of video and audio that is submitted to a website to be viewed as a downloadable digital file. A similar process to the one just described can be used to help students create podcasts.

1. Students need to consider topics for the podcasts. These can develop out of course content, so students should brainstorm as a class on possible topics. For instance, if students are reading a novel, they could make podcasts about the book (different groups could choose characters or settings, or focus on certain chapters) as well as background information or author information. Students might find references in the novel to historical or cultural events that could also be the subject of the podcast. Or students could look at some podcasts (**models**) and see how they might generate ideas for their own podcasts. Because podcasts are group projects, students should work together (**collaborate**) to determine possible topics and approaches.

2. Once a topic is selected, students should conduct **inquiry** into it. They should read the novel, conduct background research, ask questions, interview, engage in class discussions, or do anything else that will help them

understand the topic. As they inquire, students should take notes and monitor their learning and progress through **writing for content learning**. As students conduct inquiry into their topics, they should **summarize** what they find and share it with others (**collaborate**) in their groups.

3. As is true with other genres, students benefit from studying examples of the podcast genre. Students study the **models** and build a list of criteria (**product goals**) for effective podcasts.

4. At this point, students start thinking more explicitly about the **writing process**, and they set goals for that process (**writing strategies**). Teachers who have students create podcasts note that the process is more involved than it may seem. Beyond the process elements common to many L3 writing tasks, because podcasts are group projects, they require some process goals related to working with others, particularly assigning tasks. Students can still determine how much time they will spend individually on their part of the project, but they also should work together to set up a schedule for all members' parts. They can decide how to monitor themselves, and they can determine how they will reward themselves as they achieve their goals. Once their goals are set, students can begin their **prewriting**, working with others (**collaborating**) in their groups to create initial plans.

5. While students are drafting, teachers should work with them on **sentence combining**. Podcasts should sound like speech, not like a person reading a piece of writing not meant to be spoken aloud. Even though students will write their scripts, they need to be aware of syntactical concerns and make sure that their writing will reflect the unique rhythm expected of oral language. Sentence combining can help them with that. At the same time, students should have access to **word processing** for the drafting and revision of their scripts.

6. During revision, students should revisit the **product goals** established earlier in the process and work with each other (**collaborate**) to generate feedback on the effectiveness of the writing and revising choices that students are or should be making. Because of the orality of this genre, students should practice reading their writing aloud, and use that to aid in revision as well as in rehearsal for the recording. Teachers should allow some time for recording and rerecording the podcasts.

7. Finally, students should reflect on the **writing process**: on how well they used the goals for process and product they had set; and on how the work with others, the inquiry and prewriting, the model analysis, the sentence combining and word processing all helped them write the script for the podcast. They should also consider how they could use such strategies to help them write other genres in other situations in the future. In this way, students begin to transfer the **writing strategies** they use in one process for one product to other writing tasks in other situations.

As is apparent, the processes for these two writing experiences are comparable. The point is to show that teachers can adapt and integrate all eleven of the *Writing Next* elements into a variety of writing tasks.

And So . . .

In this book, we've gone in depth now into what research indicates will help our students improve as writers. We know the research, the principles, and some practices that may help us in the classroom. The rest, as the saying goes, is up to us. When I work with teachers, I often find that the bigger they see the task of changing to improve instruction, the less likely they are to do it. I know the feeling. I've sat in professional development seminars and thought, "Great idea! But I can't do that. I can't even begin to make all those changes this person described. I get tired just thinking about it." I suspect that my own musings are not so different from other teachers'.

So what do we do? I'll tell you what has worked for me: I find one thing, one thing I think I can do that I believe will make the biggest difference for my students, and I work on that. When that's going well, I work on the next idea, and so on. Do all the things I try work well? No. And that can be discouraging. Some ideas don't work because I'm not completely involved, or I haven't done my groundwork yet, or for other reasons. Sometimes, I need to try an idea multiple times, shifting a bit here and there each time until it does work. Sometimes I want to give up. But if I stick with an idea that I believe will help my students, I get there: I help my students as writers. And then the effort is worth it.

Spandel has this to say about a writer's right to write badly: "Without risk, it is nearly impossible to grow as a writer. Non-risk-takers can rise to a level of competence to be sure. [. . .] Is that enough?" (63). I have to think the same of teachers. Without risk, it's nearly impossible to grow as a teacher of writing. Certainly if we risk, students might pay a small price. But they pay a big price if we don't. So what do we do? Start now. Start with one idea, and work it until it's your own. Then move on. I hope this book has provided some options for starting—and more for when you're ready to take the next steps. What should we teach about writing next? The suggestions from the *Writing Next* report are a great place to begin.

Annotated Bibliography

Gardner, Traci. *Designing Writing Assignments*. Urbana: NCTE, 2008.

Because I mention the need to create effective (and motivating) writing assignments, I recommend this book as an excellent resource to help teachers do that. Gardner outlines elements of effective assignments and gives examples of those elements in practice. She helps teachers see ways to use technology with traditional assignments, and presents lots of resources for teachers. I highly recommend this book for teachers who need ideas to help them bring more writing into the classroom.

Graham, Steve, Charles A. MacArthur, and Jill Fitzgerald, eds. *Best Practices in Writing Instruction*. New York: Guilford Press, 2007.

The editors have collected chapters to address the design of writing programs and teaching special populations, and included strategies for teaching writing that correspond to some of the eleven elements in *Writing Next*, particularly the process writing approach and sentence combining. In addition, chapters on motivation (one I find particularly helpful) and assessment move beyond the Graham and Perin report. It's obvious that most of the contributors are aware of the research reported in *Writing Next*, but they also offer their own expertise and advice. Most of the chapters have some practical applications, and chapters deal with a wide range of student populations.

Works Cited

"Airplane Crash-Lands into Hudson River; All Aboard Reported Safe." *CNN.com/US*. Cable News Network, Turner Broadcasting System, 15 Jan. 2009. Web. 20 Apr. 2010.

Anderson, Valerie, and Suzanne Hidi. "Teaching Students to Summarize." *Educational Leadership* 46.4 (1988–89): 26–28. Print.

Andrews, Richard, Carole Torgerson, Sue Beverton, Alison Freeman, Terry Locke, Graham Low, Alison Robinson, and Die Zhu. *The Effect of Grammar Teaching (Sentence Combining) in English on 5 to 16 Year Olds' Accuracy and Quality in Written Composition*. York: University of York, Department of Educational Studies. 2005. Print.

Andrews, Sharon E. "Writing to Learn in Content Area Reading Class." *Journal of Adolescent and Adult Literacy* 41.2 (1997): 141–42.

Andrew-Vaughan, Sarah, and Cathy Fleischer. "Researching Writing: The Unfamiliar-Genre Research Project." *English Journal* 95.4 (2006): 36–42. Print.

Anson, Chris M., and Richard Beach. *Journals in the Classroom: Writing to Learn*. Norwood: Christopher-Gordon, 1995. Print.

Applebee, Arthur N. "Problems in Process Approaches: Toward a Reconceptualization of Process Instruction." Petrosky and Bartholomae 95–113.

Armbruster, Bonnie B. "The Problem of 'Inconsiderate Text.'" *Comprehension Instruction: Perspectives and Suggestions*. Ed. Gerald R. Duffy, Laura R. Roehler, and Jana Mason. New York: Longman, 1984. 203–17. Print.

Aston, Dianna. *An Egg Is Quiet*. New York: Scholastic, 2006. Print.

Atwell, Nancie. *In the Middle: New Understandings about Writing, Reading, and Learning*. 2nd ed. Portsmouth: Boynton/Cook, 1998. Print.

———. *Lessons That Change Writers*. Portsmouth: Firsthand/Heinemann, 2002. Print.

Baines, Lawrence, Coleen Baines, Gregory Kent Stanley, and Anthony Kunkel. "Losing the Product in the Process." *English Journal* 88.5 (1999): 67–72. Print.

Ballenger, Bruce. *The Curious Researcher: A Guide to Writing Research Papers*. 4th ed. New York: Pearson/Longman, 2004. Print.

Bangert-Drowns, Robert L. "The Word Processor as an Instructional Tool: A Meta-Analysis of Word Processing in Writing Instruction." *Review of Educational Research* 63.1 (1993): 69–93. Print.

Bangert-Drowns, Robert L., Marlene M. Hurley, and Barbara Wilkinson. "The Effects of School-Based Writing-to-Learn Interventions on Academic Achievement: A Meta-Analysis." *Review of Educational Research* 74.1 (2004): 29–58. Print.

Bawarshi, Anis. *Genre and the Invention of the Writer: Reconsidering the Place of Invention in Composition*. Logan: Utah State UP, 2003. Print.

Beach, Richard, Chris Anson, Lee-Ann Kastman Breuch, and Thom Swiss. *Teaching Writing Using Blogs, Wikis, and other Digital Tools*. Norwood: Christopher-Gordon, 2009. Print.

Boiarsky, Carolyn. "Prewriting Is the Essence of Writing." *English Journal* 71.4 (1982): 41–47. Print.

Bishop, Wendy. "Co-authoring Changes the Writing Classroom: Students Authorizing the Self, Authoring Together." *Composition Studies/Freshman English News* 23.1 (1995): 54–62. Print.

———. "Helping Peer Writing Groups Succeed." *Teaching Lives: Essays and Stories*. Wendy Bishop. Logan: Utah State UP, 1997. 14–24. Print.

Bizzell, Patricia. "Composing Processes: An Overview." Petrosky and Bartholomae 49–70.

Blackburn-Brockman, Elizabeth. "Prewriting, Planning, and Professional Communication." *English Journal* 91.2 (2001): 51–53. Print.

Bloomfield, Louis. "The Importance of Writing." Commentary. Philadelphia Inquirer 4 Apr. 2004. Web. *The Plagiarism Resource Site*. 21 May 2010. <http://plagiarism. phys.virginia.edu/essays/The%20Importance%20of%20Writing.html>.

Boehnlein, James M. "Explicit Teaching and the Developmental Writing Course." *Annual Meeting of the Conference on College Composition and Communication,* Washington, 23–25 Mar. 1995. Print.

Boscolo, Pietro, and Lucia Mason. "Writing to Learn, Writing to Transfer." Rijlaarsdam et al. 83–104.

Brannon, Lil, Sally Griffin, Karen Haag, Tony Iannone, Cynthia Urbanski, and Shana Woodward. *Thinking Out Loud on Paper: The Student Daybook as a Tool to Foster Learning*. Portsmouth: Heinemann, 2008. Print.

Brown, Ann L., and Jeanne D. Day. "Macrorules for Summarizing Texts: The Development of Expertise." *Journal of Verbal Learning and Verbal Behavior* 22.1 (1983): 1–14. Print.

Brown, Margaret Wise. *The Important Book*. New York: Harper, 1949. Print.

Bruffee, Kenneth A. "Sharing Our Toys: Cooperative Learning versus Collaborative Learning." *Change* 27.1 (1995): 12–18. Print.

Bryson, Bill. *A Short History of Nearly Everything*. New York: Broadway, 2003. Print.

Buis, Kellie. *Reclaiming Reluctant Writers: How to Encourage Students to Face Their Fears and Master the Essential Traits of Good Writers*. Markham, Ontario, Canada: Pembroke, 2007.

Burke, Jim. *Tools for Thought: Graphic Organizers for Your Classroom*. Portsmouth: Heinemann, 2002. Print.

———. *Writing Reminders: Tools, Tips, and Techniques*. Portsmouth: Heinemann, 2003. Print.

Burleigh, Robert. *Seurat and La Grand Jatte*. New York: Abrams, 2004. Print.

Bushman, Jonica Manak. "Summaries: Taking Writing from Notes to Summary." *50 Ways to Develop Strategic Writers*. Ed. Gail E. Tompkins and Cathy L. Blanchfield. Upper Saddle River: Pearson, 2005. 136–38. Print.

Butler, Paul. "Imitation as Freedom: (Re)Forming Student Writing." *Quarterly* 24.2 (2002): n. pag. *National Writing Project*. National Writing Project, 2010. Web. 8 May 2010.

Calkins, Lucy. *The Art of Teaching Writing*. Portsmouth: Heinemann, 1994. Print.

Campbell, Kimberly Hill. *Less Is More: Teaching Literature with Short Texts—Grades 6–12*. Portland: Stenhouse, 2007. Print.

Casazza, Martha E. "Using a Model of Direct Instruction to Teach Summary Writing in a College Reading Class." *Journal of Reading* 37.3 (1993): 202–08. Print.

Casey, Mara and Stephen J. Hemenway. "Structure and Freedom: Achieving a Balanced Writing Curriculum." *English Journal* 90.6 (2001): 68–75. Print.

Center for History and the New Media. "What Is the Web Scrapbook?" *Center for History and the New Media*. Center for History and the New Media, 2001–2005. Web. 28 Apr. 2010.

Chapman, Marilyn L. "Situated, Social, Active: Rewriting Genre in the Elementary Classroom." *Written Communication* 16.4 (1999): 469–90. Print.

Charney, Davida H., and Richard A. Carlson. "Learning to Write in a Genre: What Student Writers Take from Model Texts." *Research in the Teaching of English* 29.1 (1995): 88–125. Print.

Cisneros, Sandra. *The House on Mango Street*. New York: Vintage Books, 1984. Print.

Clark, Irene L. "Invention." *Concepts in Composition: Theory and Practice in the Teaching of Writing*. Ed. Irene L. Clark. Mahwah: Lawrence Erlbaum, 2003. 71–106. Print.

Collins, James L. *Strategies for Struggling Writers*. New York: Guilford P, 1998. Print.

Comprone, Joseph. "Syntactic Play and Composing Theory: What Sentence Combining Has Done for Teachers of Writing." Daiker, Kerek, and Morenberg 219–31.

Connors, Robert J. "The Erasure of the Sentence." *CCC* 52.1 (2000): 96–128. Print.

Crovitz, Darren, and W. Scott Smoot. "Wikipedia: Friend, Not Foe." *English Journal* 98.3 (2009): 91–97. Print.

Crowe, Chris. *Mississippi Trial, 1955*. New York: Phyllis Fogelman Books, 2002. Print.

Crowley, Sharon. "Linguistics and Composition Instruction: 1950–1980." *Written Communication* 6.4 (1989): 480–505. Print.

Cruz, Mary Carmen E. "Writing to Learn as a Way of Making Sense of the World." *Writing across the Curriculum in Secondary Classrooms: Teaching from a Diverse*

Perspective. Ed. Harriet Arzu Scarborough. Upper Saddle River: Prentice-Hall, 2001. 71–89. Print.

Cucci, Julianna, and Jamie A. Kowalczyk. "Taking Risks: Reflecting on At-Risk Teaching." McCann et al. 3–18.

Daiker, Donald A., Andrew Kerek, and Max Morenberg, eds. *Sentence Combining: A Rhetorical Perspective.* Carbondale: Southern Illinois UP, 1985. Print.

Dale, Helen. "Toward an Understanding of Collaborative Writing." *Annual Meeting of the American Educational Research Association,* San Francisco, 20–24 Apr. 1992. Print.

Daniels, Harvey, Steven Zemelman, and Nancy Steineke. *Content-Area Writing: Every Teacher's Guide.* Portsmouth: Heinemann, 2007. Print.

Dean, Deborah. *Bringing Grammar to Life.* Newark: IRA, 2008. Print.

———. *Genre Theory: Teaching, Writing, and Being.* Urbana: NCTE, 2008.

———. *Strategic Writing: The Writing Process and Beyond in the Secondary Classroom.* Urbana: NCTE, 2006. Print.

De La Paz, Susan, Philip N. Swanson, and Steve Graham. "The Contribution of Executive Control to the Revising by Students with Writing and Learning Difficulties." *Journal of Educational Psychology* 90.3 (1998): 448–60. Print.

Dickens, Charles. *A Tale of Two Cities.* New York: Signet, 1997. Print.

DiPardo, Anne, and Sarah Warshauer Freedman. "Peer Response Groups in the Writing Classroom: Theoretic Foundations and New Directions." *Review of Educational Research* 58.2 (1988): 116–49.

Donovan, Carol A., and Laura B. Smolkin. "Children's Understanding of Genre and Writing Development." McArthur, Graham, and Fitzgerald 131–43.

Dowling, Carolyn. "Word Processing and the Ongoing Difficulty of Writing." *Computers and Composition* 11.3 (1994): 227–35. Print.

Dyson, Anne Haas, and Sarah Warshauer Freedman. "Writing." *Handbook of Research on Teaching the English Language Arts.* 2nd ed. Ed. James Flood, Diane Lapp, James R. Squire, and Julie M. Jensen. Mahwah: Lawrence Erlbaum, 2003. 967–92. Print.

Ede, Lisa, and Andrea Lunsford. "The Pedagogy of Collaboration." *The Allyn & Bacon Sourcebook for College Writing Teachers.* Comp. James C. McDonald. Boston: Allyn & Bacon, 1996. 53–71.

Education Northwest. "6+1 Trait® Writing Research." Education Northwest, n.d. Web. 20 Apr. 2010.

Ehrenworth, Mary, and Vicki Vinton. *The Power of Grammar: Unconventional Approaches to the Conventions of Language.* Portsmouth: Heinemann, 2005. Print.

Eklundh, Kerstin Severinson. "Problems in Achieving a Global Perspective of the Text in Computer-Based Writing." *Instructional Science* 21.1–3 (1992): 73–84. Print.

Elbow, Peter. *Writing with Power: Techniques for Mastering the Writing Process.* 2nd. ed. New York: Oxford UP, 1998. Print.

Emig, Janet. "Writing as a Mode of Learning." Villanueva 7–16.

Englert, Carol Sue, Taffy E. Raphael, Linda M. Anderson, Helene M. Anthony, and Dannell D. Stevens. "Making Strategies and Self-Talk Visible: Writing Instruction in Regular and Special Education Classrooms." *American Educational Research Journal* 28.2 (1991): 337–72. Print.

Fadiman, Anne. *At Large and At Small.* New York: Farrar, Straus and Giroux, 2007. Print.

Faigley, Lester. *The Brief Penguin Handbook.* 3rd ed. New York: Pearson/Longman, 2009. Print.

———. "Performative Assessment of Writing Skills." Daiker, Kerek, and Morenberg 175–86.

Feiler, Bruce. *Walking the Bible: A Journey by Land through the Five Books of Moses.* New York: Perennial, 2001. Print.

Ferretti, Ralph P., Charles A. MacArthur, and Nancy S. Dowdy. "The Effects of an Elaborated Goal on the Persuasive Writing of Students with Learning Disabilities and Their Normally Achieving Peers." *Journal of Educational Psychology* 92.4 (2000): 694–702. Print.

Fershleiser, Rachael, and Larry Smith, eds. *Not Quite What I Was Planning: Six-Word Memoirs by Writers Famous and Obscure.* New York: HarperCollins, 2008.

Fisher, Douglas, and Nancy Frey. "Writing Instruction for Struggling Adolescent Readers: A Gradual Release Model." *Journal of Adolescent and Adult Literacy* 46.5 (2003): 396–405. Print.

Fleischer, Cathy, and Sarah Andrew-Vaughan. *Writing outside Your Comfort Zone: Helping Students Navigate Unfamiliar Genres.* Portsmouth: Heinemann, 2009. Print.

Fleischman, Paul. *Joyful Noise: Poems for Two Voices.* New York: Scholastic, 1988. Print.

Fleming, David. "Wrestling's Dirty Secret." *Sports Illustrated* 29 Dec. 1997: 134. Print.

Flower, Linda, and Lorraine Higgins. "Collaboration and the Construction of Meaning." Technical Report No. 56. Berkeley: Center for the Study of Writing and Literacy, 1991. Print.

Flynn, Rosalind M. "Curriculum Based Readers Theatre Scripts." *Educational Theatre Scripts.* rosalindflynn.com, n.d. Web. 30 Apr. 2010. <http://www.rosalindflynn.com/EdThtrScripts.html>.

———. *Dramatizing the Content with Curriculum-Based Readers Theatre, Grades 6–12.* Newark: International Reading Association, 2007. Print.

Foster, David. *A Primer for Writing Teachers: Theories, Theorists, Issues, Problems.* 2nd ed. Portsmouth: Boynton/Cook, 1992. Print.

Freedman, Aviva. "Sentence Combining: Some Questions." *Carleton Papers in Applied Language Studies,* vol. 2. 1985. 17–32.

Frey, Nancy, Douglas Fisher, and Ted Hernandez. "'What's the Gist?' Summary Writing for Struggling Adolescent Writers." *Voices from the Middle* 11.2 (2003): 43–49. Print.

Friend, Rosalie. "Teaching Summarization as a Content Area Reading Strategy." *Journal of Adolescent & Adult Literacy* 44.4 (2000): 320–29. Print.

Frost, Alanna, Julie A. Myatt, and Stephen Smith. "Multiple Modes of Production in a College Writing Class." Herrington, Morgan, and Hodgson 181–97.

Fulkerson, Richard. "Of Pre- and Post-Process: Reviews and Ruminations." *Composition Studies* 29.2 (2001): 93–119. Print.

Gabaldón, Salvador. "La Voz Liberada: Writing to Learn in a Sheltered English Class." Scarborough 59–69. Print.

Gage, John T. "Why Write?" Petrosky and Bartholomae 8–29.

Gardner, Traci. *Designing Writing Assignments*. Urbana: NCTE, 2008. Print.

Garner, Ruth. "When Children and Adults Do Not Use Learning Strategies: Toward a Theory of Settings." *Review of Educational Research* 60.4 (1990): 517–29. Print.

Gere, Anne Ruggles. *Writing Groups: History, Theory, and Implications*. Carbondale: Southern Illinois UP, 1987. Print.

Gere, Anne Ruggles, Leila Christenbury, and Kelly Sassi. *Writing on Demand: Best Practices and Strategies for Success*. Portsmouth: Heinemann, 2005. Print.

Giblin, James Cross. *Secrets of the Sphinx*. New York: Scholastic, 2004. Print.

Goldberg, Amie, Michael Russell, and Abigail Cook. "The Effect of Computers on Student Writing: A Meta-Analysis of Studies from 1992 to 2002." *Journal of Technology, Learning, and Assessment*. 2.1 (2003): 1–51. Print.

Goldfine, Ruth. "Making Word Processing More Effective in the Composition Classroom." *Teaching English in the Two-Year College* 28.3 (2001): 307–15. Print.

Goodman, Amy. "The Middle School High Five: Strategies Can Triumph." *Voices from the Middle* 13.2 (2005): 12–19. Print.

Graham, Steve, and Karen R. Harris. "Best Practices in Teaching Planning." Graham, MacArthur, and Fitzgerald 119–40.

———. "It Can Be Taught, but It Does Not Develop Naturally: Myths and Realities in Writing Instruction." *School Psychology Review* 26.3 (1997): 414–24. Print.

———. *Making the Writing Process Work: Strategies for Composition and Self-Regulation*. Cambridge: Brookline, 1996. Print.

Graham, Steve, Karen R. Harris, and Gary A. Troia. "Self-Regulated Strategy Development Revisited: Teaching Writing Strategies to Struggling Students." *Topics in Language Disorders* 20.4 (2000): 1–14. Print.

Graham, Steve, Charles A. MacArthur, and Jill Fitzgerald, eds. *Best Practices in Writing Instruction*. New York: Guilford P, 2007. Print.

Graham, Steve, Charles MacArthur, and Shirley Schwartz. "Effects of Goal Setting and Procedural Facilitation on the Revising Behavior and Writing Performance of Students with Writing and Learning Problems." *Journal of Educational Psychology* 87.2 (1995): 230–40. Print.

Graham, Steve, Charles MacArthur, Shirley Schwartz, and Victoria Page-Voth. "Improving the Compositions of Students with Learning Disabilities Using a Strategy Involving Product and Process Goal Setting." *Exceptional Children* 58.4 (1992): 322–34. Print.

Graham, Steve, and Dolores Perin. "What We Know, What We Still Need to Know: Teaching Adolescents to Write." *Scientific Studies of Reading* 11.4 (2007): 313–35. Print.

———. *Writing Next: Effective Strategies to Improve Writing of Adolescents in Middle and High Schools — A Report to Carnegie Corporation of New York.* Washington: Alliance for Excellent Education, 2007. Print.

Graner, Michael H. "Revision Workshops: An Alternative to Peer Editing Groups." *English Journal* 76.3 (1987): 40–45. Print.

Graves, Donald, and Penny Kittle. *Inside Writing: How to Teach the Details of Craft.* Portsmouth: Heinemann, 2005. Print.

Green, Jessica. "Adjusting the Rear View Mirror: Higher Level Reflection Strategies in First-Year Composition." Thesis. Brigham Young University, 2009. Print.

Guinee, Kathleen, and Maya B. Eagleton. "Spinning Straw into Gold: Transforming Information into Knowledge during Web-Based Research." *English Journal* 95.4 (2006): 46–52. Print.

Haneda, Mari, and Gordon Wells. "Writing in Knowledge-Building Communities." *Research in the Teaching of English* 34 (2000): 430–57. Print.

Harris, Joseph. *A Teaching Subject: Composition Since 1966.* Upper Saddle River: Prentice Hall, 1997. Print.

Heritage Makers. Heritage Makers, 2010. Web. 3 May 2010.

Herrington, Anne, Kevin Hodgson, and Charles Moran, eds. *Teaching the New Writing: Technology, Change, and Assessment in the 21st-Century Classroom.* New York: Teachers College P, 2009. Print.

Herrington, Anne, and Charles Moran. "Challenges for Writing Teachers: Evolving Technologies and Standardized Assessment." Herrington, Hodgson, and Moran 1–17.

Hicks, Troy. *The Digital Writing Workshop.* Portsmouth: Heinemann, 2009. Print.

Hillocks, George. "At Last: The Focus on Form vs. Content in Teaching Writing." *Research in the Teaching of English* 40.2 (2005): 238–48. Print.

———. "Inquiry and the Composing Process: Theory and Research." *College English* 44.7 (1982): 659–73. Print.

———. *Research on Written Composition: New Directions for Teaching.* Urbana: NCTE, 1986. Print.

———. *Teaching Writing as Reflective Practice.* New York: Teachers College P, 1995. Print.

———. *The Testing Trap: How State Writing Assessments Control Learning.* New York: Teachers College P, 2002. Print.

Holbrook, Sara. *Practical Poetry: A Nonstandard Approach to Meeting Content-Area Standards.* Portsmouth: Heinemann, 2005. Print.

Howard, Rebecca Moore. "Collaborative Pedagogy." *A Guide to Composition Pedagogies.* Ed. Gary Tate, Amy Rupiper, and Kurt Schick. New York: Oxford UP, 2001. 54–70. Print.

Ianacone, John A. "Passion and Craft in Writing: Finding a Balance." *English Journal* 85.6 (1996): 17–22. Print.

The Internet Writing Journal. Writers Write, 1997–2010. Web. 30 Apr. 2010.

Irwin, Sarah, and Cyndi Knodle. "Mandates and the Writing Curriculum: Creating a Place to Dwell." *English Journal* 97.5 (2008): 40–45. Print.

Johnson, Sabina Thorne. "The Ant and the Grasshopper: Some Reflections on Prewriting." *College English* 43.3 (1981): 232–41. Print.

Joyce, Bruce, and Marsha Weil, eds. *Models of Teaching.* 5th ed. Boston: Allyn & Bacon, 1996. Print.

Kajder, Sara B. *The Tech-Savvy English Classroom.* Portland: Stenhouse, 2003. Print.

Kellogg, Ronald T. "Effectiveness of Prewriting Strategies as a Function of Task Demands." *American Journal of Psychology* 103.3 (1990): 327–42. Print.

Kent, Thomas. Introduction. *Post-Process Theory: Beyond the Writing-Process Paradigm.* Carbondale: Southern Illinois UP, 1999. 1–6. Print.

Kerley, Barbara. *The Dinosaurs of Waterhouse Hawkins.* New York: Scholastic, 2001. Print.

Kieft, Marlene, Gert Rijlaarsdam, and Huub van den Bergh. "Writing as a Learning Tool: Testing the Role of Students' Writing Strategies." *European Journal of Psychology of Education* 21.1 (2006): 17–34. Print.

Killgallon, Don. *Sentence Composing for Middle School: A Worktext on Sentence Variety and Maturity.* Portsmouth: Boynton/Cook, 1997. Print.

Kissner, Emily. *Summarizing, Paraphrasing, and Retelling: Skills for Better Reading, Writing, and Test Taking.* Portsmouth: Heinemann, 2006. Print.

Kittle, Penny. *Write beside Them: Risk, Voice, and Clarity in High School Writing.* Portsmouth: Heinemann, 2008. Print.

Kittle, Peter. "Student Engagement and Multimodality: Collaboration, Schema, Identity." Herrington, Hodgson, and Moran 164–80.

Klonoski, Edward. "Using the Eyes of the PC to Teach Revision." *Computers and Composition* 11.1 (1994): 71–78. Print.

Lain, Sheryl. "Reaffirming the Writing Workshop for Young Adolescents." *Voices from the Middle* 14.3 (2007): 20–28. Print.

Langer, Judith A., and Arthur N. Applebee. *How Writing Shapes Thinking: A Study of Learning and Teaching.* Urbana: NCTE, 1987. Print.

Larson, Richard L. "The 'Research Paper' in the Writing Course: A Non-Form of Writing." *College English* 44.8 (1982): 811–16. Rpt. in *The Writing Teacher's Sourcebook.* 4th ed. Ed. Edward P. J. Corbett, Nancy Myers, and Gary Tate. New York: Oxford UP, 2000. 216–21.

Lattimer, Heather. "Foreword." Fleischer and Andrew-Vaughan. vii–x. Print.

———. *Thinking through Genre: Units of Study in Reading and Writing Workshops, 4–12.* Portland, ME: Stenhouse, 2003.

Lee, Gretchen. "Technology in the Language Arts Classroom: Is It Worth the Trouble?" *Voices from the Middle* 7.3 (2000): 24–32. Print.

Lee, Harper. *To Kill a Mockingbird.* New York: Warner Books, 1960. Print.

Lenhart, Amanda, Sousan Arafeh, Aaron Smith, and Alexandra Rankin Macgill. *Writing, Technology and Teens*. *Pew Research Center Publications*. Pew Internet & American Life Project, 24 Apr. 2008. Web. 26 Apr. 2010.

Lindemann, Erika, with Daniel Anderson. *A Rhetoric for Writing Teachers*. 4th ed. New York: Oxford UP, 2001. Print.

MacArthur, Charles A., Steve Graham, and Jill Fitzgerald, eds. *Handbook of Writing Research*. New York: Guilford P, 2006. Print.

Macrorie, Ken. *The I-Search Paper: Revised Edition of Searching Writing*. Portsmouth: Heinemann, 1988. Print.

Maxwell, Rhoda J., and Mary Jordan Meiser. *Teaching English in Middle and Secondary Schools*. 3rd ed. Upper Saddle River: Prentice Hall, 2001. Print.

Mayo, Margaret. *Dig Dig Digging*. New York: Henry Holt, 2002. Print.

McCann, Thomas M., Larry R. Johannessen, Elizabeth Kahn, Peter Smagorinsky, and Michael W. Smith. *Reflective Teaching, Reflective Learning: How to Develop Critically Engaged Readers, Writers, and Speakers*. Portsmouth: Heinemann, 2005. Print.

McCrindle, Andrea R., and Carol A. Christensen. "The Impact of Learning Journals on Metacognitive and Cognitive Processes and Learning Performance." *Learning and Instruction* 5.2 (1995): 167–85.

McCutchen, Deborah, Paul Teske, and Catherine Bankston. "Writing and Cognition: Implications of the Cognitive Architecture for Learning to Write and Writing to Learn." *Handbook of Research on Writing: History, Society, School, Individual, Text*. Ed. Charles Bazerman. New York: Lawrence Erlbaum, 2008. 451–70. Print.

McDougal, Littell. *McDougal, Littell English* [Orange Level]. Evanston: McDougal, Littell, 1989. Print.

McElveen, Susan Anderson, and Connie Campbell Dierking. "Children's Books as Models to Teach Writing Skills." *Reading Teacher* 54.4 (2001): 362–64. Print.

McPhee, John. *Oranges*. New York: Farrar, Straus and Giroux. 2000. Print.

"Metaphor." *Wikipedia*. Wikimedia Foundation, 28 Apr. 2010. Web. 28 Apr. 2010.

Miller, Carolyn R. "Genre as Social Action." *Quarterly Journal of Speech* 70 (1984): 151–67. Print.

Mitchell, Diana. "Writing to Learn across the Curriculum and the English Teacher." *English Journal* 85.5 (1996): 93–97. Print.

Moeller, Dave. *Computers in the Writing Classroom*. Urbana: NCTE, 2002. Print.

Morenberg, Max. "Process/Schmocess: Why Not Combine a Sentence or Two?" Annual Meeting of the Conference on College Composition and Communication, Chicago, 22–24 Mar. 1990. Print.

Murray, Donald M. *Learning by Teaching: Selected Articles on Writing and Teaching*. Montclair: Boynton/Cook, 1982. Print.

———. "One Writer's Secrets." *College Composition and Communication* 37:2 (1986): 146–153.

———. "Teaching Writing as Process Not Product." Villanueva 3–6.

Myers, Sharon A. "ReMembering the Sentence." *CCC* 54.4 (2003): 610–28. Print.

National Center for Education Statistics. "Kids' Zone." *National Center for Education Statistics*. National Center for Education Statistics, n.d. Web. 20 Apr. 2010.

National Writing Project, and Carl Nagin. *Because Writing Matters: Improving Student Writing in Our Schools*. San Francisco: Jossey-Bass, 2003. Print.

Nelms, Gerald. "Reassessing Janet Emig's 'The Composing Processes of Twelfth Graders': An Historical Perspective. *Rhetoric Review* 13.1 (1994): 108–30. Print.

Nelson, Nancy. "Writing to Learn: One Theory, Two Rationales." Rijlaarsdam et al. 23–36.

Newell, George E., Susan Koukis, and Stacy Boster. "Best Practices in Developing a Writing across the Curriculum Program in the Secondary School." Graham, MacArthur, and Fitzgerald 74–98. Print.

New York Times. *Writers [on Writing]: Collected Essays from* The New York Times. New York: Henry Holt, 2001. Print.

Nippold, Marilyn A., Jeannene M. Ward-Lonergan, and Jessica L. Fanning. "Persuasive Writing in Children, Adolescents, and Adults: A Study of Syntactic, Semantic, and Pragmatic Development." *Language, Speech, and Hearing Services in Schools* 36 (2005): 125–38. Print.

Nystrand, Martin, and Deborah Brandt. "Response to Writing as a Context for Learning to Write." *Writing and Response: Theory, Practice, and Research*. Ed. Chris M. Anson. Urbana: NCTE, 1989. 209–30. Print.

Nystrand, Martin, Adam Gamoran, and William Carbonaro. "On the Ecology of Classroom Instruction: The Case of Writing in High School English and Social Studies." Rijlaarsdam et al. 57–81.

Ostrom, Hans. "'Carom Shots': Reconceptualizing Imitation and Its Uses in Creative Writing Courses." *Teaching Writing Creatively*. Ed. David Starkey. Portsmouth: Boynton/Cook, 1998. 154–71. Print.

Overmeyer, Mark. *What Student Writing Teaches Us: Formative Assessment in the Writing Workshop*. Portland: Stenhouse, 2009. Print.

Owston, Ronald D., Sharon Murphy, and Herbert H. Wideman. "The Effects of Word Processing on Students' Writing Quality and Revision Strategies." *Research in the Teaching of English*. 26.3 (1992): 249–76. Print.

Page-Voth, Victoria, and Steve Graham. "Effects of Goal Setting and Strategy Use on the Writing Performance and Self-Efficacy of Students with Writing and Learning Problems." *Journal of Educational Psychology* 91.2 (1999): 230–40. Print.

Paris, Scott G., Marjorie Y. Lipson, and Karen K. Wixson. "Becoming a Strategic Reader." *Contemporary Educational Psychology* 8.3 (1983): 293–316. Print.

Paris, Scott G., and Alison H. Paris. "Classroom Applications of Research on Self-Regulated Learning." *Educational Psychologist* 36.2 (2001): 89–101. Print.

Parr, Judy M. "Extended Use of Technology and Students' Theories about Writing."

AARE/NXARE Joint Conference, Deakin University, Geelong, 22–26 Nov. 1992. *Australian Association for Research in Education*. Web. 07 June 2010.

Passig, David, and Gali Schwartz. "Collaborative Writing: Online versus Frontal." *International Journal on E-Learning*. 6.3 (2007): 395–412. Print.

Patterson, Nancy. "Computers and Writing: The Research Says YES!" *Voices from the Middle* 13.4 (2006): 64–68. Print.

Peck, Wayne C. "The Effects of Prompts upon Revision: A Glimpse of the Gap between Planning and Performance." Technical Report No. 26. Berkeley: Center for the Study of Writing, 1989. Print.

Perin, Dolores. "Best Practices in Teaching Writing to Adolescents." Graham, MacArthur, and Fitzgerald 242–64. Print.

Perl, Sondra, ed. *Landmark Essays on Writing Process*. Davis: Hermagoras P, 1994. Print.

———. "Understanding Composing." Perl, *Landmark* 99–106.

Petrosky, A. R., and D. Bartholomae, eds. *The Teaching of Writing: 85th Yearbook of the National Society for the Study of Education, Part II*. Chicago: University of Chicago P, 1986. Print.

Powell's City of Books. *Powell's Books*. Powells.com, 1994–2010. Web. 30 Apr. 2010.

Pressley, Michael, Karen R. Harris, and Marilyn B. Marks. "But Good Strategy Instructors Are Constructivists!" *Educational Psychology Review* 4.1 (1992): 3–31. Print.

Pressley, Michael, and Katherine Hilden. "Cognitive Strategies: Production Deficiencies and Successful Strategy Instruction Everywhere." *Handbook of Child Psychology, Vol. 2: Cognition, Perception, and Language*. Ed. Deanna Kuhn and Robert S. Siegler. Hoboken: John Wiley & Sons, 2006. 511–56. Print.

Pritchard, Ruie J., and Ronald L. Honeycutt. "Best Practices in Implementing a Process Approach to Teaching Writing." Graham, MacArthur, and Fitzgerald 28–49.

———. "The Process Approach to Writing Instruction: Examining Its Effectiveness." *Handbook of Writing Research*. MacArthur, Graham, and Fitzgerald 275–90.

Quindlen, Anna. *How Reading Changed My Life*. New York: Ballantine, 1998. Print.

———. "Look at What They've Done." *Newsweek* 3 June 2002: 68. Print.

Ray, Katie Wood. "Exploring Inquiry as a Teaching Stance in the Writing Workshop." *Language Arts* 83.3 (2006): 238–47. Print.

———. *Study Driven: A Framework for Planning Units of Study in the Writing Workshop*. Portsmouth: Heinemann, 2006. Print.

———. *Wondrous Words: Writers and Writing in the Elementary Classroom*. Urbana: NCTE, 1999. Print.

Reilly, Rick. "Give Casey Martin a Lift." *Sports Illustrated* 9 Feb. 1998: 140. Print.

Reither, James A. "Writing and Knowing: Toward Redefining the Writing Process." *College English* 47.6 (1985): 620–28. Print.

Reither, James A., and Douglas Vipond. "Writing as Collaboration." *College English* 51.8 (1989): 855–67. Print.

Reynard, Ruth. "Why Wikis?" *Campus Technology*. 1105 Media, 4 Feb. 2009. Web. 20 Apr. 2010.

Rhoder, Carol. "Mindful Reading: Strategy Training that Facilitates Transfer." *Journal of Adolescent & Adult Literacy* 45.6 (2002): 498–512. Print.

Rijlaarsdam, Gert, Päivi Tynjälä, Lucia Mason, and Kirsti Lonka, eds. *Studies in Writing: Volume 7: Writing as a Learning Tool: Integrating Theory and Practice*. Boston: Kluwer Academic, 2001. Print.

Roach, Mary. *Stiff: The Curious Lives of Human Cadavers*. New York: W. W. Norton, 2003. Print.

Rodrigues, Raymond J., and Dawn Wilson Rodrigues. "Computer-Based Invention: Its Place and Potential." *CCC* 35.1(1984): 78–87. Print.

Rohman, D. Gordon. "Pre-Writing: The Stage of Discovery in the Writing Process." Ed. Richard E. Young and Yameng Liu. *Landmark Essays on Rhetorical Invention in Writing*. Davis: Hermagoras P, 1994. 41–49. Print.

Rosenblatt, Roger. "The Man in the Water." *The Man in the Water: Essays and Stories*. New York: Random House, 1994. 168–70. Print.

Rubin, Susan Goldman. *The Yellow House: Vincent Van Gogh and Paul Gaugin Side by Side*. New York: Harry N. Abrams, 2001. Print.

Scarborough, Harriet Arzu. *Writing across the Curriculum in Secondary Classrooms: Teaching from a Diverse Perspective*. Upper Saddle River: Prentice-Hall, 2001.

Scardamalia, Marlene, and Carl Bereiter. "Knowledge Building: Theory, Pedagogy, and Technology." *Cambridge Handbook of the Learning Sciences*. Ed. R. Keith Sawyer. New York: Cambridge UP, 2006. 97–118. Print.

Schotter, Roni. *Nothing Ever Happens on 90th Street*. New York: Orchard Books, 1999. Print.

Schunk, Dale H., and Carl W. Swartz. "Writing Strategy Instruction with Gifted Students: Effects of Goals and Feedback on Self-Efficacy and Skills." *Roeper Review* 15.4 (1993): 225–30. Print.

Sexton, Melissa, Karen R. Harris, and Steve Graham. "Self-Regulated Strategy Development and the Writing Process: Effects on Essay Writing and Attributions." *Exceptional Children* 64.3 (1998): 295–311. Print.

Shakespeare, William. *The Tragedy of Romeo and Juliet*. New York: Scholastic, 1969. Print.

Shields, Charles J. *Mockingbird: A Portrait of Harper Lee*. New York: Henry Holt, 2006. Print.

Simmons, Jay. "Responders Are Taught, Not Born." *Journal of Adolescent & Adult Literacy* 46.8 (2003): 684–93. Print.

Sloan, Chris. *Central Utah Writing Project Saturday Workshop*, 20 Feb. 2010, Provo, Utah.

Smith, Michael W., and George Hillocks. "What Inquiring Writers Need to Know." *English Journal* 78.2 (1989): 58–63. Print.

Snyder, Ilana. "Writing with Word Processors: The Computer's Influence on the Classroom Context." *Curriculum Studies* 26.2 (1994): 143–62. Print.

Sommers, Nancy. "Revision Strategies of Student Writers and Experienced Adult Writers." Perl, *Landmark* 75–84.

Soven, Margot Iris. *Teaching Writing in Middle and Secondary Schools: Theory, Research, and Practice*. Boston: Allyn & Bacon, 1999. Print.

Spandel, Vicki. *The 9 Rights of Every Writer: A Guide for Teachers*. Portsmouth: Heinemann, 2005. Print.

Speck, Bruce W. *Facilitating Students' Collaborative Writing*. San Francisco: Jossey-Bass, 2002. Print.

Spinelli, Jerry. *Stargirl*. New York: Scholastic, 2000. Print.

Steinbeck, John. *The Pearl*. New York: Viking P, 1974. Print.

Storch, Neomy. "Collaborative Writing: Product, Process, and Students' Reflections." *Journal of Second Language Writing* 14.3 (2005): 153–73. Print.

Stotsky, Sandra. "Research on Reading/Writing Relationships: A Synthesis and Suggested Directions." *Composing and Comprehending*. Ed. Julie M. Jensen. Urbana: National Conference on Research in English and ERIC, 1984. 7–22. Print.

Strickland, Bill, ed. *On Being a Writer*. Cincinnati: Writer's Digest Books, 1992. Print.

Strong, William. *Coaching Writing: The Power of Guided Practice*. Portsmouth: Heinemann, 2001. Print.

———. *Creative Approaches to Sentence Combining*. Urbana: ERIC and NCTE, 1986. Print.

———. "How Sentence Combining Works." Daiker, Kerek, and Morenberg 334–50.

———. *Sentence Combining: A Composing Book*. 2nd ed. New York: Random House, 1983. Print.

Styslinger, Mary E. "Mars and Venus in My Classroom: Men Go to Their Caves and Women Talk during Peer Revision." *English Journal* 88.3 (1999): 50–56. Print.

Taylor, Marcy M. "Nancie Atwell's *In the Middle* and the Ongoing Transformation of the Writing Workshop." *English Journal* 90.1 (2000): 46–52. Print.

Thompson, Bill. *Bill Thompson's Eye on Books*. N.p., n.d. Web. 30 Apr. 2010.

Trentin, G. "Using a Wiki to Evaluate Individual Contribution to a Collaborative Learning Project." *Journal of Computer Assisted Learning* 25.1 (2009): 43–55. Print.

Troia, Gary A. "Teaching Writing Strategies to Children with Disabilities: Setting Generalization as a Goal." *Exceptionality* 10.4 (2002): 249–69. Print.

"Twitter Music Reviews: Criticism as Haiku." *npr: Music Reviews*.NPR, 2010. Wed. 8 June 2010. <http://www.npr.org/templates/story/story.php?storyId=106178234>.

Tynjälä, Päivi, Lucia Mason, and Kirsti Lonka. "Writing as a Learning Tool: An Introduction." Rijlaarsdam et al. 7–22.

Villanueva, Victor. *Cross-Talk in Comp Theory: A Reader*. Urbana: NCTE, 1997. Print.

Warshauer, Mark. *Laptops and Literacy: Learning in the Wireless Classroom*. New York: Teachers College P, 2006. Print.

Watt, Melanie. *Have I Got a Book for You!* Tonawanda: Kids Can P, 2009. Print.

Watterson, Bill. *The Indispensable Calvin and Hobbes: A Calvin and Hobbes Treasury.* Kansas City: Universal P, 1992. Print.

Weiner, Harvey S. "Collaborative Learning in the Classroom: A Guide to Evaluation." *College English* 48.1 (1986): 52–61. Print.

Welch, Marshall. "The *PLEASE* Strategy: A Metacognitive Learning Strategy for Improving the Paragraph Writing of Students with Mild Learning Disabilities." *Learning Disability Quarterly* 15.2 (1992): 119–28. Print.

Whitin, Phyllis, and David J. Whitin. *Inquiry at the Window: Pursuing the Wonders of Learners.* Portsmouth: Heinemann, 1997. Print.

"Wikipedia: Version 1.0 Editorial Team/Assessment." *Wikipedia.* Wikimedia Foundation, 28 Mar. 2010. Web. 28 Apr. 2010.

"Wiki Walk-Through." *TeachersFirst.com.* Source for Learning, 2006-10.Web. 2 June 2010.

Williams, Joseph M., and Gregory B. Colomb. "The Case for Explicit Teaching: Why What You Don't Know Won't Help You." *Research in the Teaching of English* 27.3 (1993): 252–64. Print.

Winograd, Peter N. "Strategic Difficulties in Summarizing Texts." *Reading Research Quarterly* 19.4 (1984): 404–25. Print.

Wong, Bernice Y. L. "Instructional Parameters Promoting Transfer of Learned Strategies in Students with Disabilities." *Learning Disability Quarterly* 17.2 (1994): 110–120. Print.

Wong, Bernice Y. L., Deborah L. Butler, Sherfyl A. Ficzere, and Sonia Kuperis. "Teaching Low Achievers and Students with Learning Disabilities to Plan, Write, and Revise Opinion Essays." *Journal of Learning Disabilities.* 29.2 (1996): 197–212. Print.

Wormelli, Rick. *Summarization in Any Subject: 50 Techniques to Improve Student Learning.* Alexandria: ASCD, 2005. Print.

Yagelski, Robert P. "Who's Afraid of Subjectivity?" *Taking Stock: The Writing Process Movement in the '90s.* Ed. Lad Tobin and Thomas Newkirk. Portsmouth: Boynton/Cook, 1994. 203–17. Print.

Yancey, Kathleen. *Reflection in the Writing Classroom.* Logan, UT: Utah State University Press, 1998.

Yancey, Kathleen Blake, and Michael Spooner. "A Single Good Mind: Collaboration, Cooperation, and the Writing Self." *CCC* 49.1 (1998): 45–62. Print.

Young, Carl, and Jonathan Bush. "Teaching the English Language Arts With Technology: A Critical Approach and Pedagogical Framework." *Contemporary Issues in Technology and Teacher Education* 4.1 (2004): 1–22. Print.

Young, Linda. "Portals into Poetry: Using Generative Writing Groups to Facilitate Student Engagement with Word Art." *Journal of Adolescent and Adult Literacy* 51.1 (2007): 50–55. Print.

Index

Anderson, V., 20, 25, 31
Andrew-Vaughan, S., 147, 148, 149
Anson, C. M., 54, 181
Applebee, A. N., 134, 140, 141, 144, 145, 168, 173, 174, 175
Applications
  of collaborative writing, 48
  of inquiry activities, 129–32
  of models, 161–67
  of prewriting, 112–16
  of process writing approach, 146–48
  of product goals, 64–69
  of sentence combining, 95–97
  of summarization, 31–34
  of word processing, 79–85
  of writing strategies, 15–17
  of writing to learn, 176–81
Arendt, H., 35
Armbruster, B. B., 24, 25
Aston, D., 164, 165
Atwell, N., 116, 139, 140, 149
Audience, 142

Baines, L., 138
Ballenger, B., 113, 124
Bangert-Drowns, R. L., 72, 170, 171, 176, 177
Bankston, C., 58
Bawashi, A., 102
Beach, R., 48, 49, 54, 181
Bereiter, C., 4, 57
Bishop, W., 36, 37, 46
Bizzell, P., 133, 134, 136
Blackburn-Brockman, 106

Blog posts, 189–91
Bloomfield, L., 169
Boscolo, P., 168, 169
Boster, S., 169, 173
Brandt, D., 53
Brannon, L., 172, 178
Breuch, L.-A. K., 54
Brown, A. L., 21, 22, 31
Bruffee, K. A., 37, 38, 40
Burleigh, R., 164, 165
Butler, P., 152
Bryson, B., 117
Buis, K., 114
Burke, J., 70, 116
Bushman, J. M., 29

Calkins, L., 140
Campbell, K. H., 167
Carbonaro, W., 172
Carlson, R. A., 154, 156, 160, 161
Carroll, L., 55
Casazza, M. E., 22, 30
Casey, M., 139
Chapman, M. L., 152, 153, 159
Charney, D. H., 154, 156, 160, 161
CHoMP approach to summarizing, 27
Christenbury, L., 65
Christenson, C. A., 176
Cisneros, S., 57
Clark, I. L., 100
Classroom environment, 8–9
  valued prewriting and, 107
Classroom philosophy, 183–85
Coherence, local, 24

Collaborative writing, 35–54
  applications of, 48–54
  with computers, 40–41
  versus cooperative learning, 38
  group functioning and, 39–40
  grouping issues in, 39
  interpretations of, 35–36
  overview of, 35–41
  peer review of, 50–54
  preparation for, 41–44
  principles of, 41–48
  purposefulness in, 47–48
  structure for, 44–47
  students' feelings about, 38–39
  with wikis, 48–50
  word processing and, 73
Collard, S., 123, 133, 136
Collins, J., 3, 5, 8, 9, 11, 12
Colomb, G. B., 60, 63
Comprone, J., 92
Concepts, writing about, 129–30
Conditional knowledge, 7
Connection to product, in process
  writing approach, 144–46
Connors, R. J., 87, 89
Constructivism, 183–84
Context, writing strategies and, 8–10
Contextual importance, 23
Cook, A., 73
Cooperative learning, 37–38
Copy-and-paste, in word processing,
  81–82
Copy-delete strategy, for summarizing, 21
Creativity theory, 155
Crovitz, D., 130
Crowe, C., 126
Crowley, S., 87
Cruz, M. C. E., 172
Cunningham, W., 48
Curriculum, elements of effective
  instruction and, xi

Dale, H., 36, 39, 47
Daniels, H., 169, 181
Day, J. D., 21, 22
Dean, D., 11, 57, 82, 115, 131
Debates, 109

De La Paz, S., 58, 62
Dierking, C. C., 161
DiPardo, A., 51, 52
Direct instruction, of summarization,
  26–28
Discovery, 136
Discrete skills, in summarization, 22–26
Discussion
  of models, 158
  for prewriting, 110–11
Donovan, C. A., 58, 60
Dowdy, N. S., 57, 59, 61, 62
Dowling, C., 75
Dyson, A. H., 139, 145

Eagleton, M. B., 20, 27
Ede, L., 45
Education Northwest, 43
Ehrenworth, M., 167
Eklundh, K. S., 71, 75
Elbow, P., 89, 136
Emig, J., 136
Englert, C. S., 12
Expanding ideas, 15–16
Expertise, of teacher, x
Expressivism, 135

Fadiman, A., 102–3
Faigley, L., 81, 87
Fanning, J. L., 92, 119
Feedback, in scaffolding, 28–29
Feiler, B., 26, 31
Ferretti, R. P., 57, 59, 61, 62
Fershleiser, R., 33
Find, in word processing, 80–81
Fisher, D., 20, 27, 155
Fitzgerald, J., 194
Fleischer, C., 147, 148, 149
Fleischman, P., 115
Fleming, D., 162, 163
Flexibility, in process writing approach,
  141–43
Flower, L., 42
Flynn, R. M., 178, 179
Foster, D., 99
Freedman, A., 88
Freedman, S. W., 51, 52, 139, 145

Freewriting, 109, 168
Frey, N., 20, 27, 155
Friend, R., 20, 26, 27
Frost, A., 68

Gage, J. T., 120
Galbadón, S., 175
Gamoran, A., 172
Gardner, T., 9, 10, 194
Generalizing, 26
Genre, working with unfamiliar, 147–49
Genre theory, 152–53
Gere, A. R., 36, 37, 40, 41, 42, 45, 46, 65
Giblin, J. G., 24
Goals
    effective, 60–62
    prewriting, 64–67
    product. *See* Product goals
    supported, 62–63
    task-appropriate, 63–64
Goldberg, A., 73
Goldfine, R., 71
Goodman, A., 23
Google Docs, 41
Graham, S., ix, x, 4, 5, 6, 7, 8, 10, 11, 16,
    36, 57, 58, 59, 61, 62, 63, 68, 72, 82, 89,
    100, 102, 105, 107, 118, 154, 168, 170,
    182, 184, 185, 194
Graner, M. H., 43, 50, 53
Graphic organizers, 103, 11
Graphs, 16–17
    of sentence lengths, 82–84
Graves, D., 133, 150, 140
Greene, D., 33
Guinee, K., 20, 27

Haneda, M., 172
Harris, J., 136
Harris, K. R., 4, 5, 6, 7, 8, 10, 11, 16, 57,
    105, 107
Hemenway, S. J., 139
Hernandez, T., 20, 27
Herrington, A., 75
Hicks, T., 85
Hidi, S., 20, 25, 31
Higgins, L., 42
Highlighting, in word processing, 82

Hilden, K., 13
Hillocks, G., ix, 56, 60, 93, 117, 118, 119,
    120, 121, 122, 125, 128, 132, 153, 154,
    157, 158, 159, 184
Holbrook, S., 113
Honeycutt, R. L., 135, 138
Howard, R. M., 40, 48
Hurley, M. M., 170, 171, 176, 177

Ianacone, J. A., 155
Inquiry activities, 117–32
    applications of, 129–32
    in books and journal, 4
    broad perspectives in, 125–28
    connection to task in, 128
    overview of, 117–23
    principles of, 123–28
    questioning environment for, 123–25
    writing about concept, 129–30
    writing for Wikipedia, 130–32
Irwin, S., 101

Johnson, S. T., 100, 103
Journals, for writing to learn, 176–78
Joyce, B., 109

Kajder, S. B., 77, 79
Kellogg, R. T., 104, 106, 111
Kent, T., 101
Kerley, B., 117, 164, 165
Kieft, M., 175
Killagon, D., 98
King, S., 151
Kissner, E., 21, 22, 23, 27, 28, 29, 30
Kittle, P., 59, 140, 167, 185
Klonoski, E., 71, 80, 81
Knodle, C., 101
Knowledge telling, 21–22
Koukis, S., 169, 173

Lain, S., 140, 141
Langer, J. A., 168, 173, 174, 175
Lattimer, H., 147
Lee, G., 79
Lee, H., 124, 129
Lenhart, A., 73, 78
Letters to the editor, 189–91

Levels of writing, 141–42
Lindemann, E., 106, 113
Lipson, M. Y., 13
Lonka, K., 169, 170
Lunsford, A., 45

MacArthur, C. A., 57, 58, 59, 61, 62, 63, 68, 194
Macrorie, K., 124
Main ideas, finding, 31
Marks, M. B., 5, 8, 11
Mason, L., 168, 169, 170
Maxwell, R. J., 141
Mayer, L., 169
Mayo, M., 157
McCrindle, A. R., 176
McCutchen, D., 58
McElveen, S. A., 161
McPhee, J., 124
Meiser, M. J., 141
Miller, C. R., 148
Miller, H., 135
Mitchell, D., 169
Models, 151–67
  applications of, 161–67
  integration of, 160–61
  overview of, 151–56
  principles of, 157–61
  talking about, 158–59
  for teaching persuasive writing, 161–64
  for teaching sentences, 164–67
  text selection, 157–58
  of writing strategies, 6, 11
Moeller, D., 78, 84
Moran, C., 75
Morenberg, M., 89
Murphy, S., 78
Murray, D. M., 99, 122, 134, 135, 136, 138, 142, 145
Myatt, J. A., 68

Nelms, G., 134
Nelson, N., 173
Newell, G. E., 169, 173
Nippold, M. A., 92, 11-9
Note-taking, 4, 103, 110, 168
Nystrand, M., 51, 53, 172

Outlines, 104, 111
Overmeyer, M., 57, 62, 63
Ownership, in process writing approach, 143–44
Owston, R. D., 78

Page-Voth, V., 57, 58, 59, 61
Paragraphs, in sentence combining, 95–97
Paris, A. H., 10
Paris, S. G., 10, 13
Parr, J. M., 71, 80, 81
Passig, D., 41
Peck, W. C., 61
Peer response, to computer writing, 84–85
Peer review, of collaborative writing, 50–54
Perin, D., ix, x, 36, 62, 72, 89, 100, 102, 118, 154, 168, 170, 182, 184, 185
Perl, S., 134, 136
Persuasive writing, models for, 161–64
Podcasts, 191
Poetry, as prewriting, 113–16
Preparation, for collaborative writing, 41–44
Pressley, M., 5, 8, 11, 13
Prewriting, 99–116
  applications of, 112–16
  challenges to, 106
  developing ideas, 110–11
  finding topics, 112–13
  getting ideas, 108–9
  organizing ideas, 111
  overview of, 99–107
  poetry as, 113–16
  principles of, 106–111
  purpose of, 101
  research during, 102–3
  strategies for, 108–11
  valued, 106–8
Prezi, 104
Pritchard, R. J., 135, 138
Procedural knowledge, 6
Process writing approach, 8, 133–50
  applications of, 146–49
  connection to product in, 144–46

developing sense of process, 146
flexibility in, 141–43
overview of, 133–38
ownership in, 143–44
principles of, 138–46
time and, 138–41
Product goals, 55–70
applications of, 64–69
effective goals and, 60–62
overview of, 55–60
prewriting goals and, 64–67
principles of, 60–64
problems with, 56
revising with, 68–69
rubrics and, 64–67
supported goals and, 62–63
task-appropriate goals and, 63–64
writing prompts and, 64–67
Purposefulness, 187
in collaborative writing, 47–48
in word processing, 77–78

Questioning environment, for inquiry
activities, 123–25
Quindlen, A., 160, 161, 163

Ray, K. W., 100, 121, 122, 132, 154, 155, 158
Readers theater, 178–81
Reflection
as writing strategy, 13–15
in writing to learn, 176
Reilly, R., 161, 162, 163
Reither, J. A., 37, 119
Revision strategies, word processing, 79–84
copy-and paste, 81–82
find, 80–81
graphing sentence lengths, 82–84
highlighting, 82
Rhoder, C., 24, 28
Rijlaarsdam, G., 175
Roach, M., 126
Rodrigues, D. W., 106
Rodrigues, R. J., 106
Rohman, D. G., 99, 106, 108
Rolling Exhibition, 112

Rosenblatt, R., 129
Rubin, S. G., 126
Rubrics, xi
analyzing, 64–67
sample statewide, 67
Russell, M., 73

Sassi, K., 65
Saxton, B., 120
Scaffolding
of summarization instruction, 28–31
teacher feedback in, 28
as writing strategy, 11–12
Scardamalia, M., 4, 57
Schotter, R., 112
Schunk, D. H., 59, 61
Schwartz, C. W., 59, 61
Schwartz, G., 41
Schwartz, S., 58, 61, 63, 68
Self-Regulated Strategy Development
(SRSD), 6
Sentence combining, 86–98
applications of, 95–97
benefits of, 87
context and, 91–92
decline of, 89
discussion about, 94
overview of, 86–91
paragraphs and, 95–97
principles of, 91–94
sentence play and, 97–98
supportive environment for learning, 92–93
writing starters, 95
Sentence lengths, graphing, 82–84
Sentence structure, models for, 164–67
Sexton, M., 6, 11
Shields, C. J., 124, 126
Simmons, J., 41, 42, 52
Sinclair, U., 125
Sloan, C., 32
Smith, L., 33
Smith, S., 68
Smolkin, L. B., 58, 60
Smoot, W. S., 130
Snyder, I., 73, 76, 77, 78
Sommers, N., 135

Spandel, V., 133, 135, 143, 182, 193
Speck, B., 44, 45, 48, 50, 51
Steineke, N., 169, 181
Storch, N., 36, 50
Stotsky, S., 152
Strategies. *See* Writing strategies
Strickland, B., 146
Strong, W., 87, 88, 89, 91, 92, 94
Structure, in collaborative writing, 44–47
Styslinger, M. E., 39, 50
Sullenberger, C. B., 129
Summarization, 19–34
  applications of, 31–34
  discrete skills in, 22–26
  direct instruction of, 26–28
  overview of, 19–22
  principles of, 31
  scaffolding instruction of, 28–31
Swanson, P. N., 58, 62
Swiss, T., 54
Synectics, 109

Task, connection to, in inquiry activities, 128
Task-appropriate goals, 63–64
Taylor, M. M., 140
Teachers
  classroom philosophy, 183–85
  expertise of, x
  knowledge and beliefs of, 185–86
Teske, P., 58
Text selection, for modeling, 157–58
Text structure, instruction in, xi
Textual importance, 23
Thompson, S., 33
Time
  as essential principle, 187–89
  in process writing approach, 138–41
Timelines, 108
Topics, selecting, 102, 112–13
Transfer of strategy, 5, 13
Transformations, making, 33–34
Trentin, G., 45
Troia, G. A., 4, 6
Tynjälä, P., 169, 170

Unfamiliar-Genre Research (UFG) Project, 147

van den Bergh, H., 175
Vinton, V., 167
Vipond, D., 37
Visual prompts, for prewriting, 109

Ward-Lonergan, J. M., 92, 119
Warshauer, M., 82
Watt, M., 163
Watterson, B., 99
Web Scrapbook, 110
Weil, M., 109
Weiner, H. S., 41
Wells, G., 172
Whitin, D. J., 117, 121
Whitin, P., 117, 121
Wideman, H. H., 78
Wikipedia, writing for, 130–32
Wikis
  platforms for, 49
  use in collaborative writing, 48–50
Wilkinson, B., 170, 171, 176, 177
Will, G., 161, 162
Williams, J. M., 60, 63
Wixson, K. K., 13
Wong, B. Y. L., 13
Word processing, 71–85
  applications of, 79–85
  challenges of, 74–76
  collaboration fostered by, 73
  overview of, 71–76
  peer response to, 84–85
  principles of, 77–79
  purposefulness of, 77–78
  research on benefits of, 72
  revision strategies for, 79–84
  support for, 78–79
Workshop approach, xi
Wormelli, R., 34
Writing graphs, 16–17
Writing Next, ix, x
Writing prompts, analyzing, 64–67
Writing skills, crisis in, ix

Writing starters, 95
Writing strategies, 1–18
  adapting and developing, 3
  applications of, 15–17
  assignment for engaging, 10
  context of, 8–10
  modeling of, 6
  overview of, 1–8
  principles of, 8–15
  reflection, 13–15
  scaffolding, 11–12
  transfer of, 5
  types of, 3–4
Writing to learn, 168–81
  applications of, 81
  appropriateness of task in, 173
  context of, 171–73
  overview of, 168–71
  principles of, 171–76
  readers theater and, 178–81
  reflection and, 176
  use of journals in, 176–78
  writing choice and, 173–74

Yagelski, R. P., 135, 136
Yancey, K. B., 144
Yolen, J., 86
Young, L., 46
Youth Voices, 58

Zemelman, S., 169, 181

About Deborah Dean

As a former secondary English teacher, **DEBORAH DEAN** was the odd one who always wanted to teach the writing classes. When she could, she'd teach composition, college prep writing, even journalism. Her language arts classes were always heavily focused on writing. Since she's been teaching pre-service and practicing teachers about writing instruction, she has also volunteered to teach some remediation writing courses at a local high school. In her teaching life, she is constantly trying to find better ways to help novice writers develop their skills. She is the author of *Strategic Writing: The Writing Process and Beyond in the Secondary Classroom* and *Genre Theory: Teaching, Writing, and Being*, as well as numerous articles in national and regional journals. She has presented at a variety of conferences, both national and regional, and is the director of the Central Utah Writing Project.

This book was typeset in TheMix and Palatino by Barbara Frazier.

Typefaces used on the cover include Minion Pro, Helvetica Neue Bold, and Mistral.

The book was printed on 50-lb. Opaque Offset paper by Versa Press, Inc.